James Brindley
Canal Pioneer

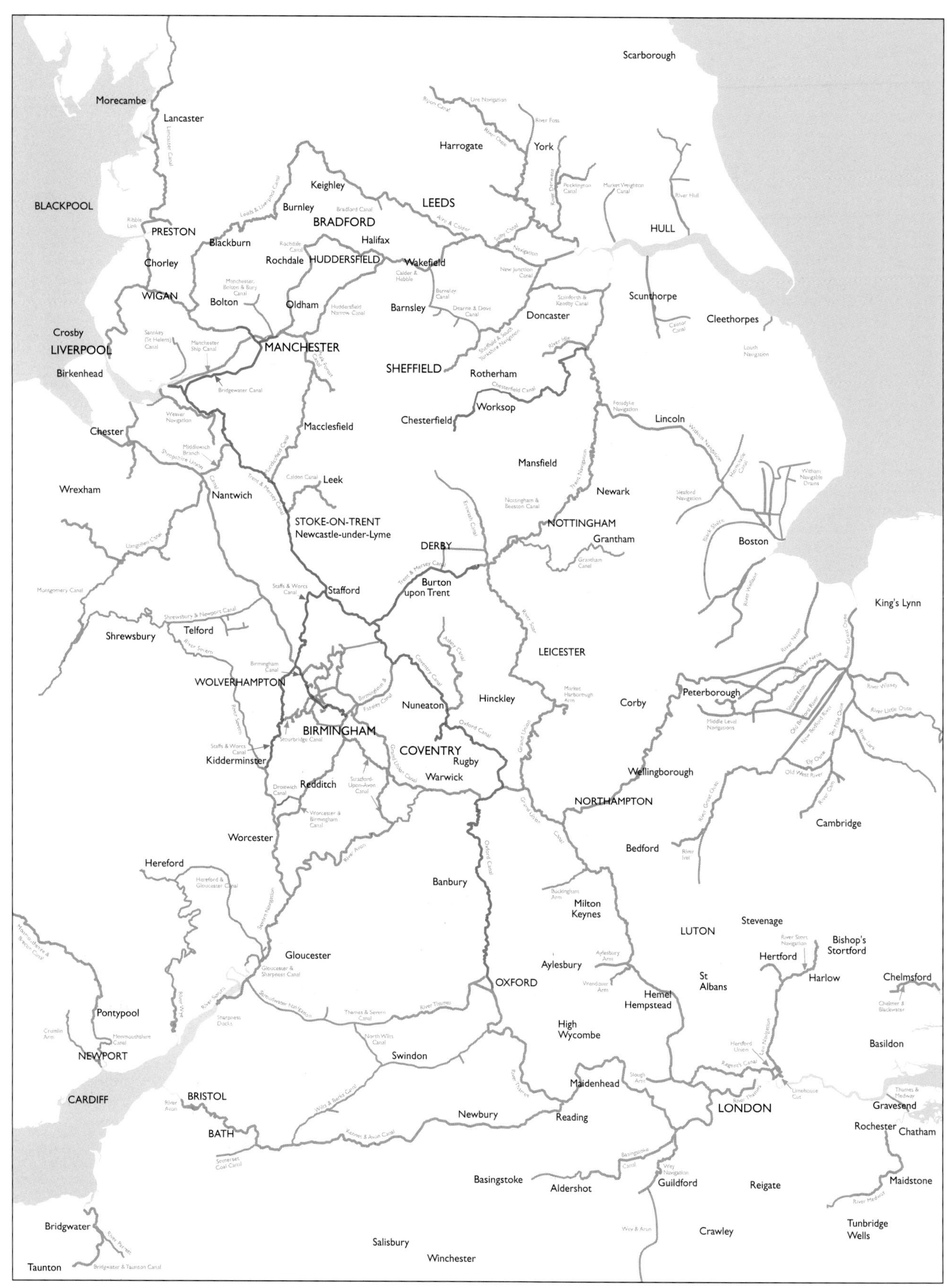

The network of inland waterways 2003 with Brindley canals shown in blue

James Brindley
Canal Pioneer

Christine Richardson

Waterways World Ltd

Burton-on-Trent, Staffordshire

First published 2004 by
Waterways World Ltd
151 Station Street
Burton-on-Trent
Staffordshire
DE14 1BG
Tel: 01283 742950

ISBN: 1 870002 95 4 (hardcover)

A CIP catalogue record for this book is available from the British Library

Printed in Great Britain by Information Press, Oxford

Cover illustration and title page: James Brindley, by Francis Parsons, 1770. (Courtesy of the National Portrait Gallery, London).

CONTENTS

LIST OF ILLUSTRATIONS

LIST OF MAPS

NOTES AND ACKNOWLEDGEMENTS

In 1995 the premier canal historian, Charles Hadfield, suggested that I should 'try to find Brindley, the man.' This book is the result, and I dedicate it to Charles' memory. I hope it encourages others to research the history of inland waterways – there is so much more to do.

I have set Brindley's personal story against a background of national events and the evolution of the pioneering era of canal construction in England, which he personifies.

To do so I have used modern systems of database storage and retrieval – and the improved archive facilities provided by national, county, borough and private associations. All of this was unavailable to previous biographers, to whom I acknowledge a debt of gratitude in keeping James Brindley's name to the fore.

Charles Hadfield (1909–96)

When quoting from eighteenth century documents I have, when necessary, amended the punctuation to aid clarity.

Many people have helped me in my research. Special thanks must go to Kathleen M. Evans for her assiduous research of the genealogy of James Brindley's family, a specialised subject of which I have little experience.

I am also grateful to the organisations and individuals who have given their permission to reproduce illustrations in this book.

Finally, an acknowledgement of the support given by my good friends John Lower and Roma Eastwood when doubts came to the fore. And, above all, to my husband Malcolm who made it all possible.

'Dare to be true …' George Herbert (1593–1633)

Christine Richardson
December 2003

Chapter 1
POTENTIAL REVEALED

Opening the patterned covers of his small pocket notebook, millwright James Brindley wrote 'Surveying the Navigation from Long brigg to Kings Mills, or inspected...12½ days'. The date was February 1758, and that early investigation of a possible route for the strategically important Trent & Mersey Canal was the first step along the path to national fame.[1]

Sheerlegs being used to install lock-gates - a method common in Brindley's era
Malcolm Fletcher

Brindley lived in a society dominated by water – as vital to the pattern of life as oil, electricity and tarmac are today. The flowing waters of almost every stream and river were used to power mills, forges and pumps, some of which contained extraordinarily complex machinery to carry out a wide variety of tasks. The transportation of raw materials, manufactured items, imported fine goods and passengers was also by water – either by coastal shipping or in river boats.

By the middle of the eighteenth century, when Brindley was in his prime, the nation was confident, internationally strong and ready for progress. It was the age of the exquisite designs and workmanship of Wedgwood, Capability Brown, Adams, Chippendale, and Hepplewhite. Our lives are still adorned with the many ancestral homes and fine town buildings erected, the magnificence of which show the constructional abilities of Brindley's compatriots. It is condescending to wonder at their achievements without the aid of JCBs. Their dexterity in the use of timber derricks, davits, cranes, pulleys, rollers, levers and muscles has been lost in our over-powered world – and they no more saw themselves as primitive, and in awe of what would be invented in two hundred years time, than do today's engineers.

In such an era it is significant that by 1772 Brindley's masterly manipulation of water had made his name known throughout the nation. He was credited with the creation of eight new canals, which had the potential to unlock the world-changing abilities of a confident age.

What he did not do, however, was invent the canal concept. Such waterways had been built elsewhere in the world for many centuries, several of them magnificent structures. Instead, Brindley's role was to lead Britain into a utilisation of artificial waterways which would eventually aid the national economy in far greater terms than had been achieved anywhere else.

The financial sources, administration, legalities, working practices and logistics of canal construction that were defined in Brindley's era would also give the lead to the promoters of Victorian railways, allowing that industry to move ahead more rapidly than would otherwise have been possible, and thereby swiftly becoming a fundamental element of the Industrial Revolution.

Today James Brindley's canals are at the heart of a network which extends throughout the nation. Once again his fame is growing, with modern statues erected and commemorative items produced, the result of a canal renaissance which is seeing the opening of many miles of waterways. This time the impetus is leisure but once again there is talk of the larger rivers taking heavy cargoes from the roads. Brindley's rise from obscurity, his genius for manipulating water, his awareness of the potential of steam-power and his subsequent identification as the figurehead of a national canal network mark him as a man of great vision – one in whom ambition was mixed with high moral integrity. Brindley's personal drive led him from obscurity to a life mixing with the nobility, industrialists, politicians and the workmen who would create his schemes. He treated them all with equal favour.

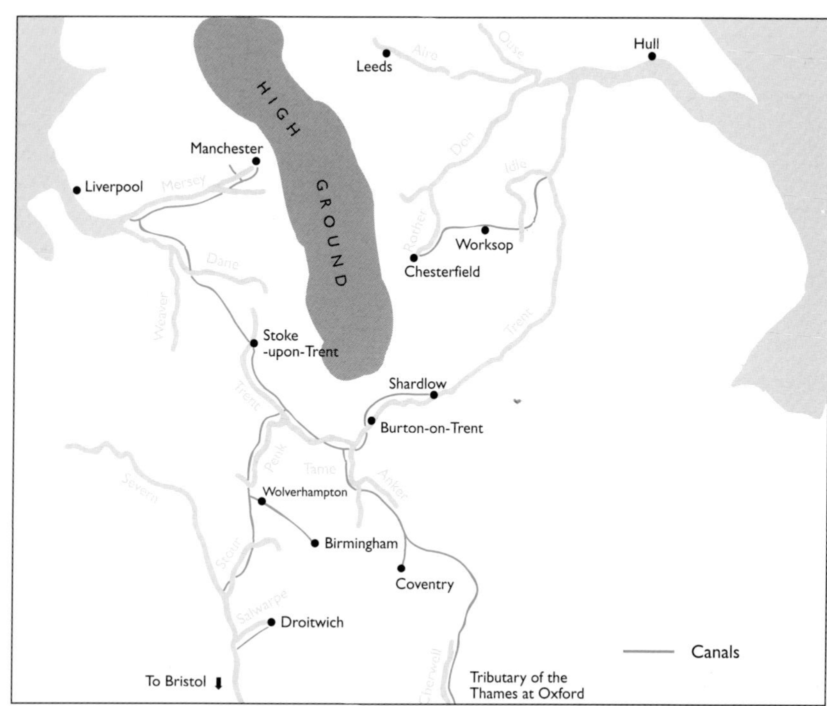

In Brindley's era canals were an unproven concept and, in general terms, they followed the river valleys

Fable has described him as a 'genius' – but has also labelled him with the words 'illiterate' and 'peasant', usually written by people he never met and some years after his death. Nevertheless, the portrayal of Brindley as illiterate has achieved wide acceptance even though it is patently mistaken. He could write and do calculations, jotting them down in his notebook as they came to mind – a methodology familiar to many modern engineers – but he always favoured the practical application of his ideas rather than the creation of documentation. He was a man born in the Derbyshire High Peak, his appearance plain with no display of finery, his speech equally so although he could be eloquent when necessary. An enquiring mind allowed him to see the potential in situations but it also drove him with an insecurity that would allow no rest.

Brindley's formative years were fundamental to his later achievements. The hills in which he spent his childhood gave an innate understanding of the behaviour of the water that flowed from them. This advantage was augmented by an apprenticeship as a millwright during which Brindley's natural talents found their outlet in the creation of an array of methods for water conservation and utilisation. His subsequent self-employed status, and a foray into steam-power, supplied the first strands of a crucial local network of contacts that ultimately led to an opportune involvement in canal construction. Furthermore, his Quaker wider family gave him an introduction to the widespread and industrially influential network of that sect, although he was not of the faith himself.

Eventually, others saw Brindley's innate abilities, making possible his transformation from an exceptional Midlands millwright into the figurehead of the pioneering age of canals and a recipient of national fame.

James Brindley was born in 1716 in the small hamlet of Tunstead, in the hills of the Derbyshire Peak District above Buxton – itself the highest town in England. He lived in that remote place until 1726 when his family moved to a farm near Leek, across the border in Staffordshire. Little is known of Brindley's first ten years in Tunstead, indeed it is difficult to know fact from folklore. Much of the story is based on Smiles' glowing biography which has his hero beset with all the disadvantages beloved by a Victorian readership – painting a picture where the one shining light in the life of young James is his mother Susanna; otherwise he is surrounded by gambling, theft, poverty, cruelty and neglect.[2]

Smiles would also have us believe that Brindley's father, James Snr, was a feckless ne'er-do-well, easily led astray by the bad company with whom he mixed at the nearby bull-running meetings – his gambling on the contests soon reducing him to poverty and neglect of his children. And all of this young James endured in 'a humble cottage' because his father was of little rank and was only allowed to occupy the dwelling and its land in exchange for his family's labour. The Victorian values of Smiles are all too apparent in his denigration of Brindley's early childhood so that his hero could be 'strong-minded, resolute and ingenious' in rising from obscurity to fame. Even the young boy's one advantage is diminished when his mother's efforts to educate her family are seen as 'but small'.[3]

It is difficult to interpret how much truth there is in this picture of remote poverty. Smiles was writing nearly one hundred years after Brindley's death so he was not close to events, but he did reflect an already well-established theme. Many years earlier John Aiken had heard tales of Brindley's early years – in a book published in 1795 he wrote of a father who 'dissipated his property … in field-amusements, and neglected his family', leaving poor James 'destitute of even the common rudiments of education'. However, there is no proof that Aiken ever met Brindley so his work is based on hearsay, and twenty years after a celebrity's death is plenty of time for factual embroidery to weave its embossed portrait. Perhaps our interpretation of Dr Aiken's opinions should be influenced by his description of Brindley at the height of his fame as 'a mere peasant' when he was patently not so.[4]

There are, however, some aspects of those early years which can be clearly seen and they are the Derbyshire hills. The high peaks are still there, moulding the lives of their inhabitants as they did in Brindley's time – the hills dictate and oversee; creating weather patterns and defining life-styles. Tunstead, Brindley's birthplace, is remote and very high. It is bleak, hard, beautiful, unforgiving, practical – and no place for finery or pretensions, no place for weakness. Brindley's formative childhood years infused hills into his soul; he was probably seventeen when he first saw a level piece of land – and that only in the distance from Macclesfield.

Brindley's working life was to be dominated by water, his whole career an endless endeavour to put the ubiquitous medium to use. He judged that uncontrolled water was wasteful, a power-source escaping before it could be channelled to mill-wheels, heated into steam, or diverted into canals. The original motivation for this attitude was formed during his Tunstead childhood when he was said to have helped on the hill-farms. The area is formed by outcroppings of pale grey limestone where motionless water is rare – in general it falls from the sky and disappears into the porous rocks. The only reason the hills are habitable is that they also contain bands of fine-grained volcanic basalt which form a barrier to the water coming through the limestone thereby creating subterranean water-tables in the hills. In the past such natural reservoirs supplied drinking water to the hill-farms of Brindley's home. However, the water produced by the bands of basalt had to be captured in troughs – the porous limestone of his youth taught James an early lesson in the control of water.[5]

Elsewhere others had been working on the control of water to provide a transport system, a process that had been on-going for many centuries. Carrying heavy or bulky goods by water transport was very much more efficient than any land alternative – an average load for a pack-horse was one-eighth of a ton, a waggon on the un-made roads of the time could carry just over half a ton per horse. On a large river a boat could carry 50 tons. It was, therefore, a blessing that Britain's major rivers reached far inland to form a natural link with the sea-ports, making them portals for all foreign commerce as well as the important coastal trading.[6] Throughout history they had been used as transport routes,

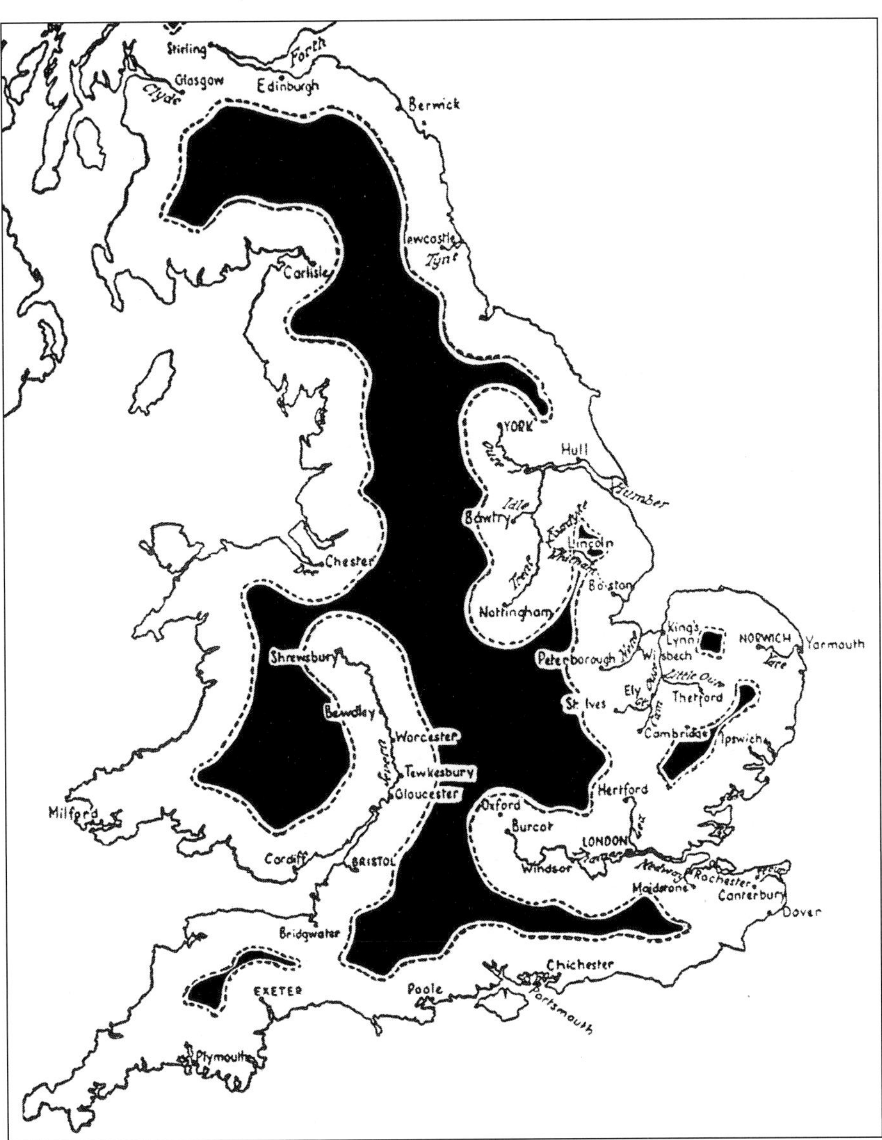

The principal navigable rivers in Elizabethan Britain, c1600. Total length 700 miles. The shaded areas were more than 15 miles from the sea or a navigable river, the distance judged to be the maximum over which land transport could be cost-effective

With acknowledgments to T.S. Willan

for example recent research has shown that the Romans probably used waterways rather than their celebrated roads to carry bulk supplies between their towns and forts. The Trent, Yorkshire Ouse, Severn and Thames were naturally navigable for many miles and others had been improved in a piecemeal fashion with the installation of flash-locks and staunches to deepen the water. Those who had invested capital in such schemes formed navigation companies, which were legally entitled to levy tolls on river craft to recoup their investment. However, these local monopolies were strangling the emergent commerce of the nation with little alternative for the carriage of heavy goods. Nevertheless, the extension of navigation was widespread – Elizabethan England and Wales had 685 miles of inland navigable waters; by 1716 – the birth year of James Brindley – improvements to major rivers had almost doubled that figure.[7]

But the navigable reaches of rivers, by their very nature, occupied the valleys and lower-lying areas leaving vast areas of the hilly core of England still without the trading advantages of water-based transport. The counties Brindley knew best – Staffordshire and Derbyshire – together with neighbouring Leicestershire, covered over two-million acres, but contained only 24 miles of navigable water.[8] Nevertheless, the extension of navigation by improving rivers was so well established it would be only when such possibilities had been exhausted that the nation would readily accept the canal concept.[9] Even then, practicalities demanded that the routes of Brindley's canals would generally follow the geography of the rivers.

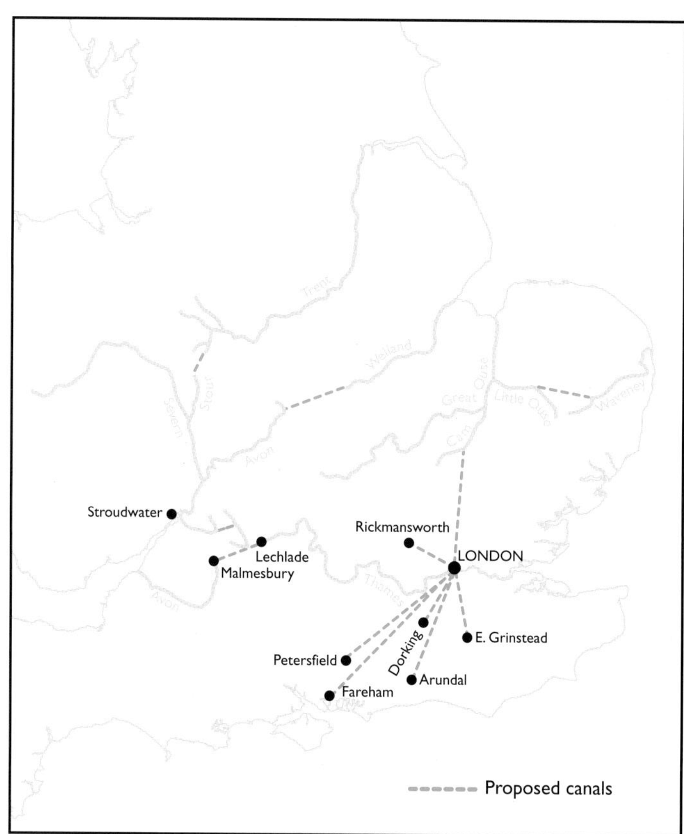

Canal schemes proposed in the period 1600–1750, but not built

With acknowledgments to T.S. Willan

However, the advocacy of canals to link the rivers had been publicised for some time, although always coming to nothing. In 1655, in a pamphlet, Francis Mathew had proposed that rivers be joined by a 'still River … with Sasses, alias Locks, or otherwise' and that the work was so important it should be undertaken by the State for the benefit of the whole nation – but two years after Cromwell took the title of Lord Protector was not the time for such proposals with the country still riven by the divisions of the recent Civil War.[10] There were many other schemes that also foundered, including one by Thomas Congreve who wrote in 1716 that the Trent and the Severn should be linked by a canal – along a route which would be taken by Brindley's Staffordshire & Worcestershire Canal sixty years later.[11]

The time was still not right for Congreve's ideas but the pressures for water transport in areas beyond the reach of the rivers was now growing. When Brindley was only four years old the industrial developments that would form the basis of his fame and fortune were already in place. Staffordshire's potteries had developed to a point where they were using clays from other areas for special effects, for example pipe-clays from Devon and Dorset which were laboriously carried by pack-horse from Chester, the nearest port.[12] At the same time an upsurge in coal demand in Manchester led the 4th Earl of Bridgewater to improve his already well-developed pits at Worsley.[13] However, he would have to contend with the extra costs inflicted by the Irwell Navigation Company, the 1720 Act for which allowed tolls of 3s 4d per ton for most cargoes on that river.[14] The triggers were in place – Worsley coal for Manchester, non-local clays for the Potteries, high monopolistic toll-charges by river navigation companies – fifty years later the young boy growing up on a Tunstead croft would play a major part in firing the first shots of the canal age.

Legend says the young James was a practical lad, helping to scare birds from the fields and working at Old Hall Farm in Wormhill, a village lower down in the Wye valley. It is also said he led grain waggons from Wormhill to a water-powered grist-mill on the Wye where his fascination with machinery began. From there fable has him making model water-wheels, operated by the fast-running streams issuing from the hillsides or in the overflows from stone troughs. The boy's natural gift for understanding machinery is always stressed, balanced with disparaging remarks about his lack of education. It is possible that he may have heard about another machine that moved water, news of which was probably spread by the hawkers of the area. Just twelve miles down the Wye water was being pumped out of a lead-mine by a Newcomen steam-engine.

The young James was very likely a sturdy lad, well used to the open-air and the practical life-style necessary to survive the topography and climate of Tunstead. He was the first of seven children, at least five of them born before the family moved. Infant mortality rates were high in the eighteenth century but James' parents did produce seven surviving children in fifteen years, so whatever their limitations they did know how to provide care and safety for their family. As the first-born, James had the benefit of some undivided attention from his parents, although his siblings followed in quick succession – Joseph, John, Esther, Ann, Henry and Mary. The standards of the household in which they all thrived is an important factor in the early development of James Brindley and, rather than repeating hearsay and fable, we should look two steps further back to find the significant influence of other relatives – and their Quaker beliefs.

In 1658 Alice and Henry Bowman, the paternal great-grandparents of James Brindley, became Quakers. They were not alone in their beliefs; in the north Staffordshire moorlands near Tunstead were the homes of a large number of followers who often met at various houses. Alice Bowman applied the good financial management of her creed to her family, establishing the basis of their wealth. Six of her seven children remained true to Quakerism – the exception being Ellen Bowman who married Joseph Brindley, and eventually became the grandmother of James. They settled near Tutbury, Staffordshire, and seem to have been ambivalent about their religion. They had their youngest child baptised, which was not part of Quakerism, but all four children were sent to the large households of Quaker relatives for a period, a common practice of the faith. There is evidence to suggest that their first-born, and only son, James – father of engineer James – was for a while sent to the wealthy Quaker household of his senior uncle, Henry Bowman at nearby Youlgreave.[15]

How much of the Bowman wealth came to James Snr from his mother Ellen is unclear. For some reason family bequests to her were always managed by her wealthy brother Richard Bowman, a task which he assiduously carried out to the ultimate benefit of his great-nephew. The effect of the significant influence of Quakerism on the early years of James Snr is also unclear, with no evidence of his continuing in the faith after his parents' drift from the sect. However, the upbringing of James Snr does cast some doubt upon the tales of fecklessness. In January 1716 he married Susanna Bradbury of whom little is known, only that she was of Tideswell, Derbyshire, and no trace of her has been found in Quaker nor Anglican records. Neither has any evidence been found of her ability to write, although that does not mean she could not. Her husband James Snr certainly could read and write – his early Quaker years ensured he could do so – and he formed his letter 'e' in the same old-fashioned way as his son would do later, that is like an 'o' with a loop on top.[16] The home they established in Tunstead was not of the Quaker faith, but their eldest son would go on to receive national plaudits for the very characteristics held so dear by that sect – James Brindley would be widely accepted as a personification of Quaker commercial ideals throughout his career.

By the eighteenth century the majority of Quakers adhered to a simple lifestyle that embraced change and development; their belief in stultifying discipline fortunately abated. A significant aspect was a tenet of experiment and observation, with practicality valued above theory. Personal failure and lengthy non-productive periods of experiment were accepted with stoicism. Allied to this was an open-minded outlook that fostered intuition and inspiration, but coupled with a mental discipline which prevented a decline into obsession and bigotry. Such controls could be overwhelmed by pressure of work, making it difficult for an individual to rest even when the need to do so was obvious to all about him.[17]

To society in general the Quakers presented an image plain in speech and dress. They practised a doctrine of universal equality, often shown as benevolent paternalism towards those who worked for them. Honesty and moderation were cornerstones of the Quaker faith, together with an urgent aversion to idleness, indulgence and the erosion of capital on worldly possessions. Quaker standards were trusted; in business their absolute integrity guaranteed dealings would be honest and truthful – a reputation which also served their own pockets.[18] By the middle of the eighteenth century James Brindley's Quaker-like plain appearance, and display of actions similar to that sect, was judged – perhaps sub-consciously – as trustworthy. Such a person also found it easy to deal with the widespread network of successful Quaker-owned companies such as the Darby family's Coalbrookdale iron foundries. There were many more, and their involvement in the early phase of industrialisation is significant in the success of James Brindley.

Although born in Derbyshire the majority of James Brindley's life was spent in neighbouring Staffordshire; his family's move to that county a major event for the ten year old boy. He may never have met his great-uncle Richard Bowman, but that wealthy Quaker was still managing the financial affairs of his relations. In c1726 he agreed to James Brindley Snr moving his family to Lowe Hill Farm, one mile south-east of Leek – a two-thirds share of which property would come to James Snr in December 1727 as a bequest in Richard Bowman's will.[19]

The journey from Tunstead to Leek may have been the first of any length undertaken by young James. The obvious

The little-changing hills of the Derbyshire Peak District viewed from the Buxton to Leek road – travelled by James Brindley at the age of ten when his family moved from Tunstead to Leek in 1726

route of fifteen miles skirted the eastern flank of Axe Edge, and the Brindleys crossed the watershed into the catchment of the rivers of Staffordshire and Cheshire – which include the Weaver and the Mersey, destined to play a major role in their eldest son's life. From Axe Edge young James would have seen magnificent distant hills disappearing to the eastern horizon, ridge after ridge, the high moorland undulating and refusing to be level. Infant streams gushed from the ground in a familiar rush of white water. The road they travelled was never level, never straight, but these characteristics would have been familiar to the eye of a boy of the hills. After ten miles the road reached its highest point, some 1,600 feet above sea level, and started the roller-coaster descent to Leek. One mile before the town their road turned-off to the left, skirted round to the south-east of the town, and reached Lowe Hill Farm. They were now in the foothills of the Peaks, an altogether greener area gently undulating and with tall trees.

The move from a moorland croft at Tunstead to a farm in a comparatively agriculturally-rich area – with Leek nearby as a market for produce – was a marked improvement in the life of the Brindley family. By 1729 James Snr could buy-out the remaining one-third of Lowe Hill Farm from his sister Hannah. They had many wealthy Quaker relatives in the area around Leek, but how much they associated with them is unknown. Nevertheless, their successful example would have been obvious to the teen-aged James Jnr. He may also have felt an affinity to them, his practical mechanical bent finding an echo in the sect's empirical beliefs. As the eldest son it may have been assumed he would stay to run the farm, and perhaps pressure was exerted to that end. However, there were no such expectations limiting his brother John who, in c1730 aged ten, was sent to Burslem (now part of the City of Stoke-on-Trent) to learn the skills of the pottery trade already well-established there – his progress a facet in his brother James' later success.[20]

Nothing is known of life at Lowe Hill but James and his remaining brothers probably helped their father with the farm, while his sisters worked with their mother in the farmhouse. There was a Quaker school in Leek, the headmaster a great-uncle of James, but the link was made remote by re-marriage and there is no evidence that any of the Brindley children attended the establishment. Neither is there evidence that they did not – somewhere James did learn to read, write, and calculate but would only go on to use those abilities to facilitate his practical skills.

A life as a farmer may have been James' future, his role as eldest son making him the major support for his family. However, matters changed with the death of his paternal grandmother, Ellen Brindley, in January 1734. Her property at Yoxall, near Burton-on-Trent, was divided between James Snr and his two sisters and this financial windfall gave freedom to his eldest son.

Released from family responsibilities seventeen-year-old James Brindley left Lowe Hill Farm during the first three months of 1734. He travelled north-west to Macclesfield, leaving Leek over the river Churnet where he would eventually return to build the mill that today bears his name. The 13 miles to Macclesfield took him through gently rolling hills, so level ground was still unfamiliar. He was on his way to start a millwright apprenticeship with Abraham Bennett at Sutton, south-east of Macclesfield on the river Bollin, over whose lower waters he would later carry the Bridgewater Canal. At this stage of his life there is no evidence that James Brindley had ever seen a navigable river, nor perhaps a sizeable boat. His knowledge was of young rivers descending from the High Peaks – stony-bedded, swift-flowing and shallow.

Fable says the apprenticeship with Bennett was arranged for James by his mother, and there is circumstantial evidence to link her Bradbury family with the area around Sutton. If his mother did find the apprenticeship, she played a fundamental role in transforming her eldest son from a farmer to an engineer, and showed an understanding of his natural talent for machinery and water management. Susanna Brindley would go on to see her other children settled into careers or married – Esther would marry Samuel Simcock, a future canal-building colleague of her brother James. Both parents reached their mid-80s and saw the fame of their eldest son.[21]

As with his childhood much of what is 'known' of Brindley's time as an apprentice millwright is based on the Smiles biography of 1861 – and once again our hero is surrounded by drunkenness, but this time he also has to deal with incompetence and lack of co-operation. At the start of the seven-year apprenticeship Brindley found it difficult to settle down, an eighteen-year-old away from the farm and his family for the first time and lodging with the Bennett family. The new apprentice spent most of his working-day with the journeymen employed by Abraham Bennett, experienced and fully-trained men who did the majority of the work found by their master. Smiles describes them as a 'rough and drunken set' who used the young Brindley as an errand-boy to fetch more beer. When he asked them for guidance on a task he often 'met with a rebuff'. Much of his first two years were spent alone in the workshop – the journeymen out on other work, and Bennett in the pub 'from which he could not easily be drawn'. Nevertheless Brindley did his bungling best, often damaging tools as he tried to carry out tasks for which he had not received the direction he sought. Throughout it all

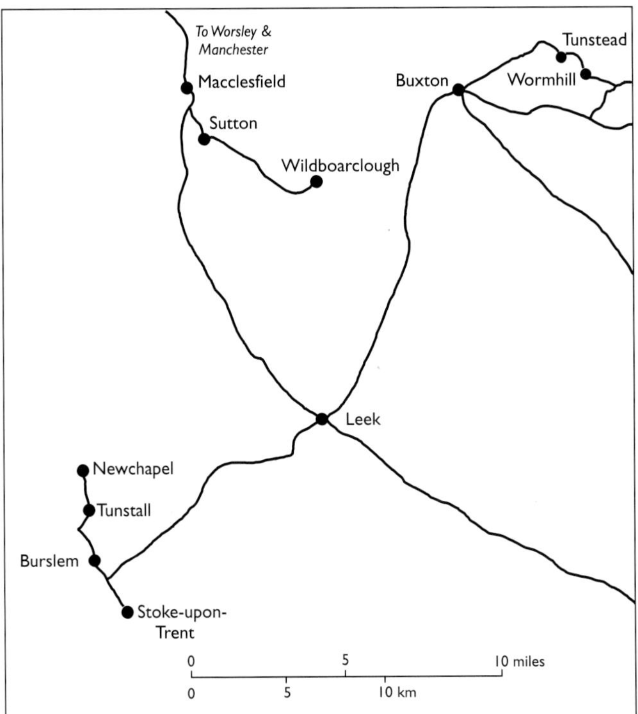

The Derbyshire–Staffordshire area of Brindley's childhood and early career

Smiles' hero was a 'brave spirit', determined to achieve 'success through defeats' and by this attitude he 'groped his way to much valuable practical information'. Such fortitude earned its reward when a mill in Macclesfield was badly damaged by fire, and Bennett obtained the contract to repair the complex machinery.

The fire at Michael Daintry's silk-mill was caused by friction in a ball-and-socket hinge within the machinery. Bennett and his journeymen manufactured the new equipment at the workshop in Sutton, leaving Brindley to remove the damaged parts of the mill under the eye of James Milner, the site superintendent. Milner was impressed by the nineteen year old's grasp of the basic concepts of mill apparatus and his ideas on how it could be designed to avoid similar fires in the future. As a result the mill-superintendent requested that Brindley be allowed to do a portion of the repair work, to which a surprised Bennett reluctantly agreed. When the mill was completed Bennett and his men celebrated in a nearby pub – Smiles, of course, writing of their drunken derision of Brindley's work. At that point James Milner famously defended the apprentice, wagering a gallon of best ale that Brindley would become a better workman than anyone else present. Truth, hindsight, or fable? However, it is said that neighbouring millers began to ask Bennett to send Brindley rather than his other men when they had repairs to be done. The young apprentice soon gained a reputation for suggesting original improvements instead of simply replacing what had been installed before. If this is so, it is an early indication of the innovative thinking that would take Brindley from local millwright to national canal engineer.

A second feature of the apprenticeship years is the source of an interesting hypothesis – was it the first time Brindley saw navigable waters and cargo-carrying boats? He was now in his fourth year with Bennett and had gained a considerable amount of experience and confidence, although major jobs were still done by his master and the journeymen. One such was a new paper-mill on the Clough Brook at Wildboarclough, in the steep foothills of the Peaks five miles south-east of Sutton. The machinery specified was a new type so Abraham Bennett went to study a similar installation on the river Irk, at Smedley, near Manchester. Once again Smiles is able to please his Victorian readership by having the returned master-millwright afflicted by a heady mixture of drink and incompetence – the practical details of his inspection almost useless. Nevertheless, not wishing to lose the contract he persevered with the construction of the new paper-mill, although it was soon obvious that neither he nor his journeymen understood the concepts involved. Brindley – perhaps concerned that the public shaming of his master would reflect on his own status – decided to resolve the situation in his own way. At the completion of his work one Saturday he walked the five miles from Wildboarclough back to Sutton – and continued overnight a further twenty miles to the paper-mill at Smedley to inspect the machinery Bennett had failed to fathom. There is no record of Brindley having been to Manchester before this but it was still a relatively small place and directions from there to Smedley, only three miles from the town centre, would have been easily found.

A fit, strong young man, aged 21, could complete such a trek overnight. There was an established road between Macclesfield and Manchester and a short summer moonlit night would not present insuperable difficulties. The intriguing question is – what did he see on the journey? Someone with the initiative to go to Smedley mill would not just trudge along, head down, ignoring the landscapes unveiled and the water-courses of professional interest. The local rivers came down from the Peaks and he must have known their characteristics very well – the flow-rates in spate and drought and the power that could be harnessed. An apprentice millwright of four years standing would naturally note all new water-courses and judge their potential – although his crossing of the infant river Mersey could not have told of its later career importance. Near the end of his walk the road from Macclesfield took Brindley to the centre of Manchester and it is possible that he saw the river Irwell, made navigable only a few months before in April 1737.[22] A millwright's professional eye would see that the deep and wide river was now controlled by a weir or a dam, as had been done to provide a head of water at many of the mills of his working life. There is, however, no evidence that he had seen how boats could by-pass such a weir via a lock, nor is it likely on this occasion as Throstlenest lock was off his route.

Brindley's presence in Manchester in 1737 is one of those points in history that sparkle in hindsight but pass by unlit at the time. The coal being produced nearby at Worsley was already in demand and a group of local business men were promoting a scheme to make Worsley Brook navigable, thereby bringing water transport within five thousand yards of the coal production. A railed-way was to carry output to the wharf at the head of the Brook, from where boats would reach the Irwell Navigation and on into the centre of Manchester. Over 300 tons would be supplied every week, with the capacity to double that figure when required. In 1737 they obtained an enabling Act of Parliament and the omens looked good – but nothing came of the scheme and Worsley coal production continued to be hampered by lack of bulk transport.[23] If it had succeeded, the need for the Bridgewater Canal twenty years later would have been doubtful. The future Duke of Bridgewater may have wished to avoid the Irwell's monopolistic tolls, but the income from 600 tons a week would have weakened the need for a capital-intensive project such as the Bridgewater Canal. The politics taking place in Manchester at the time of Brindley's visit would have a profound effect on his life.

Unaware of such developments he walked on to Smedley and on Sunday morning sought out the owner of the paper-mill and obtained his permission to study the concepts of its intricate mechanisms – spending all day on the task. That night he set off on the twenty-five miles back to Wildboarclough and on Monday morning was found working with great energy on the bungled paper-mill, with total recall of what he had seen the day before. A relieved Abraham Bennett allowed Brindley to complete the contract, which he did with great success, incorporating further improvements of his own design – and this three years before the completion of his apprenticeship.

The route of Brindley's 25-mile walk from near Macclesfield to Smedley, Manchester, in 1736, to inspect a paper mill

These two events – the paper-mill and the earlier silk-mill – highlight two of Brindley's natural abilities. Centuries of water-mill development had resulted in engineering of a high order, and the uses of water as a power-source in eighteenth century England were diverse. Nevertheless, he still saw where improvements could be made and impressed knowledgeable men with his understanding of engineering concepts – allied to a practical ability to install machinery to make more efficient use of the variations of water as a base input. To do so he must have been able to work in wood, metal, stone, brick and know the advantages and disadvantages of each material. The construction of weirs and mill-races to harness and route water required a judgement of levels, inclines, pressures and control-sluices. His systems demonstrated a profound understanding of the science of hydraulics, albeit based on intuitive understanding rather than mathematics.[24] His talent was exceptional. Brindley had made good use of the area into which he was born, the hills of Derbyshire, Staffordshire and Cheshire blessing him with a life-long affinity to the water flowing from them.

Additionally, his personality impressed both the superintendent of the silk-mill and the owner of the Smedley paper-mill. Brindley was a stranger to both men but each of them quickly recognised his honesty of intent. In a one-to-one meeting he was capable of persuasion and clarity of purpose, successfully using the direct approach in preference to the more usual channels. Often he could let his practical abilities speak for him but that was not the case with Mr Appleton, the owner of the paper-mill. On that occasion Brindley persuaded a total stranger to give him day-long access to a mill, on a Sunday, when that stranger would gain no advantage from the agreement. The integrity and strength of conviction that would impress so many others in the future were already apparent.

Brindley completed his seven year apprenticeship when he was 24, staying on with Abraham Bennett as a fully qualified journeyman millwright. When his old master died he completed the jobs in hand and wound up the business. His years at the Sutton workshop had been well spent – he acquired not only the skills that would take him to national fame, but also the first threads of a network of personal contacts that would make that transition possible. The many abilities of a millwright, trained to deal with emergencies as they arose as well as long-term projects, could be used by an innovative mind to achieve progress in many directions. In 1742 James Brindley took the first steps along that diverse path, returning to his family town of Leek to start his own millwright business.[25]

Chapter 2

THEATRE OF SUCCESS

No one lives in a vacuum and it is important to see the background against which the leading man was to perform. Something more than James Brindley's exceptional abilities was required to transform a self-employed millwright in a small Staffordshire town into a nationally famous canal engineer. Milling was an important industry, but Leek was hardly the stage from which a light would illuminate a nation – many generations may have included millwrights with engineering talents bordering on genius but nothing is known of them, their careers lost in the obscurity of time. Brindley's advantage over them was the time in which he lived. When he started his self-employed career in 1742 the country was on the threshold of the changes in social and economic life that would become known as the Industrial Revolution. It would transform the physical appearance of Britain and change the lives of the mass of the population.[1] It was Brindley's good fortune to be there at the start of a momentous age.

The first half of the eighteenth century had been a time of stability and innovation – seemingly a paradox, but in fact a partnership of latent potential. Superficially the age appears unprogressive compared with our own, but the unchanging landscape in the 1700s was a mask that covered burgeoning social and national change. At an individual level the constancy reflected the durable nature of necessities – household items, clothes and furniture were repaired and handed down; redundancy by fashion an irrelevance for the vast majority of the population. Improvements were made but only by slow evolution and, as a result, depreciation was an unknown concept for capital goods such as farm tools, waggons and mill machinery. Most implements and installations lasted a lifetime or longer.[2] Change was slow, spasmodic, and easily reversible but bad harvests, war or disease could obliterate a lifetime's progress for an ordinary family. At least 60% of the population still relied on agriculture for their living although many earned a little extra by weaving wool in sheds attached to their cottages. Specialisation is a concept of our modern world; in the first half of the eighteenth century most men worked at what was available. A jack-of-all-trades was the average way of life.[3]

Nevertheless, the fundamentals of life improved and the labouring poor had a reasonable standard of living compared to other times and other countries. In the 1730s harvests were good, so the price of food was low and there was an increased demand for labour on the farms.[4] The population of England and Wales had steadied at just over six million and the 1740s saw the start of a steady growth in numbers, so providing more manpower and consumers. This boost for the economy was the result of an increased survival rate of babies, made possible by progressive midwifery and the creation of lying-in hospitals. James Brindley himself was one of his parents' seven children, all of whom reached adulthood. However, the most important effect on a national scale was the survival of more children born to well established land-owning families. As adults they were typically younger sons – blessed with a reasonable education and bolstered by a secure financial base and able to take advantage of the abundant opportunities made possible by a stable society.[5] They dabbled in scientific theory and tested the practicality of their ideas by devising experiments on a wide range of subjects. Science became a gentlemanly pastime. Mostly they worked alone, intrigued by a problem or a phenomenon that had come to their attention and for which there was no known answer. Soon, learned societies evolved as a means of developing the ideas formed by enquiring minds.[6] The popular *Gentleman's Magazine* carried the latest theories and achievements to an erudite, but geographically widespread, readership. Change was fashionable, as Dr Johnson observed, 'The age is running mad after innovation – all the business of the world is to be done in a new way …'.[7] Overall, the society in which Brindley started his career was one where influential and affluent people were ready – indeed eager – to accept new ideas.

Science became part of a wider culture that thrived on the patronage of the royal family. As a subject it did not invoke fear. There were no laboratories where experiments were carried out in secret; instead they formed the central role of the public lectures that became a form of entertainment throughout the country. It was the dawn of the British eccentric still familiar to us – but instead of a garage or a shed they worked in rectory and country-house. Many others were willing to invest the capital required to implement the new technologies. In 1720 this produced an atmosphere of frenzied speculation, culminating in the financial crash known as the South Sea Bubble, when the South Sea Company took over the national debt in return for a monopoly of trade with the South Seas, causing feverish speculation in their stocks.

Enthusiasm had overcome prudence and almost every family in the country suffered when financial dreams became nightmares. Even the poor felt the effect when the households in which they were servants or farmhands lost money. It was a salutary lesson that investing in matters of which one knew little was not a guaranteed path to riches.

Buying shares on a street-corner was madness.[8] New parliamentary controls on the sale of stocks and shares to the public would eventually lead to Brindley's attendance at Westminster to gain the Acts required for public investment in canal construction. In addition, the prestigious Royal Society assumed the role of distinguishing between practicable industrial schemes, flights of fancy, and those aimed at unwary investors.[9] In hindsight it can be seen that the controls implemented after the South Sea Bubble created the safer financial environment necessary to encourage canal investments within living memory of the crash.

Nationally 'Britain' was a concept still new and distrusted. The Act of Union with Scotland was recent and soon a Highland Jacobite invading army would march through Leek, led by Prince Charles Edward Stuart – the claimant to the British throne known to later dewy-eyed generations as Bonnie Prince Charlie. However, that flowery name was not on the lips of Leek residents when his London-bound army of 7,000 men arrived on the 3rd of December 1745, taking over the town for night billets. Instead they later wrote to their families of 'a fierce and savage Host of Mountaineers'. Terror and astonishment filled the neighbourhood. Residents were summoned to supply forage 'upon pain of military execution'. Large buildings were 'broak open in the night and turned into a stable'. Cupboards were forced open in the search for money and food – cheese, hay and corn were carried off. Almost all of the town's horses were stolen, often their owners knocked to the ground. Fifteen cannon and fifty ammunition waggons filled the streets, there was much firing in the market place, and many families buried their plate and valuables. The leading sections of the army itself were a noble military sight with banners and well-dressed officers. Prince Charles Edward Stuart was 'straight, slender, and handsome; dressed in a green bonnet, laced with gold, a white bob-wig, a Highland plaid and broadsword'. On the other hand, 2,000 of his followers were 'meer rabble', ill-clothed 'shabby, pitiful-looking fellows ... dressed in dirty plaids and as dirty shirts, without breeches or shoes'.[10]

That army represented deep and ancient animosities within Britain but, in the modern sense, England itself was not yet a nation. Dialects were so distinct that the Devonian could not have understood the Yorkshireman, nor the Cumbrian the man from Dorset.[11] But it mattered little – there was minimal integration between the regions and cohesion was at county and town level, with events at Westminster of little consequence. County families had great local influence; an ambitious young millwright would do well if his work impressed such local grandees – in England the great families were a path to the top. Outside London the majority of the titled heads were approachable and took a keen interest in their estates. They often had no ambitions towards national politics, and those who did attend at Westminster did so as an honour for their county. Their considerable influence could be tapped so long as one remembered the ancient feuds that produced long traditions of family rivalry.[12]

Nevertheless, on the world scene Britain had reached the status of a first-class power. The start of Brindley's self-employed career at Leek coincided with a general awareness that the centuries-old fear of invasion from near European neighbours was a thing of the past. The Royal Navy was now one of the world's most formidable armed forces. Together with Britain's economic strength it had subdued the France of Louis XIV and, although wars with France and Spain would continue throughout the eighteenth century, the corrosive fear of defeat was gone.[13] Soon it became obvious that naval power also opened up world trade and the foundations of what would become the world's greatest Empire were laid. Britain's ports and rivers became gateways for raw materials from the North American colonies, exotic riches from India, Africa and the Levant, as well as the more prosaic coals from Newcastle.[14]

In the southern half of the country the Thames, Great Ouse, Wey, Warwick Avon, Severn and Kennet took boats far inland. In the north the Aire, Calder, Trent, Irwell, Mersey, Yorkshire Ouse, Don and Weaver were carrying cargoes of widening variety. Vast fleets of coastal shipping carried goods and passengers to town harbours and estuarial ports, although always having to contend with the vagaries of the weather in an age of sail. Smuggling was silently condoned in counties with remote coastlines, and the pickings were good. Compared with thirty years before, re-exports had doubled and 50% more home-production was sold abroad. Over that same period, interest rates and taxes were low and London developed into the world's greatest commercial city.[15] The banking system was in its infancy but it could supply finance to merchants, and the risks of overseas trade were covered by underwriters and insurance brokers.[16]

Times of such rapid change make comfortable viewing from future centuries, but for those involved the picture was unclear and unsettling. Society, particularly in its lower levels, was held together by tradition and, as a result, change was suspect just because it was change.[17] Enlightened men scoffed at the hundreds of superstitions but among the population there were still echoes of a belief in witchcraft. Every sort of charlatan, quack and necromancer flourished.[18] Nevertheless, Britain was not a deferential country. Few years passed without major riots, the mobs taking to the streets for a variety of reasons. Often it was prices, and the popular remedy was to seize stocks of the relevant items which were then 'sold' at what the mob considered a fair return. Turnpike routes, politics, land enclosures, new industrial processes – it needed little motivation for the masses to make their views known. They could not vote but the mobs had a collective power heard in all large towns and cities. However, such riots did not strike at the power of the state and Britain was free of the civil war which had torn it apart in the past – and the terrors of the revolution which would sweep across France in the near future.[19]

Overall, the circumstances were right for the Industrial Revolution's deluge of invention. London was the national power base – with the Royal court, the government, and the financial establishment – but it also had the debilitating effects of convoluted politics, naked ambitions, the jealousies of patronage, and the whims and flummeries of short-lived fashions. The engine-room of innovation would be elsewhere – in central and northern England where men were free of London's distractions but still able to benefit from the national stability and affluence. In Staffordshire for example, somewhere like Leek. It would be Britain's good fortune that nature had placed the raw materials of the industrial future – especially the coal, iron-ore, and clay – not only away from London but in the areas where the new thinking flourished. In 1742 James Brindley and Britain were on the threshold of great achievements – in both cases the future was viewed with confidence. But there were no great plans to follow. Things would evolve.

Chapter 3
THE MILLWRIGHT

In traditional canal songs James Brindley is often referred to as 'the millwright engineer', now an epithet of little significance but originally widely understood to describe the background from which he arose. In the eighteenth century the long-established means of producing a power greater than that of the muscles of a man, horse or ox was the turning of machinery by the natural forces of water or wind. Such was the importance of such sites that the compilers of the Domesday Book (1086) meticulously listed those in each settlement, and in the intervening centuries the power efficiency had improved greatly, with the machinery so activated becoming extraordinarily complex. The turning motion of a water-wheel or a wind-sail was harnessed to grind, lift and drain, and developments were most advanced during Brindley's era before the widespread advent of steam-power. Even so, the future use of steam would need fuel to heat water whereas in Brindley's homelands, on the meteorologically wet western side of the Pennine hills, there was always a natural and abundant supply of flowing water to turn mill-wheels.

The millwrights were the men responsible for developing, creating and maintaining these intricate sites but, although fulfilling a fundamental role in society, they were not accorded the status we would now judge them to merit. The seven-year apprenticeship they served did not turn them into gentlemen so they were still of a lower social class. In their abilities millwrights, such as James Brindley, were the equivalent of today's civil-engineers and their skill was acknowledged by society – but many doors remained closed. A 'gentleman' only dabbled in what is now termed 'engineering' as a hobby, it being beneath one's dignity to undertake such activities as an occupation – even though many of the key developments that would drive the industrial revolution would emerge from that source.[1] Nevertheless, entrenched opinion was changing and soon the dawn of the canal age would bring civil engineering to national renown and status. Even so, in its newly acknowledged ranks, millwright Brindley would be the exception, with the more usual pattern set by another prominent engineer of that era – John Smeaton.

Comparisons are often made between Brindley and Smeaton but it is invidious and futile to judge who was the more able. However, their backgrounds and early careers do illustrate the different paths trod on the way to national fame, and why Brindley's unpretentious roots became the stuff of fable and song. The two engineers had some things in common. Smeaton was only eight years younger than Brindley, they were both born in the north of England, and both showed an outstanding aptitude for machinery and constructional work – but there the similarities end. Smeaton, the son of a successful Leeds lawyer, moved to London and used his family connections and financial support to gain access to the prestigious Royal Society, listening to lectures and eventually submitting papers himself. He read French books containing the most advanced science of the day, and toured Holland to study canals and land-reclamation schemes. John Smeaton was only twenty-eight when elected a Fellow of the Royal Society.[2] At the same age James Brindley was a self-employed millwright in Leek, Staffordshire.

In different circumstances that is where Brindley may have remained, one of the thousands of millwrights whose story is lost to the passage of time. He would have been well-known locally, his trade leading to many useful contacts, but nothing other than that. What set him apart, when the opportunity came, was his willingness to try new avenues, coupled with the shrewd application of his practical skills to such challenges. As a millwright James Brindley knew about the channelling, storage and flow-control of water – often in situations requiring some ingenuity – and he lived in an area where there was an abundant supply with which to practice. In later years the planning and building of a canal would have much in common with a mill, the larger project mostly defined by the logistics of scale and the incessant politics. Both involved diverting water from a natural source along a man-made channel to a designated site, at a sustained and regulated flow-rate, and taking into account the required usage dictated by weather variations. Young Smeaton had the prestige in London, but at the same age Brindley had the greater ability to make things happen – always a valued attribute in the north of England.

Smeaton's arena was London – Brindley's small stage was Leek, a somewhat discrete location from which to launch a glittering career. The staple trade of the district was buttons decorated with silk and mohair, with ribbons a busy sideline. The main river was the Churnet, its waters having driven mill-wheels since the 11th century. On the south-western edge of the Pennines, Leek was then a small town – perhaps a large village would be a more apt description by today's standards – but its busy market brought farmers and millers in from the surrounding area. They were probably the first customers of the young millwright

Brindley, who was only 26 when he started his business in 1742. He was also a trained wheelwright, so farm waggons were a source of work, but almost nothing is known of Brindley's early trading years – he left no records of that period and, of course, no one knew he would be of interest to later centuries. Appropriately, he set up a workshop in Mill Street and the floor above may have been his home. Eating at the local inn and hiring a horse to visit work-sites, James Brindley was probably a typical un-married young man striving to make a living.

However, his innovative mind set him apart from other millwrights – instead of merely repairing old machinery he would take the opportunity to incorporate changes to improve its performance. He was also said to be adept at installing new systems for special purposes, and for completing contracts within the stipulated times – abilities for which he charged high prices.[3] Nevertheless, such methods, and the confidence to apply them, would have been valued by the more visionary of the local landowners and those with commercial interests. Recommendations via a widening network of customers resulted in Brindley's area of activity eventually extending to a neighbouring area of Staffordshire, known colloquially as The Potteries. This was indeed a fortunate adjunct to his main area of operations. Potting was well established with many predominately family-based firms and, of crucial importance to Brindley's career, it was on the threshold of becoming an industry of national and international importance. Of that, however, there was, as yet, little outward sign. The output was still predominantly produced from locally found raw materials and fired by local coal in small bottle-kilns dotted about amongst other buildings. Burslem was one of the small towns where potters worked, one of whom was Brindley's younger brother John who was well established with many contacts, including a recent marriage to Ann Rogers, daughter of another Burslem potter.[4] Instant access to this network resulted in a growing volume of work for James Brindley. By 1750 a stronger presence was worthwhile in Burslem and he hired a millwright's workshop, part of a property owned by a family with a name now synonymous with pottery – Wedgwood. Tradesmen often lived above their workshops and there is no reason to believe Brindley did otherwise – the outside yard surrounded by pot-works and gardens, with the Wedgwood's large new house nearby.[5] His neighbours employed him on many tasks and good long-lasting friendships were formed – the most significant of which was that of the 34-year-old millwright and Josiah Wedgwood.

Twenty-year-old Josiah Wedgwood was a fourth generation potter, his family well-established in Burslem under the leadership of his uncles Thomas and John. The Wedgwoods were not rich but they were comfortable enough, and had earned a high reputation for honesty and good workmanship.

A typical trail once used by heavily-laden pack-horses in the Staffordshire hills

Potting had flourished in north Staffordshire because the required clays were abundant, and the kilns could be fired with an excellent bituminous coal which was easily extracted from an unusual formation of outcroppings.[6] But evolution in fashions and styles required constant technical enhancements – and raw materials from further afield.

An ever-expanding road transport network was already in place to adjacent counties, albeit expensive, unreliable and inefficient. From Cheshire to the north-east came salt – shovelled into the superheated kilns it formed a vapour which settled on the red-hot clayware, combining with the silica in the pots to cover them with a semi-matt or shiny glaze. From Derbyshire to the east came lead ore (galena) – in powdered form it was placed on the wares before firing, also to produce a glazed finish.

All of the Burslem potters tried to make their wares as white as possible, as favoured by their increasingly affluent middle-class customers – cream-coloured earthenware was the most popular domestic tableware and the demand for it grew steadily. Unfortunately the Staffordshire clays were sometimes tainted with iron and other impurities that ruined light coloured products. Whiter-burning clays were available in the county but only in thin seams that could not supply the volumes now required. Instead pipe- or ball-clays were laboriously transported from Devon and Dorset. It was dug out in large lumps, each weighing about 35 pounds, and carried to the coast on pack-horses. The clay from north Devon sailed from Bideford, that from south Devon went via Teignmouth, and Dorset clay from the port of Wareham – all sailing up the west coast to the port of Chester on the river Dee. From Chester it was again loaded onto pack-horses or waggons for the final stretch to the potteries. This last laborious road link was shorter after 1733 when the ships could sail all the way to Winsford along the newly navigable river Weaver. In 1734 only 150 tons of ball-clay were carried up the Weaver; by the time Brindley had set up his workshop in Burslem it was 1,300 tons a year. In 1760 it would be 1,850 tons.[7]

The endless experiments undertaken had shown that products could be whitened even more if ground flint was added before firing. Unfortunately flint deposits of commercial quantity were on far away beaches: at Gravesend and at Brighton; in Lincolnshire; on the Isle of Wight and, most abundantly, at Sheringham in Norfolk. As a result the transport (via the coast, up the rivers Severn, Trent, Weaver or Dee, and again on pack-horses) was unreliable for production schedules and expensive for production costs. The use of the rivers by boats had already reached as far inland as commercially prudent but unfortunately for the potters of Staffordshire their county stubbornly remained in the shrinking central area that was still more than 15 miles from navigable waters. And in the Potteries customer demand continued to rise.

The fact that it was at this time of burgeoning trade that James Brindley became well-established and respected in Burslem is fundamental to the engineer's subsequent rise to fame, and to the development of the national canal system which would be centred on Staffordshire. Josiah Wedgwood's future role in the promotion of canals for general haulage would be crucial, but it would be only one example of the widespread achievements of Brindley's friend. He would develop into a rare man in industry – or anywhere – a visionary who was also an organisational genius, with clear judgement, production depths and talents, and natural marketing skills – together with amiability and integrity. Wedgwood was as comfortable mixing at the highest social strata as he was with his workmen.[8] Eventually his products would be of such quality that all doors would open, allowing the aristocratic and influential contacts that were so valuable to him – and to his friend James Brindley.

But in 1750 much of that was in the future and Brindley's new Burslem workshop saw a young Josiah Wedgwood still working as a junior member of the family firm. His mother was the daughter of a Unitarian Church minister in nearby Newcastle-under-Lyme and Josiah retained that faith, taking an active role in the Unitarian Meeting House in the 1770s and worshipping there with his family throughout his lifetime.[9] Brindley was not a practising Quaker but the morals and standards of that sect imbued from his family background found a ready match in those of the young potter. The Unitarian form of Christianity maintains the unipersonality of God, rejects the Trinity and the divinity of Christ, and takes reason, conscience, and character as the criteria of belief and practice. Personal integrity, trustworthiness, and egalitarianism were central to the characters of both men. Fable also has them sharing a lack of education, thereby, it is said, making their subsequent achievements even more laudable:

> Me name's Josiah Wedgwood
> and I'm Burslem born and bred,
> Not had much education
> but I've learned to me 'ead …

The principal navigable rivers of Britain c1760. Total length 1,300 miles. The shaded areas remained more than 15 miles from navigable water. The drive to build a national network of canals would come from the small area south of Manchester

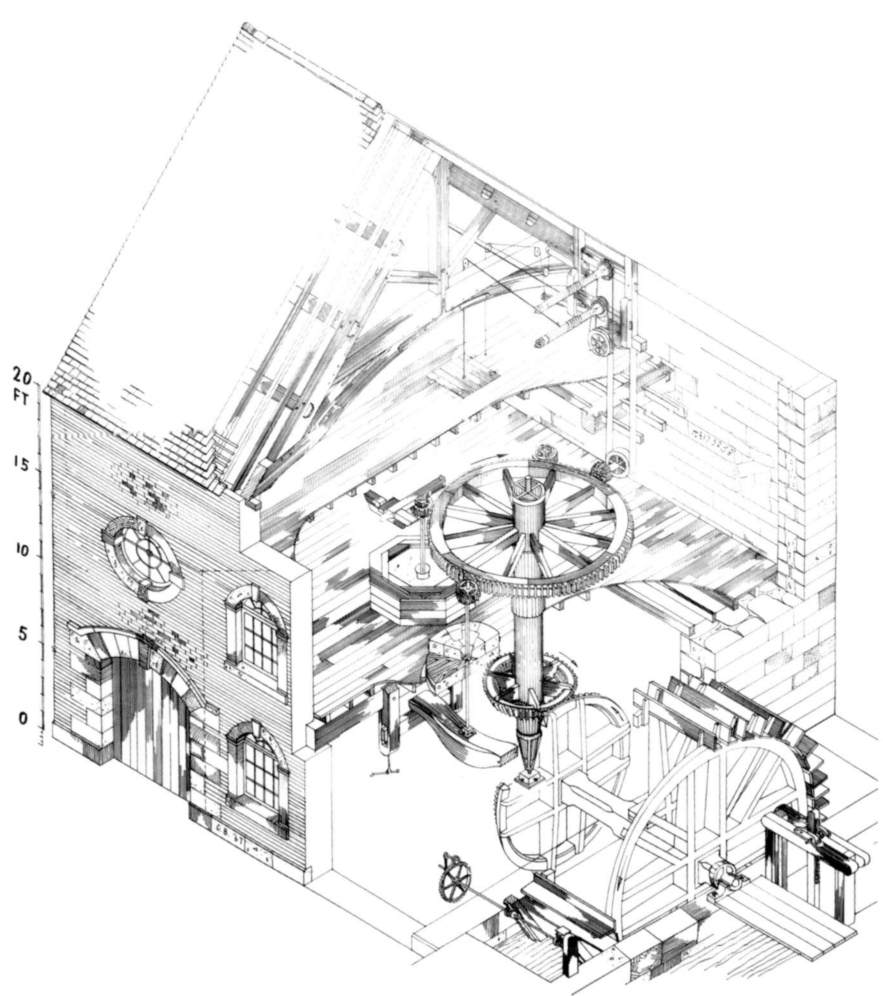

Brindley's water-mill at Leek, Staffordshire, built c1752. Two-thirds of the original building still stand and are now the Brindley Mill Museum

Courtesy of John Boucher

In both cases formal schooling was minimal but the mothers of both men ensured their sons were not illiterate. Wedgwood is said to have gone to school in Newcastle-under-Lyme when he was six, attending there for at least three years by which time his master described him as 'a fair arithmetician and master of a capital hand'. When Josiah was nine his father died and little money remained to support the family. At some time he left school to work for his brother Thomas who had inherited the family's pottery works.[10] When he was eleven, in 1741, Wedgwood was struck down by a vicious attack of smallpox, which left him in a state of deplorable weakness. His right knee was grievously harmed and when, after many weeks, he rose from his bed he found he was unable to walk because of a deadness in the limb. For a time he used crutches, but these were later discarded. At the age of fourteen a formal five-year apprenticeship was commenced, but only one year later the pain and stiffness in his right knee returned and he had to abandon altogether the potters bench with its foot-driven wheel, instead sitting at work with his leg extended before him on a stool. He was to suffer much pain during the next 22 years and his mobility was permanently hindered.[11]

Brindley found in 1750 a young Wedgwood whose vigour of mind was masked by physical weakness. Recently out of his apprenticeship and still working for his family firm, it would be another two years before Josiah became an independent potter in partnership with others in Burslem. And another two years before working with Thomas Whieldon, a highly successful potter who encouraged his prodigy to experiment and to introduce improvements in manufacturing. From these experiments it became even more evident that the importation of distant raw materials would be an on-going restriction to trade. The pressure was growing for a new transport system. The scene was set. A disabled potter and a millwright – Josiah Wedgwood and James Brindley. Only in hindsight can the potential be seen.

Chapter 4
EXPANDING HORIZONS

In the same year that James Brindley opened his Burslem workshop (1750) colliery owner John Heathcote travelled the 40 miles from Clifton, north-west of Manchester, to Hartington to attend the wedding of his nephew Michael.[1] In doing so he returned to the area on the Staffordshire/Derbyshire border where most of Brindley's work had been done, and where the millwright's abilities as an innovator were held in high regard.

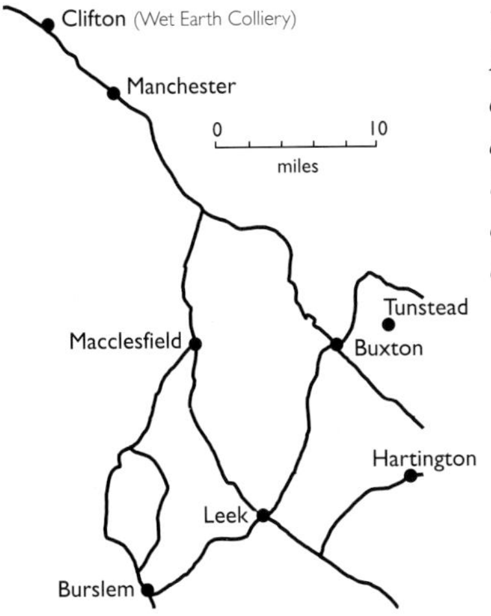

The extent of Brindley's commercial operations by 1750 and its vicinity to his birthplace at Tunstead, and his family home at Leek

The Heathcotes were an ancient north-Derbyshire family with many gentlemen in positions of administrative influence.[2] Their main area of sway was on the nearby and mighty Chatsworth estate, the home of a long line of Dukes of Devonshire – the pinnacle of land-owning power and status. An example is Geoffrey Heathcote, a lawyer of 25 years standing who, within three years, would start his tenure of 20 years as Chief Steward and Auditor to three successive Dukes – and who would later go on to play a major role in the promotion of Brindley's Chesterfield Canal.[3] To have one's name mentioned with approval in such circles was indeed advantageous, and we are told the abilities of James Brindley were discussed at the wedding to which John Heathcote travelled. There is no confirmation of this in any original documentation, but it is a credible scenario. In the centuries before instant communications, large social gatherings had an importance of almost pathetic intensity. Jane Austen portrayed in sharp detail the limitations of the rural upper-middle class – the severely curtailed association and the crushing boredom of life within a sparse population with scant transportation. For example, the Staffordshire population in 1750 has been authoritatively estimated at only 133 people per square mile. Therefore, a wedding that brought the Heathcotes together would be a valuable opportunity for the gentlemen to exchange news and gossip, and to formulate ideas on how to solve problems in their business undertakings.

The problem seriously inhibiting John Heathcote's business was the flooding of his colliery at Clifton. A single shaft, known as the Gal Pit, had been dug just over 150 feet down to the Doe seam of coal. This kind of deep-shaft mining was in its infancy, but becoming increasingly necessary as easily worked coal seams were exhausted. However, the depth of the shaft was not in itself a problem – it was the relationship between the lower levels reached and the water from the adjacent river Irwell. The soft, porous, and fissured sandstone of the river gorge allowed water to enter the mine workings. Worst of all, a great underground fault line had created steeply dipping planes into the coal measures, along which the water from the fractured river-bed flowed in great abundance. Traditional mine-drainage methods had been tried – bucket-hoists, bucket-chains powered by pit-ponies turning a gin – and steam power must also have been considered. Steam-engines were economic because they operated where their fuel was mined and they used the refuse of the coals which would not otherwise be sold.[4] In the previous thirty years many Newcomen-type steam-engines had been installed to drain collieries – in nearby Derbyshire alone, nine were already in action draining lead and coal mines, a solution still favoured in the area in the 1790s.[5] But deep mine pumping, as at Clifton, was already showing the limitations of those ponderous early manifestations of steam-power.[6] Nothing could deal with the volume of water entering the colliery. The frustration was great. Access to the deep coal had been achieved, and by the standards of the day the Gal Pit was a technical achievement of some note.[7] Nevertheless, the flooding forced the miners to work in the higher levels of the mine where the coal was only present in uneconomic quantities. As a result, John Heathcote's substantial capital investment in the Gal Pit was in jeopardy. The conditions were so bad the mine was now known as Wet Earth Colliery.

It was obvious to everyone that the flowing water of the river Irwell was a source of great power, that was as apparent then as an electricity-generation plant would be in later centuries. The power in flowing, falling water could easily be used, but where the Irwell flowed past the colliery it was 20 feet lower than the pit-head. How could it be harnessed at Wet Earth? What were the practicalities of it?

The story told is that at the wedding celebrations Brindley was recommended as the man who may be able to utilise the river to drain Wet Earth – as he was ingenious, hard working, and not afraid to face daunting challenges. It is probable that those attending would have known of Brindley's attributes, with Leek only nine miles distant. Also, the Heathcotes and their associates had many interests in north Derbyshire lead-mining and it is possible that the millwright/engineer had done some drainage work on those sites.

That James Brindley did supply the solution at Wet Earth is un-proven. Three of his biographers have told the tale, the first in 1792, but no documentary confirmation has yet come to light. The tale often told has Brindley summoned to see Heathcote, whereupon he considers in silence the plight as explained to him, eyes sparkling he announces the solution, briefly explains his ingenious plan, and is authorised to proceed to the site to put it into action. This is hardly believable. Brindley does not visit the site before announcing his plans? Heathcote does not ask for detailed cost estimates and manpower requirements? No consultation is made with Matthew Fletcher, the colliery's very able resident engineer who had sunk the deep Gal Pit in the first place? Nevertheless, there is probably some truth here, although burnished and embellished by later reflected glories. The ingenious nature of the successful scheme at Wet Earth has Brindley's hallmark on it. That he was responsible for undertaking all the work, including the tunnelling, is unlikely.

The river Irwell was unpredictable. The drainage system installed at Wet Earth would have to operate with the river at varying levels and flows, and incorporate safety features to protect the colliery from the all too common flash-flooding. During his later fame Brindley's name would become synonymous with the rigid control of water, with unstaunched flows excluded wherever possible – although this much-publicised aversion could be viewed as a prudent business promotion of what would be a new concept of stillwater canals. At this stage in his career, however, the confrontation with the Irwell at Wet Earth Colliery would bring a knowledge of the river that would be invaluable when bridging it a few years later at Barton.

However, the challenge now was a flooded deep mine and an unruly river. Accounts say Heathcote heard of Brindley's abilities in 1750 but it was another two years before work started on the celebrated drainage scheme. At the time of the initial contact the colliery owner was 55 and his on-site engineer Matthew Fletcher, although only nineteen, was a young man of great ability and of an eminent mining family. Heathcote's age may have made him cautious about more investment in an already capital-hungry project from which he had gained little reward. Brindley's boldness alone may not have sold his proposals to the older man. What is relevant is that sometime in the early 1750s Heathcote made the interests of the Clifton estate over to his young on-site engineer Matthew Fletcher.[8] A colliery closed because of flooding, with little prospect of it working again – the confidence of youth could perhaps apply a remedy. If that change of management waited for the legalities of Fletcher reaching the age of 21, then it would coincide with work commencing in 1752.

Brindley's plans for Wet Earth required a very accurate survey of the site. With long runs of flowing water as the central element it was vital that the levels of the components in relation to each other, and the capacity of each, were exactly right. To harness its power, the river at the initial point of the scheme had to be higher than the colliery's pit-head. A survey showed that by building a weir upstream of the colliery, the river's level at that point could be held higher than the pit-head, even in times of low flow – a vital requirement as water would have to be unceasingly pumped from the coal seams. The next component was a sluice on the north bank of the river above the new weir, which allowed some of the Irwell's water to drop into an 800-yard tunnel, the slope of which was less than the natural fall of the river. At the far end of the tunnel the water dropped vertically into a U-shaped complex, known as an inverted siphon. In such an arrangement water will flow through if the output point is lower than the input point, a principle known for many centuries. This feature was still in operation at Wet Earth in the early 1950s and the discharged water was noted as 'boiling up like a witch's cauldron from the hole in the ground'.[9]

In this way Brindley carried the water under the river and up onto the south bank and it was, perhaps, the origin of his epithet 'the man who made water run uphill'. From the siphon's output the water flowed along a surface channel for about one third of a mile, parallel to the river but by now 30 feet above the Irwell's naturally falling course. By staying close to the river any floodwater in the system could be released back into the Irwell via escape sluices before its disruption reached the pumping system at the colliery. When the channel was opposite the colliery it turned directly towards it for the last 700 yards. Next to the pit shaft a chamber was dug into the ground in which was installed a 22-foot diameter water-wheel. This was driven round by

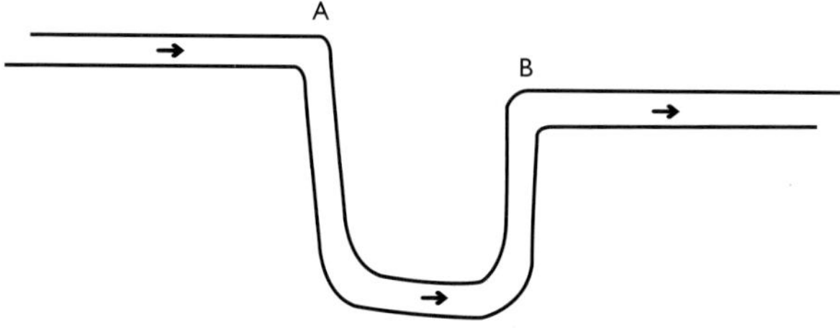

An inverted siphon - Brindley knew that water would flow through, and up from the lowest point, if the level of point A was higher than that of point B

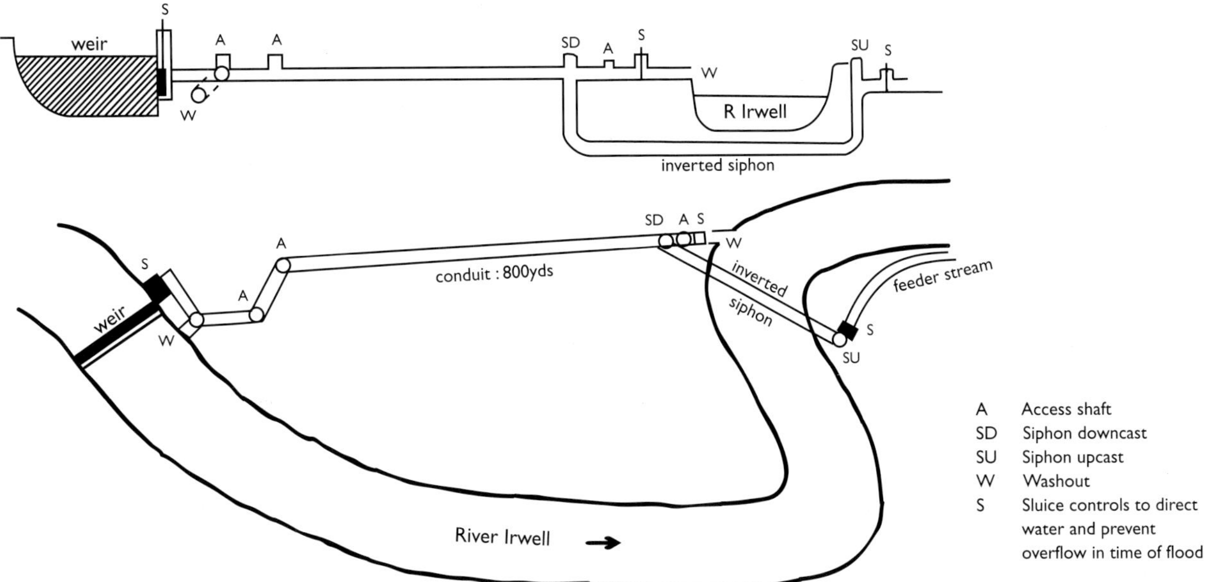

Plan of the drainage system attributed to Brindley at Wet Earth (Gal Pit) Colliery at Clifton, near Manchester

with acknowledgements to A. G. Banks and R. B. Schofield

the water arriving along the surface channels, by which means vertical wooden rods were activated, which operated bucket-pumps. The water raised from the colliery, and that which had turned the wheel, was discharged along a half-mile long channel from where it flowed back into the river.

The work was completed in 1756, four years after it commenced. The conception of the scheme, the inventive synthesis of proven components, the complete understanding of the control of flowing water, and the accurate surveying were Brindley's masterful achievements. However, there is no reason for him to have been involved in the actual construction work other than the water-wheel and its cranks and gearing. Matthew Fletcher was a very capable mining engineer who had sunk the deep Gal Pit in the first place. He and his colliers hardly needed Brindley to show them how to drive tunnels, even though these required an exactitude of incline not normally required for coal extraction. On the contrary, Brindley was presented with an important opportunity to use his natural genius for mentally recording the engineering techniques of others. It is not known how often he was on-site but the water-wheel's construction would allow him to inspect and ask about the 800-yard tunnel – built in straight sections, brick-lined, with access shafts and an accurate incline. Eight hundred yards at Clifton's Wet Earth colliery – later Brindley would build tunnels of 2,880 yards at Harecastle and Norwood.

Eminent modern engineers have rated the whole Wet Earth system highly. 'Brindley's scheme … shows a very thorough understanding of the problems of the power engineer. The prime requisites of any such water supply system must be complete reliability and exact control. The [Wet Earth] system embodies these requirements to a remarkable degree'.[10] Such praise is elevated further when the empirical nature of eighteenth century engineering is taken into consideration. Technology was local in nature, with machines and their power requirements developed for each location, even when a task was similar to elsewhere.[11] This was because the theoretical principles of hydraulics, soil mechanics and structures by which engineers may work efficiently were not correctly formulated until the latter half of the century.[12] Also, measuring machine efficiency was difficult so there were disagreements about the most suitable designs, an area in which Smeaton became a central figure with the subsequent development of evaluation procedures. As an example, views on water-wheels were widely contradictory. Smeaton pointed out that some said an undershot wheel was 6 times more efficient than an overshot one. Others said an overshot wheel was ten times more efficient than an undershot one. A difference in views of 60 to 1.[13] In such circumstances Brindley had to rely on his natural acumen, allied with experience based on careful observation, the ability to use the materials to hand, and a willingness to improvise and take reasonable risks.[14]

That he did so with remarkable success was evident by the achievements of the Wet Earth drainage scheme at Clifton. Its effect was instantaneous, and by the 1760s the colliery had been converted from one closed and almost abandoned, to one expanding into other coal seams. Matthew Fletcher's prosperity also grew and in 1763 he was able to build his imposing residence, Clifton House.[15] Overall for 40-year-old James Brindley, Wet Earth was a spectacular scheme with which to be associated and with the bonus that it was less than three miles from Worsley, the future source of his fame. There it must have come to the attention of colliery managers and land agents – and perhaps later to the ears of Brindley's future patron the Duke of Bridgewater, who was currently in Italy on the Grand Tour where he probably saw the Martesana and perhaps the Bereguardo canals with their aqueducts and pound locks.

Wet Earth colliery was exceptional in the drainage system installed, but in its pattern of ownership and funding it was a typical example of many business ventures then flourishing in Britain. Across the country local entrepreneurs, estate managers and landowners had invested their own money in enterprises of personal or local significance and their success had created a national ambience of confidence and success. But by 1750 industrial development had reached the point where the capital available to individuals was insufficient to expand the economy, no matter how assiduously they ploughed their profits back into a venture. To progress further, Britain needed major projects typified by lengthy construction timescales, and an even further period before substantial profits could be made. An example was the need for a nationwide transport system.

Elsewhere in the world such undertakings, of a magnitude beyond the scope of the business community, had been funded by the Crown, governments, taxation, wealthy aristocrats or foreign loans. The negative aspect was that those sources of finance often produced specific schemes that did not suffuse their influence throughout a country. In direct contrast, the capital-hungry projects now needed in Britain would be sourced almost entirely by private enterprise pooling its efforts to create the financial and management structures required. By coincidence, the six-year installation of the Wet Earth drainage scheme was also the period when the organisation of commerce took major steps towards the methods that would eventually make the canal age possible.

The impetus was created by the burgeoning towns. London was already a vast city dominating the southern economy, but Liverpool, Manchester and Birmingham were also growing beyond all known limits. The traditional means of supplying food for a village's inhabitants from the surrounding countryside could not meet their insatiable demands. As the agricultural hinterland grew, so the transport systems had to cope with bringing rapid and regular supplies from 30 to 50 miles away. Not only food, but also fuel both for domestic heat and for the many vital community trades – bakers' ovens, blacksmiths' forges, the vats of tanners and brewers, and brick-makers' kilns. The use of timber as a fuel had already been exhausted in most centres of population and coal was the only practical alternative in England. London drew its supplies from the coastal collieries of Newcastle, carried in fleets of vessels via the North Sea and the Thames. Ironically the growing inland northern towns had coal relatively nearby, but the local transport was either inefficient because of the hilly terrain, or constrained by monopolistic high charges – or both. If the logistical problems were not solved, the industrial potential of the area could not be realised and, in hindsight, would not break out of its northern heartland to change the world. It was vital that the economy find a way of activating a collective initiative, thereby supplying the capital required to break the transport bottleneck.[16]

Eventually the solutions evolved from precedents already set, rather than as a bolt of brilliance hitting one individual. Since the middle of the previous century some roads – by permission of Acts of Parliament – had been made into turnpikes where the Justices of the Peace in the area levied tolls on the traffic, the money being used to employ labourers on a part-time basis to maintain the road. It was only a partial success, with tolls easily evaded and highways not much improved, but it was an indicator of what could be achieved if the turnpike system was improved. The answer was the creation of Trusts to manage the turnpikes, the first of which gained parliamentary approval in 1706. The trustees of that first example were 32 men of status from the local community – landowners, lawyers, gentlemen, churchmen, inn-keepers, manufacturers – who took over the legal and practical responsibilities for a stretch of road from the Justices of the Peace. The tolls were not easily evaded as they were charged at turnpike gates, with the revenue paying the salaries of professional surveyors who in turn employed a paid workforce. The charging of tolls on public roads is always a contentious subject but it was gradually accepted that the roads must be improved and that this was the best method to date. In the first half of the eighteenth century there were, on average, ten Acts each year authorising the creation of Turnpike Trusts. London led the way with 57% of the miles making up its thirteen main routes to the provinces Trust-maintained by 1730. At the opening of the crucial period starting in 1750 it was 88%, with the industrial impetus in the north spreading the idea further afield. Such was the pressure by now for improvements to the national transport system that 1751 became the first year of the 'turnpike mania' which, by the time it abated in 1772, would see 389 Trusts in operation.[17]

The turnpiked roads were not all good but the majority were, and they tended to be the primary routes to and from the busy towns. They were capable of carrying a continuous traffic of heavy wagons and were usable throughout a normal winter, an aspect not only important for the carriage of goods but also the passing of news along the route. More passengers travelled and spread the word of developments taking place elsewhere; more newspapers were printed and circulated speedily around the country, often with inn-keepers reading them out loud to those who could not read for themselves. Traders and businessmen could more easily ride between towns to attend meetings and enhance their professions – the solitude imposed by bad communications was giving way to an economy of a larger scale. Such developments had a widespread effect and it has been estimated that by 1755 the cost of land carriage was lower than it had been at the start of the century. Furthermore, those trusted to hold the turnpike funds often fulfilled the role of a community banker, making business loans available before the professional banking system became widely established outside London. In the near future many of these financially adroit gentlemen would be appointed Treasurers of Canal Companies.[18]

However, the large scale development of the road network was in competition with the carriage of goods and passengers by water. Britain's major commercial advantage over her European rivals was her island status; moreover, an island with a coastline generously endowed with the estuaries of rivers flowing from far inland. A phenomenal tonnage of goods was carried around the coast to the ports and their inland river tendrils. For example, long distance travellers in the Midlands could make their way to the Trent, from where boats ferried them down to the Humber for transfer to coastal craft at the great port of Hull.

The Romans, Danes and Vikings all used the rivers to reach far inland, and their examples had been followed for all of the intervening centuries. However, navigation was often hindered by the weirs built across rivers to give the head of water necessary to power mills. In the Middle Ages milling was generally given priority and boats sometimes had to wait two or three days before the miller would deign to open his weir, after the payment of a fee.[19] Before the introduction of pound-locks, boats changed level at weirs by the use of water-inefficient flash-locks, a method in itself also responsible for many delays (Appendix C). Improvements were gradually made but developments were often piecemeal in nature – a well-established landowner would see the local advantages and financial returns of such an undertaking and would personally plan and supervise its construction. This approach did extend navigation further inland but it also resulted in a hotchpotch of standards, rules, tolls, and capacities. However, the standards achieved could be laudable and those responsible for the engineering were often men of great ability – Andrew Yarranton, George Sorocold and Thomas Steers were three – but the economy was not yet ready to allow their abilities to flourish at a national level. Eventually, private but powerful navigation companies evolved on many of the major rivers, their controls and tolls for boats using their waters a source of much aggravation to those dependent on them as a heavy-cargo transport route between a port and its hinterland. Some rivers were maintained by Navigation Trustees in a method similar to the turnpiked roads. The trading advantages conferred on the towns and cities on such rivers would later be the goal of those promised a canal – the scale of river engineering now taking place giving confidence to those asked to invest in such pioneering waterways. Levels deepened by weirs, pound-locks, improved banking, water–road transhipment links – all were prototypes for the future. A typical example of the large schemes now coming to the fore in the north of England was that on the Ouse in Yorkshire. The river had been made navigable to York in 1732 by the old well-proven methods, but by 1752 the new techniques of management and capital provision made major improvements possible. Competition in the area was already intense with the river Aire now navigable to Leeds, the Calder to Wakefield, and the Don to the outskirts of Sheffield. Now the Ouse Navigation Trustees agreed to fund a tidal-barrier weir at Naburn with an adjacent lock to give access to a deepened and widened river above it.[20]

However, there were two major defects in using rivers as transport routes. One – they flowed in naturally formed valleys and often not conveniently between the source of a commodity and the market for it. Two – they did flow, and boats struggling upstream found great difficulties after the winter rains, as did those carried downstream on swollen and flooded waters. Summer droughts created other problems. Typical were the Mersey and the Irwell – linking the coast and the thriving cities of Liverpool and Manchester but by-passing the almost un-tapped Lancashire coalfield. Two turnpike roads had been built, but not carefully enough to ensure their surfaces could stand the wear and tear of the volume of heavy traffic carrying coal to Liverpool, and there were vociferous protests about the resultant acute fuel shortages. Prices were also unpopular as the turnpike trustees raised their

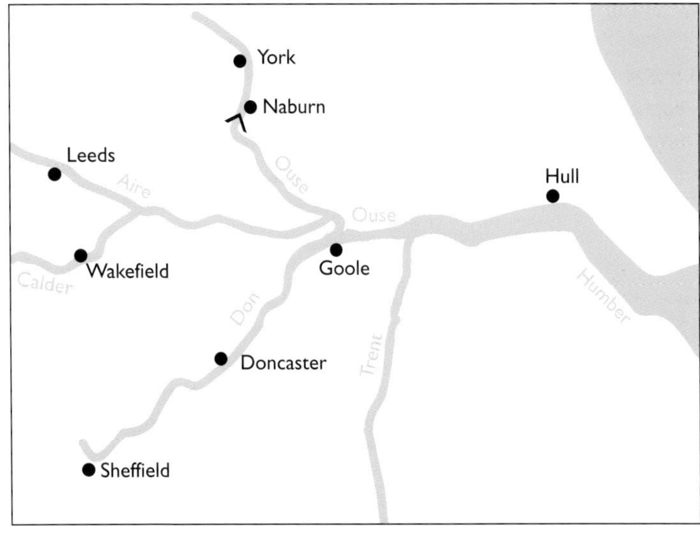

The location of the tidal-barrier weir and lock at Naburn and the major rivers flowing down to the Humber estuary

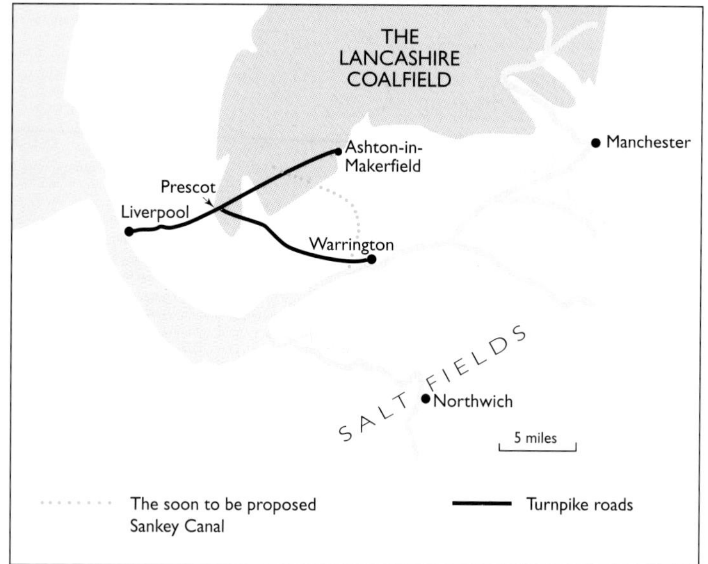

The strategically important Lancashire Coalfield and its inefficient transport system in 1753, soon to be improved by the construction of the Sankey Canal

tolls and the colliery owners loaded all their development costs onto the consumers. There was no competition to force them to do otherwise.[21]

What tended to happen in such pressurised circumstances was the extension of the tried and trusted river system. If a main river did not flow to where it was required, it probably had a tributary that did so. This was pushed to the limit with the navigation companies reaching into their catchment areas via the fine filaments of brooks and streams. This was seldom efficient, cost effective or practical – but it was nevertheless familiar and comfortable to those supplying the enabling capital. It was therefore greatly to the credit of Manchester that in January 1754 a group of its traders placed a petition before Parliament for a radical 'stillwater' canal, on which the slight flow engineered in would be insignificant when compared with natural rivers.[22] Stealing a march on their Liverpool rivals they planned a twenty-mile artificial waterway from Salford to the coalfields of Worsley, Leigh, and Wigan. If it could be achieved, the magnitude of a stillwater navigation would be difficult to comprehend as the delays and damage caused by the wayward nature of rivers had been an insurmountable fact of life for many centuries. But the promoters of the Salford Canal were politically naive. They had secured the backing of landowners along the route, including the Bridgewater estate at Worsley, but had taken no actions to quell the erroneous belief that by-passing twenty miles of the Irwell in Manchester would permanently take water from the mills, machines, engines and fisheries along that stretch of the river. Nor had they sought the opinions of those with access to power in London. The Salford Canal, portent of the future, was swiftly crushed under an avalanche of opposition in the House of Commons (Appendix D). Those who planned stillwater canals in the near future would learn from this failure – taking time to avoid anticipated objections and spreading their support networks beyond a local core before publicising their intentions.

One scheme, however, took a more surreptitious approach. Sparked into action by their rivals, and learning from their failure, the Liverpool merchants took the conventional course and looked towards the Sankey Brook as a route into the Lancashire coalfield. At its inception this appeared to be a normal scheme and the 120 shares were taken by local traders, many of them members of Liverpool Corporation. In the summer of 1754 a summary survey had been done by Henry Berry, the city's Dock Engineer. He was a confidence-inspiring choice who had been brought up near the upper reaches of the Brook and was now a locally trusted civil engineer of great ability. The lower reaches of the Brook were already navigable up to Sankey Bridges and it was assumed that this would be extended, although it was winding and, far-upstream, shallow for most of the year. The Act of Parliament necessary to carry out all such works was obtained on the 20th of March 1755 (28 Geo.II, cap. 8). It gave no hint that it would be used to create a new concept in waterborne transport and, therefore, there were no objectors to the scheme. It simply gave permission for 'making navigable the River or Brook called Sankey Brook and the Three several Branches thereof'. There were the usual clauses allowing the making of 'such new cuts ... as they shall think proper ...' – no one realised that 'such new cuts' would be linked together to form a canal independent of the Sankey Brook.

On the 5th of September 1755 work began on a waterway that would mark the transition from the improvement of rivers to the construction of canals. It would soon be seen that canals have two major advantages over rivers – but only one would be achieved by the Sankey. Liverpool was going to create a stillwater canal. No more battling against flows, no more varying water speeds around bends, no more floods – and a capacity for craft up to 68 feet long and 16 feet 9 inches wide. It would be at a higher level than the brook so weirs and sluice-gates could drain excess water from one to the other. For the first time a constant water-supply was a necessary facet of the planning process. For some lengths the canal would cling to the side of the brook's valley, climbing 60 feet from the Mersey via nine locks. The bridges would swing clear to allow boats to sail when there was enough wind. Soon warehouses and wharfs would rise along its straight, man-made banks. The advantages would be many. Nevertheless, the existing methods of water transport were so entrenched that it is likely that, had Berry's plans become known, many investors would have removed their funding, the recent frightening

Manchester example making opinions even more immovable. But he confided in, and was supported by, one of their number, probably John Ashton who held 51 of the 120 shares. Ashton's backing was vital and allowed Berry to proceed with his bold plan without further recourse to Parliament for added permissions.[23]

So by some subterfuge the Sankey Canal had, by the end of 1757, reached into the Lancashire coalfield and was efficiently and cost-effectively carrying coal down its ten miles to the Mersey from where it was taken to satisfy Liverpool's constant craving. Soon the tolls charged by the turnpike trustees were lowered, but too late – the future was almost upon them.

The Sankey Canal – innovative, but still duplicating the course of a natural waterway

However, the Sankey went only halfway to achieving the canal breakthrough because it was still bound to the course of the brook from which it took its name. The further step to a canal striking out to take an artificial course was a few years away. In the same year as the Liverpool promoters of the Sankey Brook ostensibly received parliamentary permission to improve a natural waterway (1755), the merchants of that same city teetered on the edge of a much bolder move. The idea was to link the Mersey to the Trent and, thereby, Liverpool to Hull. The two ports were thriving – both were vital access points to internal and coastal national trade, and both were crucial portals for the transhipment of international cargoes. Liverpool looked west to the rich and productive American colonies – Hull east to Europe, war permitting. If goods could be carried safely between them without the delays and dangers of an 800+ mile sea passage then there would be great gains to be made; not only for the two ports but also the towns along the route that would gain access to them – Chester, Stafford, Derby and Nottingham. The concept was proved to be practicable by a survey carried out by Mr Eyes of Liverpool and Mr Taylor of Manchester. In 1755 the idea was right, but the time was still wrong – lack of widespread belief that such a project was viable preventing investment. Two years later a second survey gave the door another push. The vision was there – they were not alone in knowing what was required – but without a successful example to follow, the financial risks involved in a full-scale canal scheme proved to be unacceptable.[24]

How matters would develop was still in the balance. The pressure was intense – the new transport schemes frequent and ambitious. The north-west of England was going to produce some answer, the powerful rivalry of Liverpool and Manchester would ensure that. There had to be some way of quietening the loud protests about incessant shortages. Many looked to new ideas, many others preferred the proven route. For every futuristic concept there was one looking backwards – such as the previous year's (1754) discussions about a second scheme to carry the coal from the Duke of Bridgewater's Worsley mine down an improved Worsley Brook, the first having come to nothing in 1737. Again the Mersey & Irwell Navigation Company was in favour because it would bring more coal to their rivers for onward carriage with the subsequent increase in the volume of toll income. Again the plan failed. If it had succeeded, the impetus for the Duke of Bridgewater to build his canal would have been reduced, thereby removing the successful example that eventually blew open the door to the canal age. When its time came, the Bridgewater would be a clarion call to action – a stillwater canal that would boldly take its own route, crossing rivers and valleys on its artificial way from the Worsley coalfield to the city of Manchester and then towards Liverpool.

The country was changing rapidly. Soon canals would transform the navigable lengths of rivers into a linked network of waterways. We can only surmise what James Brindley saw of the new Sankey Canal whilst travelling to see customers. There was as yet no hint of his future path to fame, but as a millwright he would have had a trained interest in locks with their water controls and level-setting weirs. Aware of the opportunities created by the thriving business atmosphere, he had an open mind about the type of work he should undertake. Mills would continue to be his basic stock in trade but it is indicative of his acceptance of bold fresh ideas that he now strode along a new avenue; not to waterways – but to steam-power.

Chapter 5

ON THE BRINK OF FAME

In 1756 Brindley was a self-employed craftsman working for many different customers in a relatively small area near his Burslem and Leek workshops. So far the picture of his life has had to be assiduously pieced together from various sparse sources, with care taken to avoid the cursory look often dazzled by subsequent fame, but an unhindered view of the next nine years comes into focus because his personal notebooks have survived. They show that as he became busier he employed men to carry out some of the work, although still maintaining a close control over each project. To keep track of personal finances he jotted down reminders – how many days work done, for whom and at what cost, how much paid to his workmen, and outgoings for lodgings and stabling.[1]

After the winter months of January and February it was a year of high productivity with working days accounting for 66 per cent of the remaining ten months, including Saturdays and Sundays. It was as a millwright that Brindley continued to earn most of his income, with the majority of his time charged to mill owners in Ashbourne, Bucknall, Congleton, and Abbey Hulton. Although his skills in such work were exceptional, it was James Brindley's acceptance of new challenges that showed him to be a man of very special qualities. He was an artisan and in its strictest sense that denomination is accurate; Brindley certainly was a skilled craftsman, but in current usage it also has unwarranted connotations of traditional methods and materials, an aversion to change, an unawareness of the latest technologies. In Brindley's case it is often used as redolent of a 'north-country bumpkin' when compared to the engineering methods of his contemporary, the Royal Society groomed John Smeaton, who was undertaking European tours, studying the French language and producing erudite scientific papers. An acceptance of this patronising judgement does a disservice to both men.

James Brindley was a successful mill engineer with a highly valued reputation for fine work. Many would be content with those achievements, but at the age of 40 James Brindley embarked on a different means of carrying out his life's work – that is moving water from where it was unharnessed to where it could be productive – by designing and installing steam-powered pumping engines. The concept was not new, as engines of the type developed by Thomas Newcomen had been working in the coal-bearing regions of the country since early in the century. Nevertheless, some saw that the efficiency of such engines could be improved and it was this aim that Brindley now approached with his usual confidence.[2] New principles had to be understood but when compared with the technology of water-driven mills, which was at its pinnacle, steam-power was still in its foothills.

The lumbering machines had a great beam of timber that rocked high above the ground on a pivot supported by masonry. One end of the beam was connected to a piston

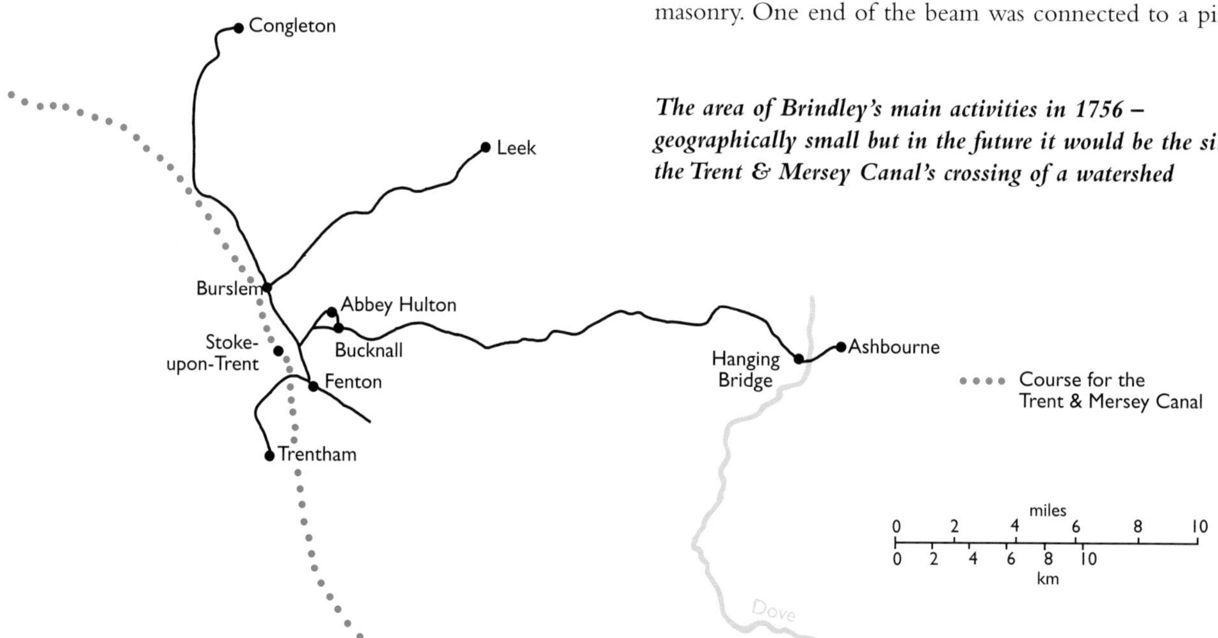

The area of Brindley's main activities in 1756 – geographically small but in the future it would be the site of the Trent & Mersey Canal's crossing of a watershed

that moved up and down in a cylinder as steam was injected and condensed, so the timber beam rocked, thereby also moving up and down the pump-rods attached to the other end of it. The movement of the pump-rods drew the flood-water up a pipe in the mine-shaft.[3] Once above ground the water could either be used to create the steam for the engine or put to some other use. Either way, it was out of the colliery where it had been hindering coal extraction. It was a circle of power, which would have appealed to Brindley – the engine needed water and coal, from them it produced steam, by which it made available water and coal in greater quantities than it used. There were already a number of such engines in his home area of the Staffordshire–Derbyshire borders and it is almost certain he would have found the opportunity to inspect, mentally record and discuss the machinery involved.

The first steam commission Brindley received was to build an engine to drain Thomas Broad's colliery at Fenton, near Burslem. The learning curve was steep but fulfilling, although it would entail a good deal of travelling.

In the middle of March 1756 two days were charged for going to and from Knypersley for a pump. A little over a week later it was to Bakewell for boiler plates – another two days. At the end of the month it took three days to visit a forge somewhere in Cheshire. Interspersed among these were two visits, of three days each, to work on a mill for George Goodwin at Ashbourne, which was another large project. Back to Fenton on the 1st of April to spend a day counting the bricks for the engine-house pit – this so-called ill-educated man able to add the 1,630 needed for the 'firehole' to the 1,550 in the foundations. Then another two days at Bakewell 'about the boiler plates to be made', to the Ashbourne mill for four days, and then immediately off on a long ride to Nottingham to obtain more parts. Juggling the two substantial assignments was arduous, with work on Mr Goodwin's mill lasting until October, during which time Brindley had at least four men working for him on that site.[4]

It is not known what this busy period was doing to his health – riding long distances in all weathers, eating when he could, facing the pressures of a new challenge – but during that year he did write in his notebook cures for 'the gravel', the ague and a painful back. It is to be hoped that he did not suffer from all three at the same time.[5]

Meanwhile, the steam project needed more knowledge. After one day at the Ashbourne mill, probably to check that the work there was well in-hand, Brindley made a final assessment at Fenton before riding on a circular tour of the Midlands to see engines already at work.[6] The first destination was Bedworth and the most obvious route was along the valley of the river Trent, via Great Haywood which would later become the junction of his Trent & Mersey and Staffordshire & Worcestershire canals. Travelling on horseback at the slow pace of a long journey a rider is part of his surroundings and sees it as geography rather than scenery. From the road, which kept to the ground a little higher than the river, Brindley would have been able to see the levels and water-flows of the central section of the Trent's valley. A millwright with his natural talent for such matters could hardly do otherwise.

The first stop was Lichfield, then one of the largest and wealthiest towns in Staffordshire with its beautiful cathedral and an erudite population – clerics, lawyers, scholars, men of science. One of its sons, the oft-quoted Dr Samuel Johnson, would soon say 'We are a city of philosophers. We work with our heads and make the boobies of Birmingham work for us with their hands.' Brindley would visit Lichfield again when it became the source of much of the funding for the Trent & Mersey Canal. But now he merely bought a pair of shoes and carried on to Bedworth for an overnight stay.[7]

The 28th of April 1756 was a busy day for James Brindley. It is thought that in the morning he went to Bedworth's Exhall Colliery to look at an engine, the cylinder of which had been cast at Coalbrookdale. Perhaps he met Henry Beighton, the steam-engine expert who lived nearby at Griff.[8] Later he rode on to

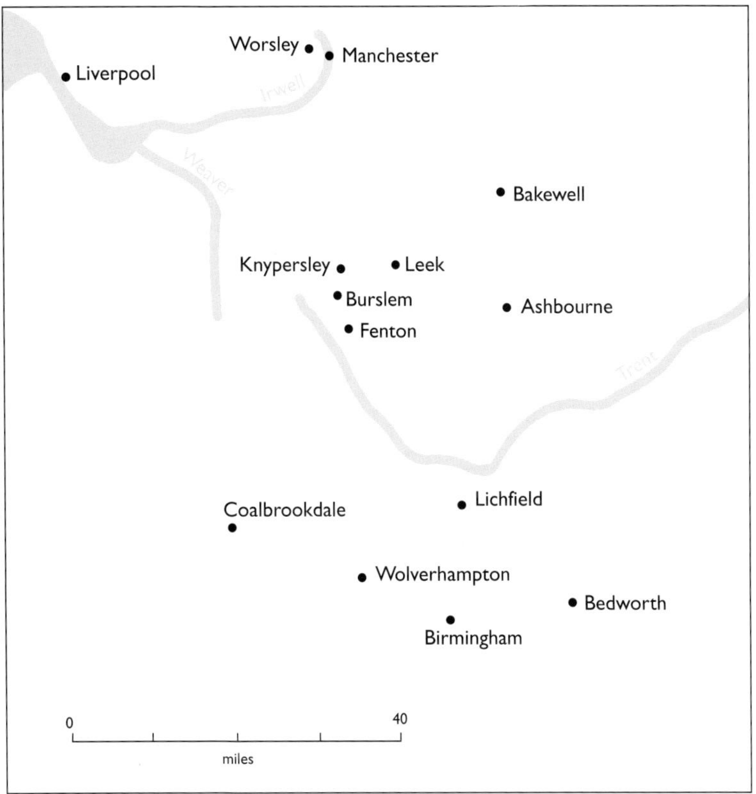

Brindley's travels in April 1756

Birmingham and then to Wolverhampton, via Tipton, which was the site of Newcomen's original engine. The next day he returned to Fenton.

It was a successful tour and the enlightenment was more valuable than Brindley could yet know. The solutions incorporated into his engine at Fenton over the next six days were uppermost in his mind, but stored in his memory was the topography of the country through which he had journeyed. In addition to the strategic central section of the Trent valley, he had ridden from Birmingham to Wolverhampton along the future route of his Birmingham Canal. The collieries of Bedworth and Griff would gain the benefit of his Coventry Canal. And the journey home from Wolverhampton was along the river Penk valley, which would form the northern part of the Staffordshire & Worcestershire Canal.

Work continued on the steam-engine for Thomas Broad – in July 'felling big trees' took three and a half days, and Derby was visited for some unknown reason in September. On the 3rd of October 1756 James Brindley had a meeting with Mr Broad that may have marked the completion of the construction phase, with an £80 per annum agreement for the next fifteen years to cover all repairs and the provision of men to operate the engine (Appendix E). It must have been a success because although mill work still took up most of his time it was not to be that way the next year. Miss Clara Maria Broad, possibly a relative of Thomas Broad, commissioned a steam-engine for her colliery at nearby Fenton Vivian. The 26th of February 1757 was the start of two years very hard work, the first ten months especially so. At the end, when Brindley calculated his account he would charge £164 for the first year, noting that it was for 'night and day'.[9] But, not knowing that at the outset, he also started work on a new flint-mill for Mr Baddeley at Tunstall, the other side of Burslem. One day 'drawing a plan' for the mill, the next day making pipes for the engine.[10]

Brindley was employing more men now, so work continued while he was busy elsewhere. His home was still at Leek but Brindley was hardly ever there.[11] He stayed in lodgings, which was cheaper than prolonged stays at the inns that generally catered for those travelling through. On his longer journeys, overnight stays at inns would have meant meals with the landlord and his family in a parlour or a kitchen, after personally ensuring his horse was comfortable and well fed and watered. Many visitors to England commented on the kindness shown to horses by their riders, blacksmiths and stableboys.[12] At the end of April 1757 he stopped at the flint-mill for a quick inspection of the building foundations before riding to Coalbrookdale, one of the many places since hailed as 'the birthplace of the Industrial Revolution'.

The improvements made in the iron trade had required considerable periods of experimentation with little return on the capital invested. As such, it was well suited to the sound business judgement of the Quakers whose ventures into industry were carefully thought out to ensure compliance with their sense of social and spiritual truth.[13] For over fifty years the Darby family had assiduously tried different methods of smelting and casting iron – originally making pots, kettles and other small objects for sale at fairs and markets.[14] Gradually the trade changed to producing large cast-iron items for a wide range of newly emergent industries. The technology of steam was still at the experimental stage with engineers trying different construction materials for the most problematic elements – the boiler and the cylinder. The first had to hold the steam under pressure without bursting or losing heat; the second had to be made with fine accuracy, not allowing steam to escape past the piston that moved up and down within it. Various combinations of wood, iron and brick were tried in construction and cladding. Every engine was different in size and design so every component had to be made to order – with Coalbrookdale the leading source of what was made from cast-iron.

Iron-master Abraham Darby II was the current head of a family of sincere and scrupulous Quakers that had

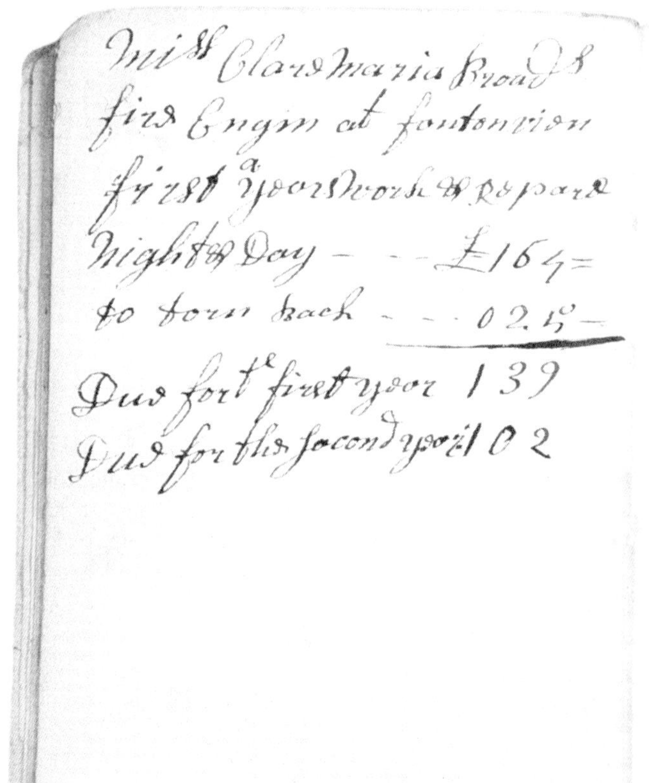
Miss Clara maria Broad Dr
firs Engin at fonton vion
first a years work & Repare
night & Day - - £164 =
to torn back - - 02.15 -
Due fort first year 139
Due for the second year 102

In his notebook for 1758–60 James Brindley calculates his charges for work done for Miss Broad at Fenton Vivian

Courtesy of the Institution of Civil Engineers, Archives

drawn others of the sect to Coalbrookdale as workmen, partners and managers. There was fellowship and equality among them within a structure almost domestic in nature.[15] Abraham's wife Abiah invited all visitors to her table, be they merchants, technicians, retailers – or a millwright building a steam-engine. She said a few words of advice or ministry before meals and those present accepted the simplicity and grace of the household.[16] Although all were welcome, the natural affinity of Quakers was to those who shared their beliefs, or at least their ethics and standards. James Brindley's upbringing and background must have been advantageous on his visits to Coalbrookdale – perhaps leading to talk of the Leek household where Abraham and Abiah first met, and where their hosts were friends of Brindley's Quaker relatives.[17] Such affability was important as the Darby family was also the hub of a vast network of visiting Quaker business contacts who also attended their religion's monthly meetings wherever they travelled. Coalbrookdale was a clearing-house of knowledge, finance and personality assessments. Opportunities would come to those who were like-minded.

Often present on business matters was Joseph Whitfield, a leading Quaker and a close friend of Abraham Darby. As the London Lead Company's agent in Derbyshire he was interested in improving the transport from Chesterfield, a town in which there was an influential Quaker presence.[18] His attention turned first to turnpikes and the river Idle; later to a canal – which would have to be built by a man of proven ethical Quaker-like values.[19]

The work on Miss Broad's steam-engine commenced after the winter when materials could more easily be moved to the site at Fenton Vivian, five miles south of Burslem. After two visits to Coalbrookdale everything was at hand for three weeks of making pipes and cylinder-hooping. The engine-house was built in late spring and trees were purchased to provide the large timbers required. In the long summer days progress was swift with five days hooping the piston and another five raising the 'great beam', which was fortunate because the last six months of 1757 would be full of frustration. For six weeks in July and August the notebooks contain only the terse comment 'about the boiler'. Everything was taking more time. The workforce employed was now quite numerous but the problems being experienced meant Brindley was continually on site – his horse permanently out to grass. By November the engine was in steam but there were serious problems with the cistern – the component vital to efficient operation. 'Bad luck' was all he could bring himself to write on two occasions. But they were followed by six days of 'middling luck'. During the short daylight hours of December Brindley worked on the cistern continuously for 22 days.[20]

Somehow a few days were found to do various tasks at Mr Baddeley's new flint-mill near Tunstall: drawing plans, setting out the millrace, employing a brickmaker, paying £2.6s.0d for cow-hides, which were used to line buckets and parts of a pump. He also calculated that 38 pounds of brasses, at 14d a pound, would cost him £2.4s.4d.[21]

Finally, on the 19th of March 1758, Brindley could write 'engine at work – 3 days', which it continued to do for another three weeks until he thought it in 'good order' in the middle of April. A few days later, among a list of payments made to his workmen, Brindley wrote 'to running about and drinking, 1s.6d'.[22] Whether he bought drinks for himself, his men, or everyone together, it matters not. It was a well-earned celebration at the end of an arduous, but successful, enterprise.

Although still describing himself as a millwright, James Brindley was now a successful and ambitious businessman who had moved into another sphere of operations – while prudently maintaining his core profession. He had a workforce of about 20 men on a freelance basis and was purchasing materials from a wide variety of suppliers, including items to the value of almost £100 from Coalbrookdale within a few months, an amount equivalent to around £8,000 today. On-going maintenance contracts, including the provision of a permanent workforce, brought an income guaranteed for a number of years. That safeguard allowed him to promote his engines as the way forward. Five months after the celebrations at Fenton Vivian, and knowing there were business opportunities beyond draining mines, he lodged a patent for a steam-engine the benefits of which, he stated, would include pumping water along pipes to supply cities, towns and ornamental gardens. (Appendix E).[23]

Looking forward with confidence over a wider field, he could not know that steps towards his future fame had already been taken. The previous year his future patron, the Duke of Bridgewater, had reached the age of 21 and had taken direct control of his Worsley estate.[24] Furthermore, in February 1758, in the midst of the darkest days when his second steam-engine was causing so much frustration, James Brindley had been employed to survey the central section of the Trent & Mersey Canal.

Chapter 6
A CANAL FOR THE NATION

When considering inland navigation in Brindley's era it is necessary to understand the interconnection of not only canals and rivers but also the sea. The trade carried by coastal shipping was very great, with vessels calling at ports of varying status all around Britain's shores as well as sailing inland up the largest rivers. Although paradoxical, the sea should be viewed as the third element of the network of inland navigations, its waters so important to the nation, both economically and logistically. Only when this is realised can the development of canals be seen in its correct perspective. 'From the point of view of inland navigation the sea becomes merely a river round England, a river with peculiar dangers, peculiar conditions, and peculiar advantages' (T.S. Willan).[1]

The course of a potential water route across England to link the great ports of Liverpool and Hull was obvious – the gap between the already navigable river Weaver and the river Trent was only ten miles geographically. In practice it was wider, as the Trent was generally navigable only to Wilden Ferry, and to a lesser-used extent to Burton. How two rivers flowing to the west and east coasts could be linked across the watershed near Burslem remained open to question, although the Liverpool-financed preliminary surveys in 1755 and 1757, by Taylor and Eyes, had shown the project was viable. Now, in 1758, there came a further impetus from the east with Henry Bradford's proposal that the Trent be made navigable as far as Stoke, by the traditional method of extending the use of rivers. To lend credibility to this plan it was referred to John Smeaton who estimated eight locks and one staunch would be required.[2]

But schemes emanating from either end of the route had the disadvantage of being planned and judged from the biased viewpoint of those with vested interests to the west or east of the watershed. Those with capital invested in the infrastructure of river navigations saw a link across the hills as an opportunity to increase their own returns, as did the various merchants and manufacturers who were reliant on the Mersey, Weaver or Trent as trading outlets. Whereas the clearest picture, metaphorically and actually, was seen from the hills of Staffordshire, which divided the two river systems. Here too the clearest need was identified – by those who had no water-borne transport of any kind to aid their business ventures. In their hilly central position they were relatively free of other influences and had no wish to import the natural problems and monopolistic practices of river navigations. Instead, the Staffordshire gentlemen saw the advantages of stillwater canals and as an initial step asked James Brindley to survey the Trent valley from near Burslem to Wilden Ferry.

At this early stage the impetus was provided by Earl Gower and Lord Anson – typical examples of the nobility of the time, members of which often used their influence to promote projects that brought benefits not only to themselves but to the local area where they continued to reside. Brindley was well placed to win the surveying assignment – he had installed pumps on Earl Gower's Trentham estate and had built a steam-driven engine for another leading advocate of the scheme, colliery owner Thomas Broad.[3] Installing pumps and building steam-powered engines may not sound like qualifications for surveying for a canal but Brindley's millwright's eye for levels and

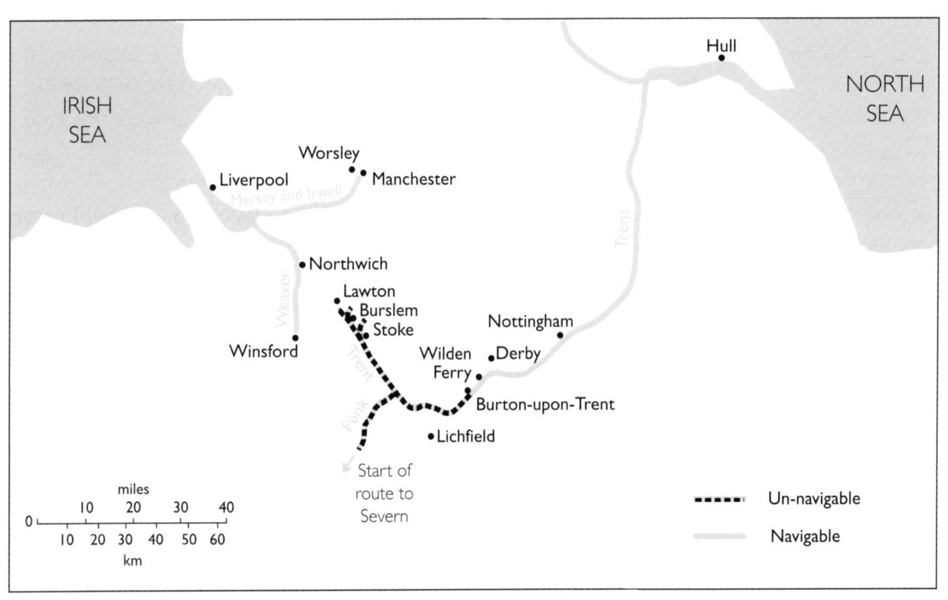

The close proximity of the rivers Trent and Weaver and their navigable state in 1758

water supplies was just what was needed. He also had the benefit of being the local engineer.

The outmanoeuvred backers of the aborted Salford Canal had shown how not to promote a radical and capital-hungry project such as a stillwater canal. On the other hand twelve miles of the new Sankey Canal were there as an example of how to achieve that aim. By employing their own city's docks engineer to survey and build their canal, the merchants of Liverpool had curtailed public discussion until they deemed it expedient. In the same way a well-established millwright could ride through the countryside and cast his eye over the landscape – seeking out small watercourses, checking flows, noting the type of soil, the availability of timber and stone. It was what millwrights always looked at. Later Brindley would be famed for his ability to see the best route for a canal by riding to look at the countryside, leaving his surveyors to do the detailed work. For Earl Gower and the small group of Staffordshire gentlemen quietly examining the feasibility of a Trent & Mersey Canal, trustworthy and local James Brindley was just the man.

Paper in the eighteenth century was expensive and as a consequence it was not used in today's profligate manner. A typical personal notebook of the time eventually had every page covered with jottings or diary entries; every inch used including later thoughts vertically in the margins. Brindley's notebook was no exception and he only started a new page when he thought it would be justified by on-going work for a specific project, thereby making the charges for his work easier to calculate with all the entries grouped together. He had done so for Miss Broad's, by now infamous, steam-powered engine. Now, on the 18th of February 1758, he turned to a new page, at the top of which he wrote the heading 'Surveying the Navigation from Long brigg to Kings Mills or Inspected' (on the river Trent near Burslem to just upstream of Wilden Ferry). Under which the first entry was a note to charge for 12½ days work. Not only did he start a new page, he even left the next one blank as well – a clear indication that he thought the canal work would bring a significant amount of work over a period of time.[4] It eventually did – but not before he had started a new notebook, leaving the two blank pages to tell their story.

That judgement of the potential success of the Trent & Mersey scheme was mirrored by the other gentlemen involved. However, with past lessons in mind, they took their time – quietly gathering opinions and priming those in positions to help, until, ten months after Brindley's survey, they were eventually ready to make a public announcement. On the 7th and 8th of December 1758 newspapers in London and around the country carried a prominent account of what was proposed. It was a masterpiece of political expediency. Prudent national figures, and that included Earl Gower, do not publicly put their name to anything radical that may fail at the first hurdle – instead the headlines were of 'Mr Broade's Scheme' which was anonymously supported by 'other publick spirited Gentlemen' in Staffordshire. Another name missing was that of their millwright surveyor – an astute move because it meant nothing to the national readership and an unknown in such a vital role would have aroused otherwise dormant doubts.[5]

At this early stage the Trent & Mersey as it would eventually be built was far too complex an idea. Instead it was suggested that a canal be constructed along the Trent valley between Stoke and Wilden Ferry, as surveyed by Brindley. This was to be 40 miles long, 24 feet wide, and 3 feet deep, with pound-locks to make the water 'as dead as the Canals in Holland', and aqueducts to allow the disorderly waters of rivers and streams to pass underneath. The commercial virtues and financial rewards that would come to all the towns near the Trent were extolled in some detail before a further tempting element was introduced. It would be possible, it was stated somewhat coyly, to make this Trent canal 'communicate with the Cheshire Rivers', by which they meant the Weaver and subsequently the Mersey. It was not stated how this could be done, not only because that sort of detail would have frightened possible investors, but also because, as shown by later correspondence, no decision had yet been made on how a canal could cross the watershed. Undaunted, the article hastened on like an over-eager salesman – explaining that if the expense of linking to the Cheshire rivers was thought too great then the Trent canal could be extended to Burslem, and a second canal dug from Northwich, on the river Weaver, to Lawton. The two canals would be linked across five miles of the watershed by 'a new road for Carriages and Horses ... through Harecastle-Vale'.[6]

Having covered the main Liverpool–Hull route another component was mentioned – again diffidently, almost as an after-thought – although it must already have been an integral part of their wider vision. In 1716 Thomas Congreve, a Wolverhampton doctor, had published a pamphlet on making a navigable link between the rivers Trent and Severn, tributaries of which would be used wherever possible with very short lengths of canal joining the upper waters.[7] This proposal was obviously well known because it was referred to with no explanation of what it entailed. However, the advocates of water transport had already divided into two exclusive factions – one favouring the extension of navigation along rivers, as in Dr Congreve's pamphlet, the other rejecting such old methods, instead proposing the new concept of totally artificial stillwater canals that would eventually form an inland network linked only to the most major of rivers, and thereby the coastal trade. Firmly in the second camp, Thomas Broad and his associates used Dr Congreve's name to introduce the long accepted idea of a Severn–Trent navigation but amended it to suggest a stillwater canal could be built along the same route at a quarter of the cost. By adding that waterway to their proposals they could bring the industrial areas of Wolverhampton and Birmingham into the picture, promising them an easy trade outlet to the 'Western Nations' via Liverpool.[8]

How the funding capital for either scheme was to be raised was left unsaid. Even at the optimistic estimate of £40,000 for the Trent canal alone it was beyond the means of the Staffordshire promoters, therefore subscriptions would be needed, but where such investors could be found was still unclear. The response to the newspaper announcement would give an indication of the country's favour, disapproval or inertia. To round off matters the account ended by extolling the virtues of the scheme to the nation, one of which was said to be a ready supply of men familiar with boats to augment the Navy in times of war, instead of their 'becoming Vagabonds, Poachers, and Thieves'. Finally it was hoped that 'this truly useful and noble Design' would meet with 'all possible Encouragement and Support from every publick-spirited Person'.[9]

Involvement in this project of national significance, and the implied trust of the influential men driving it forward, marked a turning point in James Brindley's career but there was little he could do in 1758 to take it further. Having done the survey, it was now being fought over in the commercial and political arenas where the outcome of this particular bout was still uncertain. Nevertheless, he had joined the stillwater canal camp and would make its creed his own, becoming known for his adamant condemnation of uncontrolled running water. Conversely John Smeaton had become the professional voice of the rivers' lobby and was currently discussing an engineering contract to improve the Calder & Hebble Navigation in Yorkshire. Notably, Smeaton gave credit to the profession of millwright by choosing one to be his on-site assistant, the man who would be responsible for the practical day-to-day engineering work – Joseph Nickalls having shown his skill by carrying out difficult sluicework in a masterly fashion.[10]

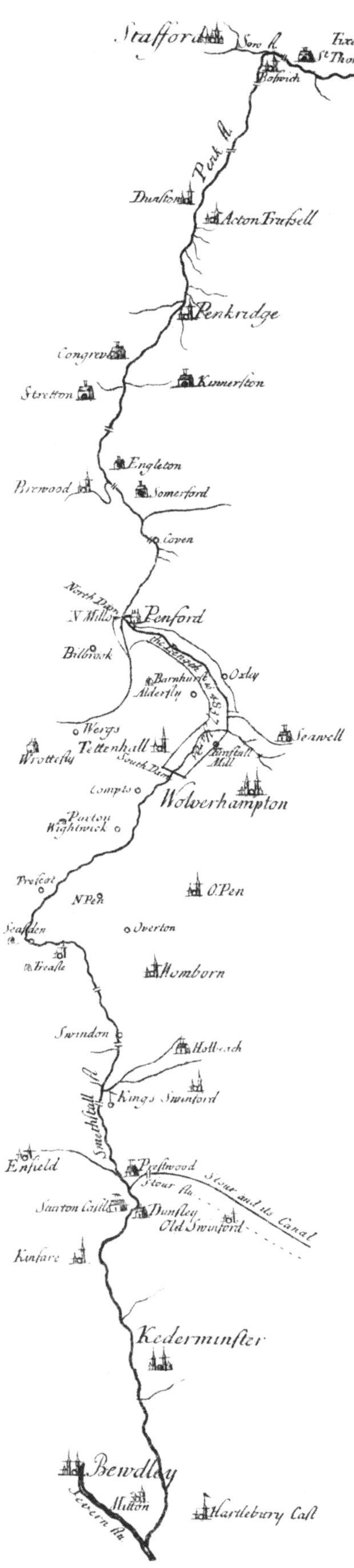

Meanwhile, self-employed Brindley had to earn a living. The flints used by the pottery trade were first heated to burn off impurities then taken to water-mills to be ground down to a fine powder before being added to the clay. The dust produced was injurious to health so the grinding process was done in vats of water, an innovation often erroneously credited to Brindley. What he did do, whilst waiting for news from the canal lobby, was design an ingenious 'stamping' system to increase a mill's crushing power.[11] In addition three mill contracts, steam engine maintenance, and pump inspections on Earl Gower's estate near Burslem, added to the success of Brindley's business ventures.[12] His contacts in Burslem were not yet significant in the promotion of canals as the pottery trade was not at the forefront of matters. His friend Josiah Wedgwood, who would later play a pivotal role when the Trent & Mersey project came to fruition, was now only 28 years old and although having established an excellent reputation locally had yet to start his career as an independent potter.[13] It is said, however, that Brindley built a flint-mill powered by the wind for the Wedgwoods, although there is no mention of this in his notebook. Of greater power than any yet known in the district, it also supplied water to the grinding-vats from a well within its walls. Its sails were like those of a yacht and were unusually large. Having exceeded conventional tolerances the mill failed in the first high wind when the sails were blown away. The repairs were somewhat lengthy but in time the windmill became one of the most valuable in the Potteries, producing high volumes of ground flints for the expanding Wedgwood range of products.[14]

A section of Thomas Congreve's map, showing his 1716 proposal for a waterway link between the rivers Trent and Severn

Flint, used by potters to whiten products. In its natural state** (left) **and after heating and ready for grinding at a water-mill** (right)**. Brindley designed a system to increase a mill's crushing power

The first half of 1759 also had many days with steam-engines, including a number of visits to Coalbrookdale to discuss and order various castings for them. These seem to be less innovative than those installed for the Broad family, with Brindley spending little time on site at Cheadle in Cheshire, and Bedworth and Little Wyrley near Birmingham.[15] Picking up business wherever he could, Brindley would have known the significance to his career of an intriguing reference in his notebook in another's handwriting for 'Mr Brindley to be at J Gilbert's' on the night of 7 March 1759 to travel to Ecton the next day.[16] The importance of the meeting as an opportunity for advancement would have been obvious. John Gilbert was Agent for the Duke of Bridgewater's Worsley estate near Manchester, and the owner of limekilns at Ecton, the meeting an opportunity to solicit Brindley's opinions and abilities on engineering matters.[17] The millwright would have known of the duke's intention to build a canal as it had already been announced and the Royal Assent to an initial Act of Parliament was imminent, although the magnitude of the proposals which would eventually be of national consequence were still a closely held secret. That Brindley was known at Worsley is not surprising – his influential supporter Earl Gower was married to the Duke of Bridgewater's sister and had been one of the duke's three guardians. Also, the Earl's estate at Trentham on which Brindley often worked was managed by Thomas Gilbert, brother of John at Worsley.

Even so, Brindley cautiously continued to keep high volumes of the type of work to which he owed his success. Altogether this was a period of consolidation with the 43-year-old millwright securing contracts, and contacts, on great estates. He had a workforce to carry out on-going tasks but a great deal of travelling was still necessary – to Coalbrookdale in Shropshire, Worsley near Manchester, a silk-mill at Congleton in Cheshire, steam-engine installations near Birmingham and to Gloucestershire to order pipes.[18] And he was wise to do so. At the close of the 1750s the construction of a canal to link the Trent and the Mersey had been judged physically possible – but it remained politically unproven, both locally and at Westminster, and was still hindered by uncertain public acceptance. How the finance could be raised was also an unresolved fundamental problem. Essentially the scheme was floundering because England was not a nation in the modern sense, instead it was still a collection of parochial interests within which local advantage had traditionally been channelled into funding turnpike roads and river improvements. The magnitude of a plan with strategic national ramifications was far too bold to herald the canal age. Instead of the well proven social channels of change there would be a need for complex management structures and widespread capital investment to carry the project through, both of which were unfamiliar, adding to the general doubts. That a canal of the type proposed could be seen in France – the Canal du Midi, with its aqueducts, locks and tunnels – was of no consequence. A virulent dislike of the Catholic French had thrived through many conflicts, and the two countries were again at war after battles in the American colonies. Recently Admiral Rodney's fleet had bombarded Le Havre, destroying a French force preparing to invade Britain. Brest was still blockaded, and in October would come news of General Wolfe's great victory at Quebec, which pushed the French out of Canada. Flags were flown, fireworks set off, crowds sang in the streets, and the taverns stayed open all night.[19] It was no time to suggest that people should follow the lead of Europe. The intolerant national mood was dangerous, with any person heard talking other than English often challenged physically with a snarled 'speak your damned French if you dare'.[20] The only foreign example of canal building that was acceptable was that of the Protestant Dutch, but their flat country only added to the doubts regarding waterways crossing hills.

A sceptical public needed a successful home example that they could see with their own eyes, to overcome the uncertainties surrounding the Trent & Mersey proposals. They wanted to see a high-profile artificial waterway that would prove the trading and, more to the point, the financial benefits to be gained by those involved in its construction. A canal that would not shadow a natural watercourse, as the Sankey had done, but one that would strike out to take an independent course between the source of a marketable product and a voracious market. Such an immense project would, of course, have the same capital funding problems as the Trent & Mersey scheme. It was, therefore, an impasse, which could have delayed the canal age, leaving the country starved of coal and the heavy goods necessary to retain the impetus of the industrial revolution – but in 1759 the solution was already underway on the Duke of Bridgewater's estate at Worsley, and once again James Brindley would be entrusted with a central role.

Chapter 7

A CANAL FOR THE DUKE OF BRIDGEWATER

It had always been known there was a substantial amount of coal below the surface of the Duke of Bridgewater's estate at Worsley, near Manchester. Unfortunately flooding of the colliery workings had been constant. Eventually, in 1647, a new drainage system was excavated. It was made possible because the coalfield ended in a high vertical sandstone quarry rock-face called Worsley Delph, which gave easy access to levels that were geologically lower than the valuable underground coal-seams. A sough (a mine-drainage tunnel in northern England) was dug between the coal-seams and the delph, sloping downwards so that gravity would cause the flood-waters to flow along it for discharge at the cliff-face. Thereafter the flooding was continually, and cost-effectively, alleviated by gravity causing the water to flow down the sough until it was discharged at the cliff-face. The system was expanded in response to nearby Manchester's increased coal demands and by 1731 the sough reached more than a mile into the hillside.[1] Production had been increased substantially, but its full potential could not be realised because transport of the coal to prospective purchasers was still a problem. Long lines of pack-horses plodded between the colliery, Salford and Manchester and profits slumped.[2] In 1737 plans were made to alleviate the problems by making it possible to carry the coal by water. To do so it was proposed to make the Worsley Brook navigable to Barton but the scheme foundered in a morass of local politics, its effectiveness hindered by the fact it would take cargoes down to the Mersey & Irwell Navigation, the monopolistic nature of which would allow the controlling company to levy high tolls on the coal-carrying boats. The Mersey & Irwell was a river navigation of the traditional sort with inland Manchester's Irwell flowing into coastal Liverpool's Mersey to span the distance between the two cities. It had been completed only one year before the Worsley Brook proposal although it had been opened in stages since 1724.[3] Eight locks allowed craft to cover the 20 miles from Quay Street, Manchester, to Warrington, beyond where the Mersey was tidal – and free of tolls.[4]

This was the situation in 1757 when the Duke of Bridgewater left London to live at Worsley. Aged 21 he would rely to a great extent on his agent, John Gilbert, who had taken over direct management of the estate from his brother Thomas in June of that year. It was Gilbert's responsibility to maximise the output of the Worsley estate and to that end his first major task on taking up his appointment was an evaluation of the coal deposits and how they could be extracted and transported. Evidence was gathered from detailed studies, added to which were the findings of bore-holes and topographical surveys of the surrounding areas.[5] John Gilbert and his brother, who had a deep knowledge of the estate from his years there, discussed the needs of Worsley with the duke. Significantly the three men each had an informed knowledge of canals. The family and management ties between Worsley and Earl Gower's seat at Trentham meant that the Gilbert brothers had been closely involved with the Trent & Mersey plans, becoming convinced adherents of the stillwater canal creed. The duke was not only influenced by the opinions of Earl Gower – his ex-guardian and brother-in-law – but also by the canals he had seen in France and Italy during three years on the European 'Grand Tour', then undertaken by most young noblemen and from which he had returned less than two years before. John Gilbert talked to anyone who had any knowledge of Worsley's coal extraction and transport problems, and then retired to his room at the Bull Hotel in Salford for two days, refusing all visitors while he worked out a brilliant colliery/sough/canal plan.[6]

His financial calculations showed that an increased tonnage would have to be produced to earn the profits that would justify building a canal to carry the coal. To increase the colliery's output sufficiently, still-flooded coal-seams lower in the hill would have to be drained and worked. John Gilbert had the engineering knowledge to know that it could be done by digging another sough into the lower coal-seams, one that would discharge the removed flood-waters near the base of the quarry face at Worsley delph. So far, little was involved other than an expansion of earlier solutions, but the brilliant move was to make the level of the new sough's outfall and that of an adjacent canal the same, the output of the first filling the second. After that it was obvious that the sough should be made larger than usual so that boats could float along it into the hillside to be loaded near the coal-faces. From the results of a single undertaking the Worsley estate would gain the benefit of improved colliery drainage, an efficient usage for the water thereby removed, an increase in the tonnage of coal available for extraction, cost-effective transport by water from the coal-face direct to the market-place and a method of carrying goods back to the estate. The advantages were so great that the Duke of Bridgewater agreed to finance the construction himself, thereby avoiding one of the crucial obstacles confronting the promoters of the Trent & Mersey. As early as the following year [1758] the duke was telling associates 'that he was inclinable to make a water road from Worsley Mill to Salford, at his own expence …' so that he could sell his coal there at a reduced price.[7]

As publicly announced, the canal to be built would be of little national significance, going eastwards from Worsley to Salford, and south-westerly to Hollin Ferry to join the Mersey & Irwell river navigation. In form it would be similar to the nearby Sankey Canal, although it would be bolder as it would not follow a watercourse and would instead have to face the engineering challenge of crossing Chat Moss, a large area of boggy, low ground. Privately it was known that it was to do no such thing. Already the duke's ultimate, but cloaked, target was a canal to the Mersey estuary to capture the lucrative and burgeoning Liverpool–Manchester trade.

Meanwhile, leaflets were written, produced and distributed to the landowners along the publicly announced route of the canal, seeking their 'approbation and concurrence'.[8] In December 1758 the political case came to a head with evidence given before Parliament in support of the Bill for an enabling Act, necessary to obtain rights of access, land purchasing powers, the setting up of conciliatory bodies and the protection of others' trading interests. John Gilbert told the House of Commons he was present when the surveying had been done, the result of which showed that the canal could be built without any locks. The whole length would be 15 miles and 591 yards, one third through land owned by the duke. Of the remainder, only the owners of four and a quarter miles had withheld their agreement, some of whom would lay a counter petition before the House.[9] Nevertheless the Royal Assent was granted to the first Bridgewater Canal Act on 23rd March 1759.

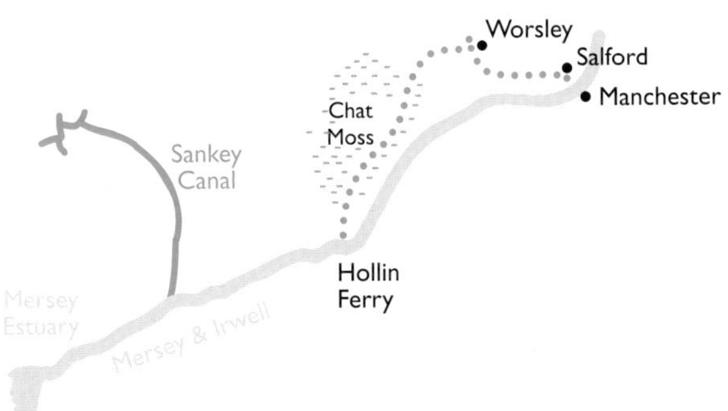

Route defined in the first Bridgewater Canal Act, 23 March 1759 from Worsley to Salford and Hollin Ferry

Even at this early stage it was apparent that it would be impossible for one man to organise the day-to-day engineering operations and carry out the administrative management, in John Gilbert's case in addition to his estate duties. The necessary re-organisation of the works at Worsley dates from 23rd June 1759 when specific account books were opened to record canal expenditure.[10] All was ready; the discussions with Brindley since the March meeting (Chapter 6) having borne fruit. Two days later the millwright went to Worsley Old Hall for a six day visit[11] during which time his goods and clothes were brought there, along with those of three of his workmen and their families: Samuel Addimand, George Harrison, and Samuel Bennett.[12] The triumvirate of the visionary and wealthy 23-year-old Duke of Bridgewater, the trusted and progressive 35-year-old manager/colliery engineer John Gilbert, and the bold, ambitious, and immensely practical James Brindley, aged 43, had been formed.

Over the intervening centuries a myth has flourished that James Brindley was responsible for all of the engineering aspects of the Bridgewater Canal, as well as being the source of the original concept. To allow for this inflated role the other members of the famous Bridgewater triumvirate were relegated to supporting players – the duke simply providing the money whilst John Gilbert managed the workforce and administered the paperwork. Twentieth-century research did much to correct that erroneous scenario but it has proved to be a hardy survivor much to the chagrin of canal historians amongst whom the balance has perhaps now become over-weighted on the opposite side. Supporters of the duke and John Gilbert have produced well-researched books that clearly advocate the crucial roles played by each of them in the conception, promotion and construction of the Bridgewater Canal, but in doing so an impression has been created of James Brindley as a consultant engineer who undertook a minor role in the overall project. The actuality is that they were a team of three, each of whom contributed vital abilities of different dimensions. Any two of the team could not have succeeded without the third.

Nevertheless, the leading member was the splendidly titled Francis Egerton, Baron Ellesmere, Marquis of Brackley, Eighth Earl, and Third Duke of Bridgewater.[13] He was a determined, single-minded young man with a clear vision of what he wanted to achieve. Art and aristocratic finery had never taken his attention; instead practical problems became the focus of his independent will.[14] The decision to build the canal, and to incorporate the challenge for the lucrative Liverpool–Manchester transport trade, was his alone. Financially it was he who would also face the challenge, but in the political arena he did have family allies, necessary as each of the three Parliamentary Acts needed to complete the canal would become more contentious in turn. They would not be the first to incorporate compulsory purchase powers, but it was one thing for a turnpike road to be built through one's land – that could be crossed with ease – it was quite another for an estate to be dissected by a wide water-filled channel. The political opposition would come from landowners along the proposed route but their importance would escalate as they took on the mantle of defenders of the sanctity of private property on a national scale.[15] Fortunately the duke's Egerton family were part of a mainly Whig powerbase, its influence bolstered by his brother-in-law Earl Gower and his uncle the Duke of Bedford. To garner support the duke sent out 750 letters to MPs, some of whom were in sympathy with his plans whilst others were still unsure of how to vote. Westminster was the place where the votes would be counted but influence was used at behind-the-scenes meetings in private houses and clubs. Individual antagonists could have been overcome reasonably easily but the threat to sacrosanct private property, and the fear of the precedent it would set, provided the various opposition lobbies with a powerful point of convergence, the blunting of which required the duke to be politically powerful and adroit.

His second challenge would be an acute financial burden, under the weight of which any hesitation or lack of resolve would result in failure. Even though he was a rich man, capital funding was difficult to find without bleeding dry his estates. Instead, extra money was raised by issuing bonds which gave a return of 4 per cent, redeemable at will and secured on the duke's own titles and land. In this way many local people lent their savings to the canal venture. By 1762 the canal debt would be £28,000, three years later £60,879 and growing daily – not until 1786 would a small, but increasing, profit be made.[16] Only a man of steely determination would be able to withstand such financial peril in a venture of unproven worth.

Although the duke has become synonymous with Worsley, it was only one of his twelve landed estates, all of which were administered centrally at Ashridge in Hertfordshire. Overall management was in the hands of Thomas Gilbert who was also the duke's legal advisor and personal secretary. As he also served Earl Gower in a similar role at Trentham, it meant the two estates were run in a close alliance. John Gilbert was one rung lower on the management ladder, responsible for the individual estate at Worsley. He was a practical, persevering and industrious man with an engineer's understanding of mines and underground works, although it would be incorrect to view him as a man whose whole career was centred on Worsley. He owned and directed a blacklead mine at Borrowdale in the Lake District, operating a factory for its output at Worsley. He also had saltworks at Marston in Cheshire, limestone quarries at Caldon Low and Astbury, limekilns at Hem Heath and Ecton, and a colliery at Meir Heath. In addition in 1767 the duke would help him to buy the Clough Hall estate, immediately above Harecastle Tunnel, as a reward for his services.[17] As with Brindley, he would also eventually gain from being associated with the successful Bridgewater Canal, being offered freelance work as a consulting land-agent and engineer – such as the drainage of the Martin Mere bogland near Southport in 1778 for Thomas Eccleston.[18]

However, it was his mining expertise that would be in greatest demand as he would be the rightful recipient of the plaudits for the tunnels at Worsley – an example being the 1774 contract to construct the Speedwell boat tunnel in a lead mine near Castleton, Derbyshire.[19] Because of his many interests John Gilbert had to have the ability to delegate tasks. The administration at Worsley was done by Robert Lansdale, his personal assistant and cashier, to whom other staff submitted their accounts for work done – including mining engineer John Royle and master-miner Ashton Tonge. When a specific problem required expert knowledge Gilbert called in consulting engineers, but the timing of Brindley's recruitment indicates that he was chosen to fulfil a more fundamental role. The work already done on the declared Salford route had proved that the duke and John Gilbert could complete that project with only minimal outside help. But they could not do the still undisclosed extensions to Manchester and to near Liverpool to capture the rich prize of taking the trade of those cities away from the river navigation company nor the incorporation of a link with the proposed Mersey–Trent canal. To do both, the duke's canal would have to face the onerous engineering challenges of crossing the rivers Irwell and Mersey, and the boggy ground of Trafford Moss. It was to achieve those ends that Brindley was recruited by the duke at John Gilbert's suggestion.[20] Overall he would work consistently on the Bridgewater Canal for only three of the seventeen construction years – but they would be the years of the scheme's ultimate challenge and brilliance.

By 1759 the upheaval of a major construction site had already come to Worsley with the present village green as the centre of operations. James Brindley added his expertise to the collection of specialisations on site – miners, boat-builders, masons, labourers. All worked amongst noise and bustle, hot forges shaping tools, and amidst a sprawl of workshops and living accommodation, with the horses and wagons of suppliers constantly delivering food and raw materials.

John Gilbert was the duke's man and earning a salary of £200, soon to be increased to £300, per annum.[21] Brindley, on the other hand, retained his independence and joined the scheme as a consulting engineer, charging fees and expenses agreed on a long-term basis. He was his own man, with his own freelance workforce operating the steam-engines already installed elsewhere, and a widespread customer base of valued clients. Canals were not yet an obvious career move so Brindley continued with his other work during his involvement with the

The Bridgewater Canal at Worsley – the entrance to the mineworkings is beyond the bridge

Bridgewater Canal. Although not part of the Worsley establishment, his status was such that he was always referred to as 'Mr Brindley' in estate records, rather than the first- and surnames used for all the other skilled men on the canal.[22] Their differing pasts and future personal objectives would lead to some discord between Gilbert and Brindley. One viewed the canal as a great advance for his master and the Worsley estate; the other saw that a job well done would create great opportunities for personal advancement – as would any of today's self-employed consulting engineers. John Gilbert's central role would include getting the best from a man eight years his senior, a man who was used to making his own decisions and being master of his own destiny. James Brindley would have to be a team-player for the first time in his adult life. One important commonality shared by the Bridgewater trio was that they had all been involved in the politics of the stalled Trent & Mersey Canal. They knew the doubts voiced. They knew landowners on a proposed route could be intransigent. They knew that those with opposing business interests could cause delay – but only if they knew what was planned. They knew the magnitude of the proposals had created difficulties otherwise avoided. Experience had shown it was prudent not to show one's hand and they had the advantage of not having to do so as the duke was providing the finance.

During the first months of Brindley's involvement three miles of level canal were dug towards Salford.[23] It was relatively straightforward work although a flash-flood did cause damage in November.[24] Ostensibly those miles were part of the announced plans – actually they were the first part of the still private larger scheme. During the second half of 1759 Brindley spent many days at Worsley Old Hall. The canal digging did not need his personal attention and it is probable that the time was spent with the duke and John Gilbert planning their ultimate objective. In his notebook Brindley wrote that he was at the Hall – but nothing of what was done or said there;[25] very different from the later years of construction work on the Bridgewater Canal when he would detail many names and tasks.

In many ways 1759 was an auspicious year in which to start an immense project. Britain was straddling the Atlantic, confident, bursting with ambition, reaping the riches of successful conquests.[26] The dominating political themes were India and America and there was little organised opposition to industrialism, the development of which did not seem nationally significant.[27] Conversely, the country was embroiled in the Seven Years War against France, a conflict that would change the course of events in Europe in a way comparable to the two world wars of the twentieth century. And the price of iron moved suddenly upward.[28] Nearer to home the French were still a threat and imports and the crucial east-coast trade route were disrupted by the imposition of convoy sailings. It was Britain's good fortune that the infant Industrial Revolution was growing far inland.

As successful and outwardly confident as the age in which he lived, James Brindley set out to ride to London on 23rd January 1760, to join the duke who was already there garnering political support for the passage of a second Act for the Bridgewater Canal.[29] It was probably Brindley's second visit to the already huge, bustling, noisy capital city, his first having been to lodge his steam-engine patent. The journey usually took three days, which would have him arriving late on Friday 25th January. Earlier that day a petition was placed before the House of Commons, asking if a Bill may be presented to change the route of the canal. The decision was referred to a committee of the House which formed and adjourned at 5pm.[30] Early the following week Brindley gave evidence to the committee in the Speaker's Chamber, his first experience of parliamentary procedures – with many more to come in the future. The preliminary moves for the first Act had been presented by John Gilbert, but now the duke's newly appointed engineer was the expert witness, his comprehensive statements convincing the committee that the new route was practicable and that the duke's canal should go to Manchester instead of Salford.[31]

He told the gentlemen that the new drainage sough at Worsley colliery would give access to coal 30 to 40 yards deeper than was before possible, adding that work had already begun with the tunnel 7 feet 6 inches high, 5 feet 6 inches wide and, so far, 150 yards long – through which the canal's new route would receive three times as much water as would have been available to the old. Furthermore, the previously authorised way to Salford would be arduous as it would have to be carried for about 2½ miles through rock, and on the side of a very steep hill, thereby making it difficult to make the canal hold water. It would also pass through valuable, enclosed land whereas going to Manchester would cross two miles of the boggy Trafford Moss which was of no value, with the added benefit that the canal would drain it and bring marl and manure to improve the land.[32]

On the crucial point of carrying the canal across the river Irwell at Barton, Brindley was confident, saying it would present no difficulty, 'the Foundation being good'. There was already a road bridge at Barton, a substantial three-arched structure high enough to allow navigation of the river below. The boats were hauled by men passing under the bridge on a towpath of planks through one of the arches. Brindley said that the canal's aqueduct would be built nearby and would also have three arches, with each of similar or greater breadth than those of the road bridge, and higher by seven or eight feet, one or more of which would also have a planked towpath for the river traffic.[33] Further information was included in the subsequent Act, some of which may indicate that the confidence was not unbounded. Permission was given to 'fix and adjoin' Barton aqueduct's piers and arches to those of the road bridge 'if they or others shall think fit'. There is no evidence that they did so, but the inclusion of such a clause has the hallmark of Brindley's belt-and-braces philosophy, his aptitude for not taking more chances than necessary, and a preference for gaining advantage by incorporating features already on site.[34]

Some members of the Commons committee were still not convinced that such a thing as an aqueduct was technically possible. No record has survived at Westminster, but it was said that Brindley cut through their confusion by bringing a large round cheese into the room, from which he made a reasonable model of an aqueduct. Having seen what the structure would look like there were still doubts about how it could be made to hold water. When he was called at the next session, the MPs were surprised to see him enter with containers of sand and clay, and a large jug of water. Having formed a trough from the clay he poured some of the water into it, and it ran out over the floor. Then he kneaded the sand and the clay with more of the water until it was saturated or 'puddled'. From this material a second trough was made, into which the remainder of the water was poured, and from which it did not leak. Although anecdotal, this ability to make a strong personal impression

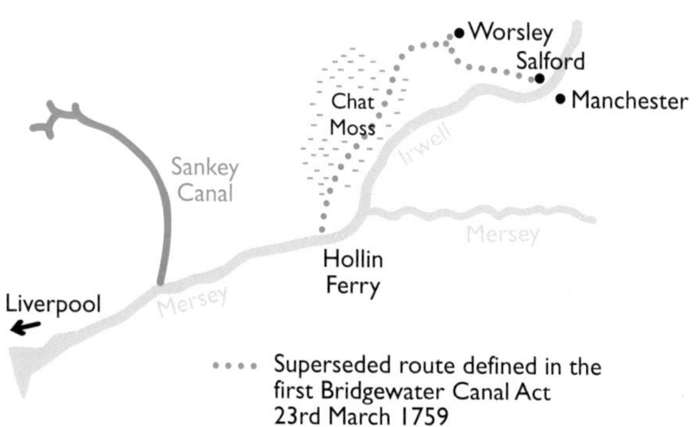

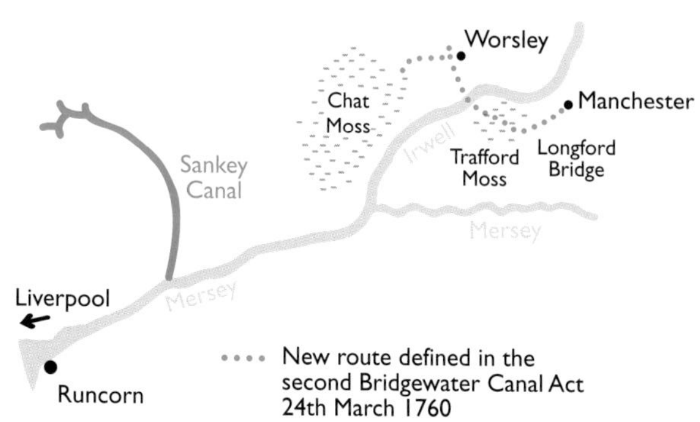

The Bridgewater Canal's routes as defined in the first and second Bridgewater Canal Acts. The route defined in the second Act includes a small section of the old route, already built to Chat Moss

when promoting a project would also become the hallmark of other engineers and inventors whose names would enter the public domain: Watt, Telford, Brunel, Stephenson. Their perceived infallibility was an aura created by themselves and others for commercial and professional reasons. James Brindley's boldness and larger-than-life persona was promoted similarly, but as with the others there had to be a kernel of character around which it could be fashioned. The duke must have been confident that his engineer had the personality as well as the knowledge to win over sceptical politicians. The more memorable the methods, the better.

In addition to Brindley's evidence the Commons heard petitions of support from the traders and merchants of Manchester, Altrincham, Knutsford and Stretford – all of whom saw the advantage of the duke's canal coming to their side of the Irwell. After a well-fought passage through both Houses the second Bridgewater Canal Act received the Royal Assent on 24th March 1760.[35] Authorisation had been given to construct a canal from or near Worsley Mill, over the river Irwell, to the town of Manchester, via Longford Bridge.[36] It is not known which of the Bridgewater–Brindley–Gilbert triumvirate should receive the praise for the idea of crossing the Irwell on an aqueduct, which at that time was a phenomenal concept in England. But the duke wanted a canal without locks and the level of the canal at its source at the colliery sough was just right for the aqueduct and the rest of the route to the Mersey estuary. The aqueduct idea may have been the duke's as he had seen the Languedoc Canal in France, along which three river-crossing aqueducts had been built in the 1680s.[37] Brindley's evidence to the Commons indicated his knowledge of its planning, and that its style and dimensions were dictated by the nearby road bridge over the river. John Gilbert's role is open to question but he had set the levels for the sough so he must have allowed for the canal's planned extensions. What is beyond doubt is that only one of the three would be able to use it to further his career. The aqueduct at Barton would capture the public imagination and Brindley's association with such a stunning success would subsequently be used as a marketing gambit by those promoting his later canals – a perception of professionalism used to advantage. An example is the story that the aqueduct had been considered 'a wild and extravagant project' and Brindley had therefore asked that the opinion of another engineer be taken before construction work commenced. 'A gentleman of eminence' was brought to the site and exclaimed 'I have often heard of castles in the air, but never was shewn before where any of them were to be erected'.[38] This first circulated when the aqueduct was successfully in use and, of course, it reflected well on Brindley and to the detriment of the 'gentleman of eminence', rumoured to have been Smeaton – otherwise known as Brindley's main civil engineering business rival. But they were future legends – the current situation was that the Bridgewater Canal would reach the south bank of the Irwell, from where the still concealed Liverpool and Trent & Mersey destinations could be more easily achieved.

On returning to the north from London, Brindley gave some time to his old work – supervising the foundations of a mill.[39] Prudently he maintained his reliable income from mills and steam-engines for at least another two years. But canals were taking up most of his time with his recent recruitment to the Bridgewater cause not precluding his continued involvement with the Trent & Mersey which, in December 1759, once again came to the fore after discussions with interested parties raised the possibility of including branch canals to Newcastle-under-Lyme, Lichfield and Tamworth. Once again Brindley optimistically headed-up a page in his notebook ready for the new work – 'About the Navigation in Staffordshire', the first entry under which was three days inspecting the countryside for the new side-cuts.[40] Two of the three days were spent in the vicinity of Burslem, a fact that may be relevant to an event eight and a half months later. It has filtered down through the intervening centuries that the infant John Bennett,

Brindley's notebook 1758–60

Courtesy of the Institution of Civil Engineers, Archives

baptised in Burslem on 31st August 1760, was Brindley's illegitimate son. The baby's mother was Mary Bennett, aged 33 and un-married, but no documentary proof of paternity has been found, although many have searched for it.[41] Nor has any evidence been found linking Mary to Samuel Bennett who moved to Worsley with Brindley in June 1759. That Brindley was 'about the Navigation in Staffordshire' at a supposed time of conception is known, but if being in the same county can be viewed as proof of paternity then every male reader will have cause to worry. Through the generations the Bennetts continued to make the claim of Brindley's involvement, with it coming to national attention via the author Arnold Bennett, who was John's great-great-grandson. In 1928 he wrote in the *Daily Express* that he had grown up believing 'the genius' Brindley to be his forebear but not knowing with what justification. His biographer Margaret Drabble wrote, 'perhaps there is no truth in the story at all – it is a well-known habit of ordinary families to lay claim to distinguished … predecessors, especially when they are too far removed to cast any real shame on existing members'.[42] The truth, however, may be discovered by DNA profiling, and one bearer of the name Brindley is attempting to have his Y-line DNA compared with a direct male descendant of John Bennett.[43]

Whatever else he was doing, Brindley's involvement in two separate canal schemes now placed him at the forefront of the waterways' revolution and it is this dual role that broke the previously accepted pattern of engineering. Up to now rivers had been mostly improved by local landowner/engineers who employed a surveyor and the other skilled men required, and undertook a scheme of local advantage. In general they carried out one work only. Others were part-time civil engineers, mainly earning their living in unrelated ways.[44] But now there were two major canals in the pipeline, and both had the same engineer – thereby inextricably linking his name to such waterways in the minds of those anticipating future investment.

In the furtherance of one of his schemes, the majority of May 1760 was spent on an accurate survey of the route for the Trent & Mersey Canal east of the watershed. Brindley did not personally do the theodolite surveying of the proposed line, that was delegated to his senior aide, Hugh Henshall, with a team of assistants. It was referred to as 'levelling', or 'taking the levels', with water depths measured from boats where a Trent tributary had to be crossed, and distances measured with a surveying wheel.[45] They began high up on the watershed at Harecastle and worked their way downstream for four days. Brindley's presence was needed wherever judgements had to be made, such as at the crossing of the Trent at Alrewas, a situation complicated by the prior call on water supplies made by two mills there.[46] Almost every stream, brook, and river drove mill-wheels, with the millers and owners vociferous in their objections if it was thought a canal may take the water on which they relied. The choice of a millwright as canal engineer had many benefits.

The new survey was at the sole expense of Earl Gower who continued to play a leading role, although not openly so. Generally the project was still too formidable to garner widespread support with the majority unconvinced of the advantages to be gained.[47] It was, therefore, expedient to break the overall plan into smaller, more digestible, pieces for public consumption. A link across the watershed to the Mersey was still too much to swallow, so the first bite offered was simply a stillwater canal shadowing the Trent along its valley, in much the same way as the successful Sankey Canal had followed its brook, albeit for a much shorter distance. The new canal would stretch for 55 miles from Longbridge, near Burslem, to the navigable Trent at Wilden Ferry via 47 locks – with the new side-cuts adding another 17 miles and 11 locks.[48] Viewed from Staffordshire, at the headwaters of the Trent, this one aspect of the overall plan was seen as an objective of some magnitude, but with obvious commercial advantages. Viewed from elsewhere it was still too much to take. In these circumstances there was a need to add credibility to the proposals and John

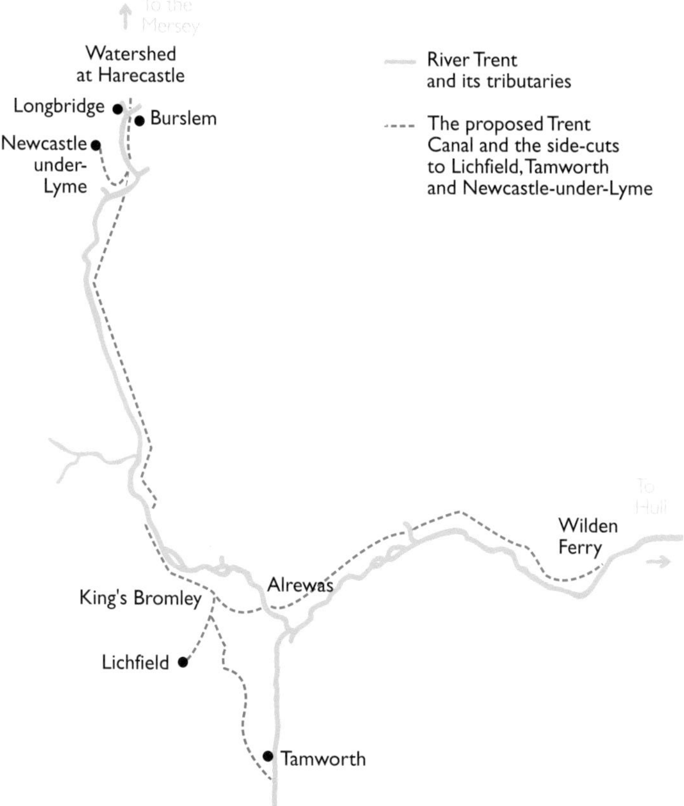

The reduced scheme for a Trent Canal, with side-cuts to Newcastle-under-Lyme, Lichfield and Tamworth – promoted and surveyed in 1760

Smeaton, Fellow of the Royal Society, was brought in to do so. If he had been the 'gentleman of eminence' who had, only two months before, disparaged the Duke of Bridgewater's planned Barton Aqueduct, would his opinion have been sought on Earl Gower's Trent canal? Probably not. After all, seeking an independent opinion when one is uncertain of receiving approval is negligent conduct. Accordingly, Smeaton rode over the proposed route with Brindley and surveyor Henshall in November 1760.[49]

They compared the various tracts of land to the plans and levels previously measured and inspected the Trent and lesser watercourses. At this stage the major concerns were identifying the land through which the canal would be built, making judgements on the sources of water to fill it, calculating how many locks would be needed to cater for the rise or fall of the land along the route, and making round-figure estimates of the costs. Upon that information an engineer would judge the practicability of a proposed canal. Details such as lock locations, how to cross rivers, the number of bridges, and where to obtain construction materials, were left to later – on Brindley's canals, much later. The two engineers agreed that the locks would have an average rise-fall of between 5 feet 7 inches and 6 feet with approximately £500 allowed to build each one, and an average of £1,000 allowed for each mile of level canal. Also that the canal should be eight yards wide at the waterline to allow navigation by the boats now trading on the river Trent up to Wilden Ferry. The depth was to take account of 'fording-places', a method of crossing watercourses that would remain a familiar part of life until the first half of the twentieth century, although public roads across the canal would have 'carriage bridges'.[50] The water at the 'well-paved and sloped' fords was to be 2 feet 6 inches deep, in keeping with the general view that such crossings for pedestrians were acceptable up to 3 feet deep.[51] Elsewhere the depth of the canal was to be up to 3 feet 6 inches. Such fords may have been incorporated to alleviate the type of opposition voiced during the passage of the Bridgewater Acts – that to move their animals between pastures landowners would have to take lengthy diversions. Even with such depth restrictions it was estimated that a boat on the canal would be able to carry double the cargo of one on the shallow Trent on the approach to Wilden Ferry.

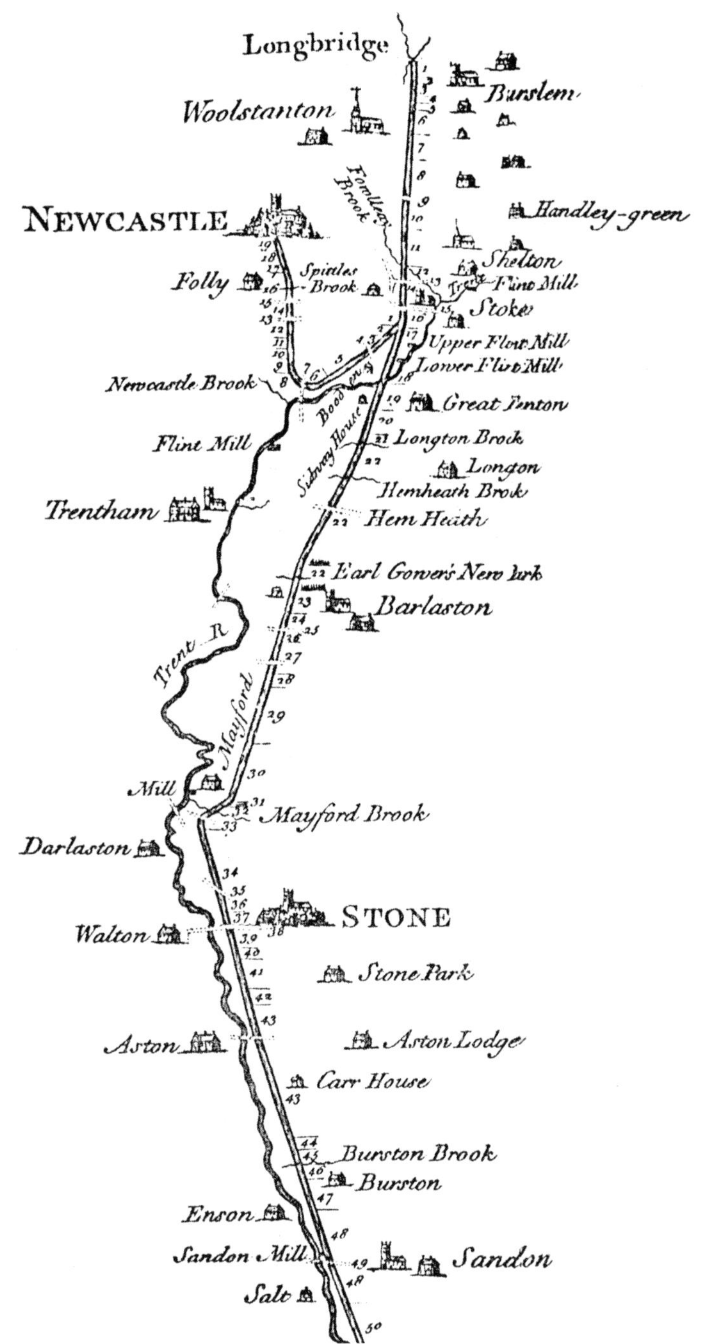

Part of the original map of the Trent Canal route, as inspected by Brindley and Smeaton in November 1760. The numbers identify various landowners Courtesy of Stoke on Trent City Archive

Smeaton found no fault with Brindley's work, describing the course as 'well chosen, and for the greatest part well adapted by nature for such a purpose ... Mr Brindley having judiciously designed the course ... to pass through a great number of level commons and waste grounds, and, in general, through the most barren lands that could be found in any wise to agree with the course thereof'. Smeaton knew his subsequent report would be used to assuage London opinions and he therefore reduced the main channel of the canal to only 25 miles, from Wilden Ferry to King's Bromley, treating the 30 miles from King's Bromley to Longbridge as a branch canal and, thereby, implying it was optional. However, having thus minimised the scheme, Smeaton then astutely offered the concept of a link to the west coast as his own inspiration, although there seems to have been no shortage of people available to supply local topographical information. He favoured a deep cutting across the watershed near Harecastle – through a meadow between two higher hills, from which natural drainage would provide water for a reservoir. In dry seasons, he suggested, supplies from the lower levels of the canal could be pumped up to the summit by a steam-engine, an idea which could have emanated from steam-engineer Brindley – or at least the possibility had his agreement.[52]

Smeaton's approval was important as he was arguably the greatest English civil engineer of the eighteenth century – his research papers in London were already augmented by major works in Plymouth, Scotland, and many points between.[53] In this instance, however, he had no more personal experience of surveying or building a stillwater canal than did Brindley although he had the advantage of having seen such locks in Flanders and Holland – even so, they were not relevant to taking a canal across a high hilly watershed.[54] And that was now required because the decision had already been made privately to build a single canal, rather than one on either side of the hills linked by a road as in the first public proposal. The motivation was the passage of the second Bridgewater Canal Act earlier in the year, which meant the extension of the duke's canal to near Liverpool was probably going to succeed – a junction with which could simplify this canal's route to the Mersey from the Trent. The brave decision to tunnel through the watershed may have been made before Smeaton's visit, regardless of his preference for a deep cutting. If so Brindley must have been involved in such a fundamental conclusion. Any canal is at its most vulnerable where water is scarce – if the surveying does not take account of that fact, the volume of boats will be severely curtailed with a resultant loss of trade and income. And when it is anticipated that the canal is to form the spine of a national complex then the bold decision to tunnel at Harecastle is of monumental importance.

By the end of 1760 all that could be done to advance a canal to link the rivers Mersey and Trent had been done – but the time was still not right. The scheme would now slumber for four years, during which period the banner of stillwater canals would be carried triumphantly forward by the Bridgewater, its success eventually proving the validity of a new transport system in which many could, indeed should, invest.

Chapter 8
A PHENOMENAL SUCCESS

In England the aqueduct at Barton became a wonder of the age. Well-informed people knew that such structures had been built in France and Italy in previous centuries but that did not lessen the awesome effect of seeing it with one's own eyes. Those who knew something of engineering from their own estate management appreciated the magnitude of the approach embankments, and marvelled at the weight of water contained without leaks. Many more gazed at the effortless transport system carried across the aqueduct and compared it with the struggle to move boats on the river below it. Ever since the Romans, Danes and Vikings had used the rivers to found and supply their settlements it had been accepted that transport by water was unavoidably subject to lengthy delays, and often losses. Around the coast storms, tides and adverse wind directions kept ships in harbour for many days, sometimes weeks. When at sea a destination was often ruled out for the same reasons. Inland, rainfall or lack of it caused swift river currents or shallows. When in wooded areas or passing through gorges boats were sheltered from the wind and had to be pulled upstream by gangs of men. When a river was too narrow to allow tacking upwind, boats were once again man-hauled. With no towpaths this involved scrambling through undergrowth and bushes, balancing on steep riverbanks and making allowances for differing lengths of rope to allow a boat to use varying deep channels. The physical effort was immense.

The Duke of Bridgewater, age 29, pointing at the Barton Aqueduct. In the foreground is the road bridge that pre-dated the aqueduct. On the left the road tunnel through the aqueduct's embankment

Visitors to Barton saw such gangs on the river Irwell struggling to pull partially loaded boats slowly through the arches of the aqueduct and the nearby road bridge, also along the precipitous banks between. Such scenes were as familiar then as traffic jams and exhaust fumes are to later generations, indeed more so as they had been unchanged in England since the dawn of time. Familiarity had bred unthinking resignation. Now eyes could be raised to higher things – metaphorically and actually. Across the top of the aqueduct the still water of the duke's canal carried fully loaded boats, each pulled by one animal walking on a smooth and level towing path. Serenely, silently. Too much wind or lack of it made no difference. Too much rain or lack of it, the same. Day or night, cargoes were being carried safely and to a schedule. It was this startling difference between the river below and the canal above that made Barton Aqueduct a national phenomenon while clearly demonstrating to even the most sceptical the benefits canals could bring to elsewhere in the kingdom. It was the first canal structure built by James Brindley. Hindsight shows that as a springboard to national celebrity and a new career it could not have been bettered. Future investors would be confident that the man who had built Barton Aqueduct could complete a canal from their town, no matter what was involved. However, at the time of construction, Barton was the site of considerable worry and stress.

The aqueduct was built in approximately fourteen months, from June 1760 to July 1761. The work was done under the general surveillance of John Gilbert but it was Brindley who tested the river bed for sound foundations, as he had done many times elsewhere when building weirs and dams to store water to power his mills. It was his expertise that created piers strong enough to withstand the flow of the river around them. Although familiar, everything was on a far larger scale than Brindley had experienced before, including the number of men involved. Fortunately, he was popular with the workforce because he understood their superstitions and working practices. It was only 25 years since witchcraft had ceased to be a capital offence and among the populace belief in such practices still flourished, along with a hundred other superstitions, catered for by numerous necromancers, quacks and adventurers.[1] Brindley sympathised with the problems of his men and allayed their prejudices, typically dealing with the frustrations of working with a foreman bricklayer who waited for the planets to indicate a lucky day to start work.[2]

In spite of such delays, a massive embankment was built on the north bank, which carried the canal from Worsley, at its ordained level, out into the river valley. At its far end the water channel was sealed and, when filled, it allowed canal boats carrying baskets of Worsley coal to float out onto the embankment high above the Irwell. From here the cargo was lowered by crane to river barges, in which it was taken upstream for sale in Salford and Manchester.[3] Traffic tolls had to be paid to the river navigation authority, but the income earned by the Worsley estate was greater than that from the meagre tonnage carried by pack-horses over the same route and the duke needed to increase his estate's income in every way possible. An added bonus was that on their return trip the river barges brought construction materials to the site, their cargoes – timber, stone, bricks, and limestone for mortar – lifted to the canal's boats by the same crane.[4]

Eventually, immense stone pillars rose from the riverbed, the individual blocks linked by iron staples set in lead. The pillars' great strength was indicative of the volatile nature of the river Irwell with its penchant for flash-floods – known to Brindley from his work further upstream on the Wet Earth colliery scheme in the previous decade. At their tops the pillars were linked to form arches, the centre one of which was 63 feet wide and approximately 38 feet high so that the largest of the river craft could pass underneath with mast and sails standing. The channel across the top was some 200 yards long with stops at each end, these could be lifted to seal off the aqueduct from the rest of the canal so that it could be drained, via a wooden tube, into the river below by drawing a plug. The approach embankments from both sides of the Irwell were vast, each approximately half a mile long, 112 feet across the base, 24 feet wide at the top and 17 feet high, the one on the Worsley bank pierced by a road tunnel. Beyond the south bank 400 men worked to take the canal across the boggy ground of Trafford Moss, in itself a challenge of some magnitude.[5]

At the main work camp around Worsley Green vast quantities of bricks were made. Nearby, a water-wheel turned by Worsley Brook powered a multi-functional mortar-mill into which limestone from near Leigh was shovelled to grind it into powder after it had been burnt in kilns to soften it. The same wheel drove a tapered drum of various sized meshes that graded sand and gravel. Finally, a further function with vertical rollers in a trough mixed the sand and the powdered burnt-lime with water to produce lime-mortar.[6] Overall, the scale of the canal project was far in excess of anything in which Brindley had previously been involved – overwhelming because he could not give it his full attention, the latest survey for the Trent & Mersey Canal being done simultaneously, including the crucial on-site meeting with John Smeaton. Time also had to be found in early 1761 for visits to Congleton, 30 miles away, where Brindley's men were still developing a complex mill.[7] At the age of 45 it was a wearing overture to the dramas of canal construction.

The surviving northern embankment for Barton Aqueduct, refaced in 1821

Unmarried, with his family far away in Leek, Brindley had no one in whom he could confide to ease the pressure, and between mid-March and mid-July 1761 he was subjected to a high degree of stress. His whole attention was given to the completion of Barton Aqueduct and its embankments. No one had any experience of building such a structure and sceptical voices could be heard from all quarters. In what must have seemed another lifetime, the construction of a steam-powered engine for Miss Broad had been fraught with problems but its failures before success had been of solely local consequence to Brindley, his professional reputation, and his client. And

The road-arch originally through the Barton embankment, later moved to this position to allow for road widening

impossible. A further gossipy anecdote told of Brindley's horse, the mare to whom on long journeys the somewhat lonely engineer probably confided many of his thoughts, being turned out in a field, which was common practice in the summer to reduce stabling costs. One night John Gilbert's stallion broke into the field and got the mare in foal. Brindley was furious, accusing Gilbert of allowing it to happen to prevent him riding the mare in pursuit of his non-canal business interests. There is usually a grain of truth in such tales and it is an indication of the discord emanating from the differing attitudes of the two men towards the great project. John Gilbert was the duke's man and committed to the Worsley estate, and he resented Brindley's absences on mill business. Brindley, on the other hand, was tetchy about Gilbert's comfortable long-term security of tenure at Worsley, seeing him as uncomprehending of a more precarious career.

In July 1761 Brindley deemed Barton Aqueduct and its southern embankment ready to take the weight of the canal's water. The blockage at the end of the northern embankment was removed and the water flowed over the aqueduct to the other side of the Irwell. The strains on the aqueduct and Brindley were immense – the former showed signs of buckling, the latter fled to bed at the Bishop Blaize tavern in Stretford.[9] The eccentric, pro-Bridgewater, source of the other anecdotes wrote that Brindley locked himself into his room where he had a nervous breakdown.[10] The problem was the system used to make the aqueduct watertight. Using puddled, or saturated, clay to make a water-retentive channel was not new, the Romans having used the same method. It was, therefore, well proven but had the disadvantage of being heavy because the thick, multi-layered, saturated clay was required on the sides as well as the bottom of the channel. At Barton one of the arches was barely supporting the weight when the water was added. In Brindley's absence, John Gilbert had the aqueduct drained into the river below and either added more clay over the arch to aid compression, or removed some clay to lighten the load over the arch; both actions would be reported in later years.[11] However it was done, Barton Aqueduct was ready for its official opening on 17th July 1761. Local newspapers reported that the duke was accompanied by his friend and neighbour the Earl of Stamford and several other gentlemen. A crowd of spectators watched as the

although such matters were of consequence to a self-employed engineer, they paled into insignificance when compared to the calamity of a failure of Barton Aqueduct with its ramifications for the Bridgewater Canal and the consequential impact on the other schemes dependent on its success. If the aqueduct collapsed under the weight of the water it would do so in the full glare of the national spotlight and James Brindley's career as a canal builder would be at an end. Furthermore, the duke would probably find it impossible to obtain parliamentary approval for the Act necessary to extend his canal to the Mersey estuary and Liverpool – the goal that was to make his current expenditure worthwhile. Brindley knew that if his name became associated with such a public debacle, he would afterwards find it difficult to obtain contracts for work, even when he had a proven ability. He also knew that damage limitation would ensure that it would be his name, and not those of Bridgewater or Gilbert, that would bear the blame. The famous trio would very quickly become a one-man-band.

Years later it would be asserted by one of the Bridgewater family, trying to reclaim the duke's share of the glory, that when Brindley had been housed at the duke's Worsley Old Hall his habit had been to drink a basin of milk in the morning before going out to the works. However, it was said that when he moved to an inn at Stretford 'he became drunken'.[8] Judgmental statements, especially when made by someone with a hidden agenda, are difficult to quantify. Certainly, drunkenness cannot have been a fundamental trait, otherwise Brindley's on-going acceptance by Quaker business contacts and his later friendship with the church-going family of Josiah Wedgwood, would have been water filled the aqueduct's channel and marvelled as 'a large boat carrying upwards of 50 tons was towed … over arches over the river Irwell which were so firm, secure and compact that not a single drop of water could be perceived to ouze thro' any of them …' [12]

Such newspaper reports, augmented by private correspondence and word of mouth, spread a national awareness of what had been achieved at Worsley. A constant stream of visitors arrived and bought tickets for boat-trips into the underground mine workings. The boatmen became adept at relating the facts and figures that were avidly remembered for future dissemination. The boats were 'fifty feet long, four and a half broad, two feet three inches deep' and floated for 'near three miles' underground. In the candlelight passengers saw niches in the side of the arching, which were openings through the rock to the top of the hill 'in order to preserve a free circulation of fresh air … and to let men down to work in case of accident' and in some places there were 'gates to close up the arch, and prevent the admission of too much air in tempestuous and windy weather'. Progress was made by 'towing the boat on each hand by a rail'. The visitors watched as output from the coalfaces was brought to the underground quays in little low wagons, each holding almost a ton, and pushed on a railed way to a stage over the canal where the contents were shot into a boat, which held about eight tons. When fully loaded a boat was linked to others, 'from six to twenty at a time' and moved by one man, by means of the hand-rails, to the tunnel's entrance before being drawn along the canal towards Manchester by a horse or two mules.[13] The credit for such wonders was rightly attributed to the Duke of Bridgewater and John Gilbert. At this early stage the duke also received the plaudits for the aqueduct, but within two years the popular recipient of Barton's fame was James Brindley, awareness of his name becoming widespread outside the Midlands. After all, it was he who had boldly told Parliament that such a structure was feasible, and there it was – to the amazement of many. London newspapers contained letters telling of Brindley's achievement in 'erecting a navigable canal in the air; for it is as high as the tops of trees'. One correspondent admitted that he 'almost trembled to behold the large river Irwell underneath … this extraordinary bridge' upon which he 'durst hardly venture to walk'.[14] All who saw Barton Aqueduct viewed it with a blend of awe and fear, deliciously flavoured with profit potential. It was a compelling mixture that propelled its nationally accepted creator to fame – as 'Rocket' would do for George Stephenson at the start of the next transport revolution.

Having successfully crossed the river Irwell the Bridgewater Canal could now be extended towards Manchester in accordance with its second Act of Parliament. The triumvirate, meanwhile, was covertly planning the canal's major extension to the Mersey estuary, for which the passage of a third Act would be required. The resolution to build the canal at one level without locks would be maintained, with the resultant need for embankments and aqueducts to cross another two substantial rivers and their valleys – the Bollin and the upper waters of the Mersey.

The challenge for the rich Manchester–Liverpool trade started with a battle of pamphlets. In his publications the duke deprecated the tendency of the area's turnpike roads to run alongside navigable rivers, both therefore confined to boggy lowlands and circuitous routes, making neither

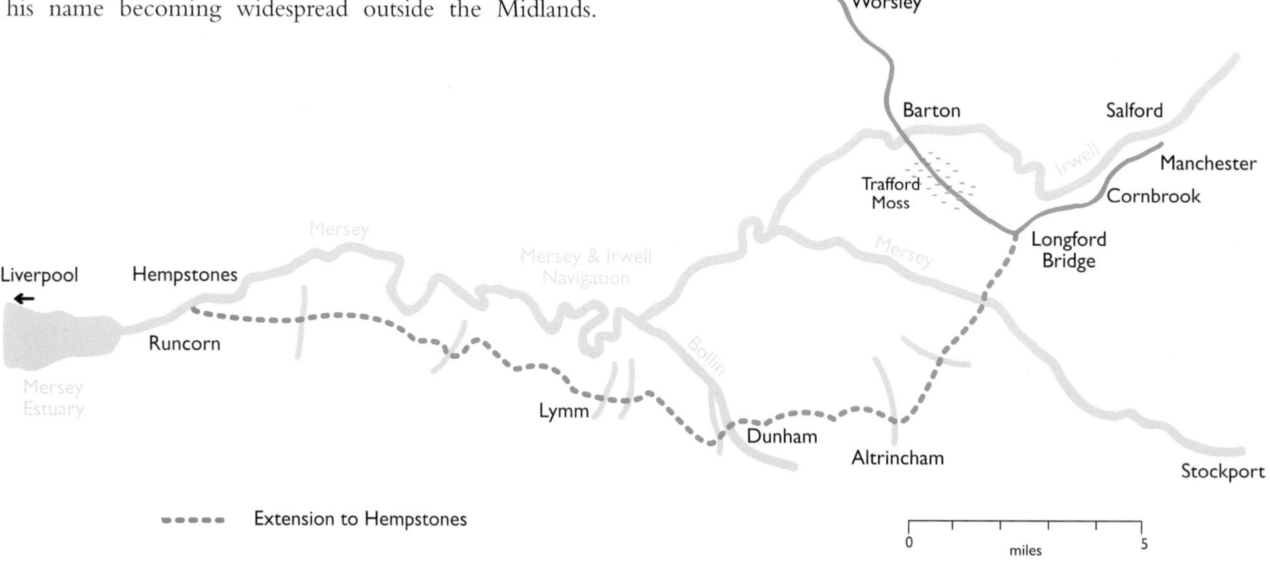

Bridgewater Canal – the extension to Hempstones as defined in the third Act, 24 March 1762

efficient. The supporters of the established river lobby were referred to as the 'Old Navigators', their opposing pamphlets answered by more from the duke.[15] Gradually, public opinion began to back the duke's arguments, swayed by the success at Barton. The priority now was to gather the facts to be used in evidence at Westminster where the entrenched opinions of the river/road lobby would form a vigorous opposition. For James Brindley it would mean the last four months of 1761 becoming a period of almost continuous winter travel on horseback. The second and third weeks of September opened with three days in Liverpool, probably furthering the duke's plans for the canal's approach to that city, but thereafter it was a time of consolidation of Brindley's pre-canal business. Three days at Congleton mill, then across to Newcastle-under-Lyme followed by a day working on one of the steam pumping-engines installed for the Broad family at Fenton, then back to Congleton mill for another three days. Eventually, Brindley was free to return to Worsley, only to leave again to start two weeks surveying the route towards the Mersey estuary.[16] For near 20 miles the canal's constant level would have to be maintained not only across two rivers but also across numerous brooks and lesser watercourses that followed the natural fall of the land towards the Mersey. The necessary embankments would hinder the canal traffic's access to the towns and villages along the route, but that was not as important as the duke's requirement for a level canal that was as straight as possible between two flourishing cities and his colliery. He had no shareholders or committees of management to mollify by providing a wharf at every village. His single-minded aim was the port of Liverpool and the onward transportation of its coastal and Atlantic trade – to be carried in the boats that had taken his coal to the booming city. Eventually, the only locks on the Bridgewater Canal would take it down to the Mersey, an unavoidable conclusion as the level canal could not otherwise link with the river, which had continued its natural fall. The result would be a canal unlike any other built in the Brindley era: one that had all the hallmarks of those that would be built in the following century – wide, relatively straight, embanked, with time-consuming and expensive locks avoided wherever possible. It is clear that the engineering technology of the time could build such a waterway and that Brindley's later circuitous canals were the product of the involvement of myriad shareholders, coupled with a requirement that a waterway must serve the varied political, financial and commercial agendas of those investors.

By the middle of November the route to the Mersey had been surveyed and Brindley added up the number of days he had spent in the duke's employment to date, making the total 133. There may have been some dispute about his claim because from now on Brindley would write in his notebook each day where he was on behalf of the duke, and often what he was doing. The almost continuous travelling of this period culminated with another journey to London, through the cold and damp of the early winter. Riding his mare, Brindley set off on 19th November 1761, arriving on the 23rd. The duke and Earl Gower had remained at Worsley until the completion of the surveying towards Liverpool, and had then gone to London a month before Brindley.[17] The reason for the summons to their engineer was to assist with preparations for the submission to Parliament of the third Act, work which had to take account of recent events. In the eighteenth century the monarch was still actively involved in the political scene, so royal circumstances were of profound importance to the Duke of Bridgewater. Two months previously, the coronation of the 22-year-old George III had taken place, two weeks after his marriage to Princess Sophie Charlotte of Mecklenburg-Strelitz, aged seventeen.[18]

James Brindley stayed in London for one week before starting his journey back to Worsley. The weather was very cold, the daylight sparse. On the second day, while making for an overnight stay at Coventry, his faithful mare slipped and had a bad fall in the frost. Fortunately she was only bruised and shaken. After a night's rest in a stables they were able to carry on, taking a further three days to reach Worsley. Something of what had been discussed in London can be deduced from Brindley's activities immediately after his return. After only one day's rest the 45-year-old engineer rode to Dunham and Hempstones, presumably to further define route details, before reporting to Henry Tomkinson, the duke's Manchester solicitor.[19] It had been learnt that opponents to the third Act would assert the view that there was insufficient traffic between Liverpool and Manchester to warrant the construction of a canal.[20] To quash that theory Brindley spent two days in December counting the loaded carts and horses using the road. As that was a somewhat mundane task for a highly paid consultant engineer one can only assume that it was considered important for a parliamentary witness to state that he had seen the facts himself. Even so, it is surprising that one of John Gilbert's clerks did not carry out such an assignment. As the days shortened, Brindley – and his horse – had a rare rest from travelling with the last two weeks of 1761 spent at Worsley, but such leisure was not to last. The first two weeks of the new year would be a busy time of measuring and checking information before returning to London for the passage of the third Act. A crucial political battle was about to take place, the outcome of which would determine the future of canal construction in Britain. Success would blow a hole in the defences of the river and road lobby – a hole through which would pour the progressive waters of the first Canal Age. James Brindley was now at the heart of a development of national importance.

Brindley set out for London in the early morning of 13th January 1762. The journey was difficult in the short daylight hours, travel at night not only being dangerous unless there was a full moon in a cloudless sky but the approaches to London were still plagued by highwaymen. He arrived on Sunday 17th, bringing with him the data he had measured since the start of the year: facts and figures to parry the predicted thrusts of the opposition – not only road traffic levels but also the heights of the tides in the Mersey estuary at Hempstones.[21] It was obvious that the 'Old Navigators' would claim that an enlarged canal would be filled by taking excessive amounts of water from tributaries of their rivers, thereby decreasing the depth in the Mersey and the Irwell and hindering their boats. Already the supplies from the underground colliery at Worsley were bolstered by the diversion of water from Worsley Brook and the river Medlock.[22] To counter their assertions, Parliament would have to be convinced that the proposed extension would have sufficient water without harming others' interests. As there was no method of accurately measuring water flows and volumes, one had to be developed. To do so, John Smeaton's high reputation was again harnessed, this time to work with Brindley in devising a calibrated water-gauge[23] – a task they undertook with such success the product would still be considered an accurate method two centuries later. Eventually, the Duke of Bridgewater's party was ready to submit its evidence to a committee of the House of Commons, made up of MPs all of whom had a vested interest in the outcome.

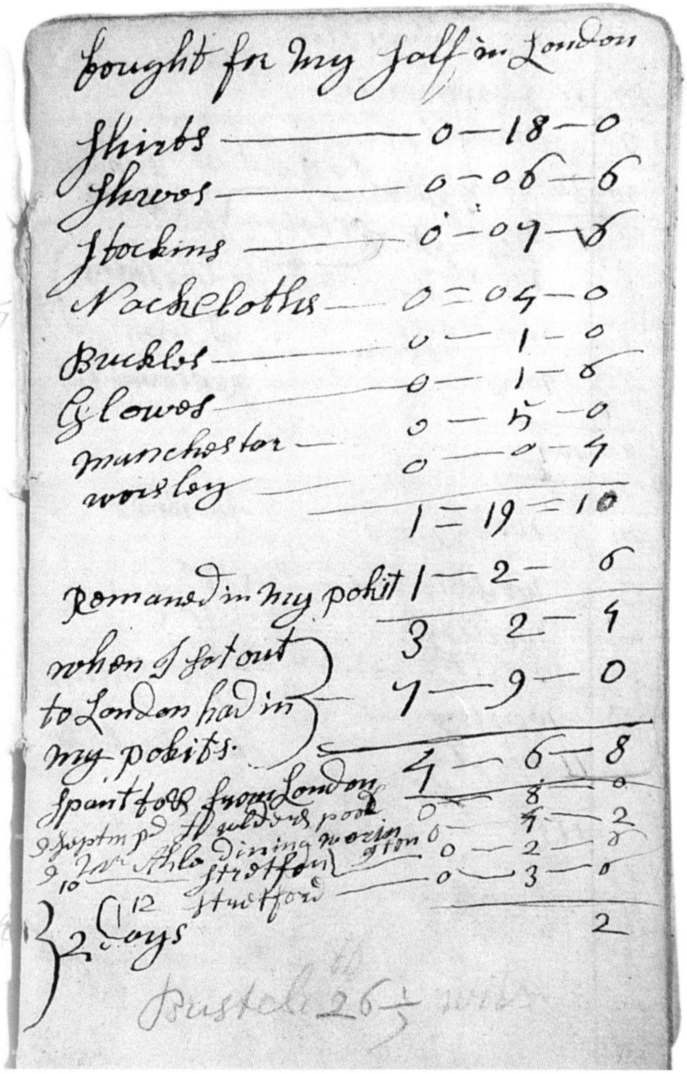

James Brindley used his visits to London to buy new clothes for himself. This page from his 1762 notebook details the purchases made on a visit during that period

Courtesy of the Institution of Civil Engineers, Archives

It was said of Brindley that his mind was always occupied with his business and that he was incapable of relaxing 'in any of the common amusements of life'.[24] In an endeavour to lighten Brindley's mind John and Lydia Gilbert took him to Drury Lane theatre on the evening before battle was to commence at Westminster. There they saw David Garrick, the greatest actor of the age, perhaps in his legendary role as Shakespeare's Richard III. If so, they would have seen a play in the English tragic style, that is 'very bloody', with Shakespearean tragedies and histories typically reviewed as 'the most barbarous cruelty and the most refined wickedness'.[25] Probably never having been to such an event before, it was said to have disturbed Brindley so much he was unfit for business for several days – semi-derogatory comments made of the unsophisticated Brindley by others who considered themselves more refined. In forming a judgement we should not imagine a theatre audience as the quiet, reserved body of this century. Instead, the London theatres were raucous places where the nobility were treated with little respect, especially so during the long intervals between acts. If that was not enough, Puritan hostility to the theatre was not dead. Actors were considered to be dissolute while actresses were seen as little better than whores. Theatreland was the haunt of pick-pockets and ladies of the town – the 'nuns' who worked for a 'Covent Garden abbess' not giving their lives to prayer! For such reasons, Garrick had held back from an acting career while his mother was alive, and during 1762 there would be serious disturbances known as the 'half-price riots' at London theatres.[26] It is therefore understandable if Brindley, with his Quaker roots, was disturbed by the experience but there is no evidence that his discomfort lasted for a number of days, although he may have regretted the nine shillings expenditure – £33 at present values.[27]

The Bridgewater Canal's extension to Hempstones would duplicate the route of an established river navigation and was the first to lay down a forceful challenge to an old regime. There was, therefore, great interest in the Westminster committee sessions where the first public debate of the merits or otherwise of rivers and canals as transport mediums was heard. The opposition to the duke, the Mersey & Irwell Navigation, was fighting the cause of all such river enterprises in the country. Joshua Taylor, a miller, stated that the two rivers could carry all the cargoes necessary and that the canal would be of no service. Others argued that the slow-flowing waters of the canal would freeze up in the winter and halt traffic whereas the running water of the rivers would remain clear. Throughout February 1762 the battle raged on although Brindley was ill for the first two weeks of the month, eventually recovering and giving thanks at the church of St Mary Axe in the City of London.[28] Taking his place in the duke's ranks he listened to the 'Old Navigators' giving reasons for opposing the canal extension, their assertions parried by Henry Tomkinson, the duke's solicitor, who presented Brindley's traffic survey figures during four and a half hours of intense examination.[29] Leading the opposition was Lord Strange, an able politician who had formed the established landowning and navigation interests into a formidable anti-canal force. His family owned swathes of land near Liverpool and in Cheshire, and they also had special ancient links with Salford.[30] Behind Strange's banner the landowners themselves were stridently led by Sir Richard Brook whose Norton Priory estate was on the proposed canal route, south of Warrington. He had commercial interests in river navigation and considered the canal superfluous, moreover, he had recently spent £20,000 rebuilding his house and laying out magnificent gardens and lakes. That anyone should be given the right to enter his land to build a canal, along which a towpath would allow general access, was anathema to him. He would become the Duke of Bridgewater's strongest opponent – delaying the completion of the canal by years. Even though the Act would give the duke legal rights Sir Richard would fight on, knowing that delays cost money – and the delays he would cause by arguing about the cost of the land would almost bring the duke to his financial knees.[31] The obdurate landowner would delay the completion of the canal through his land until 1776.[32] It was to be a long and bitter dispute.

John Gilbert opened the case for the Duke of Bridgewater, giving an outline of what was intended. However, the star witness was John Smeaton, for the first time standing squarely in the canal camp. Before this he was associated solely with the 'Old Navigators' through his on-going engineering responsibilities for the Calder & Hebble Navigation in Yorkshire – a substantial project for the time but solely an old-style improvement of the two rivers in its name. Now he told the committee that 'those who have experienced Canals would chuse to Navigate in them when they can'. Although his role was solely to lend authority and status to the assertion that the canal's water supply would be adequate, Smeaton was uncompromising in his opinion that canals were vastly superior to rivers. Astutely he mentioned that the volume of the flow from the colliery sough at Worsley would result in the canal overflowing into the Irwell, to the benefit of that river. However, the locks that would eventually have to be built down to the Mersey estuary concerned the members of the committee greatly. If they leaked, perhaps the water supply would be inadequate. Smeaton confirmed that such locks should suffer only a little leakage, the rate dependent on how they were constructed, covering his position by reminding the gentlemen that he was not the engineer who would carry out the work.[33]

Thomas Unsworth, a boatman on the Irwell, explained that the efficiency of his craft was hindered by the fact that skippers had to estimate the varying depth of water in the river and load their craft accordingly. In the winter they could carry 35 tons, but summer water shortages restricted them to 18 tons. Another boatman, John Bradshaw, who had sailed vessels on the Irwell for 25 years, was forced to admit that even with a light cargo he had never done the voyage from Liverpool to Manchester in less than one week. It was generally agreed that boats regularly waited at Liverpool for two to three weeks before being loaded, thereafter taking an average of two weeks to reach Manchester. It was quite usual for delays at Warrington to stretch to four or five days because of summer low water levels.[34] Highlighting these problems Brindley, in his usual confident manner, stoutly asserted that the canal's relatively straight route would be eight or nine miles shorter than the river's meandering course, its deep water and towing-path allowing boats to make the journey from Hempstones to Manchester in one day – every day, if necessary. Scornfully he compared that picture with what he had noticed at Barton – boatmen on the river throwing anchors ahead of them and then pulling on the anchor-ropes to kedge their craft over the shallows. Again the subject of water supply was raised, to which he replied that he had 'as much experience about defending water as anyone'.[35] That was a claim Brindley could substantiate, unlike his assertions on the construction of locks, of which he had no experience at all. Notwithstanding that minor matter, he boldly held forth on the subject. There is a fable that he took a piece of chalk from his pocket and drew pictures on the floor to further clarify his methods. Asked how long river locks lasted he replied 'Perhaps a twelve month, and perhaps not two months', which was a claim with little justification. Whereas, he said, his locks on the canal would last 'ten years or more without repairing in that state of perfection as not to lose more than one gallon in an hour'.[36] Who could cast doubt on that imprudent declaration? In the past he had told an unbelieving

Commons committee that he could build an aqueduct to allow a canal to soar over a major river – and he had. The MPs saw a witness presenting the image of a successful man; dressed in britches, shirt, neckerchief, a broadcloth waistcoat, gloves, and black shoes with shiny buckles – all purchased a few days before.[37]

But the practicalities of building the canal were in the future. The task in hand was to persuade MPs to vote for the Act, thereby setting a precedent for the legislation which would follow to build other canals. In an age without document-copying capabilities, the duke massed his clerks to write letters to 200 supporters, followed a week later by 250 more. Eventually all the evidence had been given and a great debate took place in the Commons on 26th February 1762, culminating in a vote that the canal lobby won by 127 to 98. But that was not the end of the matter. March started with 250 more letters and a crucial debate on the 4th of the month before three separate divisions of the House, all of which were won by the duke. Having fought its way through the Commons, the Bill still had to pass through the House of Lords but there its passage was smoothed by the awaiting Bridgewater–Gower–Bedford powerbase. Brindley was summoned before a Lords committee but there was no opposition. The Third Reading took place on 15th March, nine weeks after Brindley had set out from Lancashire. The following day he started the ride back to the north.[38] The Royal Assent would not be granted until 24th March, but the parliamentary battles had been won.

The ride back was arduous. By the time Dunstable had been reached for the first night at an inn, Brindley noted that his mare 'had almost lost the use of her limbs'. The next day they trudged through the cold March weather to the edge of Towcester, the next morning on to Coventry. Three days later Brindley reached Congleton, having gone there via Newchapel in his Staffordshire homelands.[39] It is significant that even though he had just been embroiled in the national politics of canal construction, and had acquired fame for his work on Barton aqueduct, Brindley's priority after a prolonged absence was to work on the complex gears of a silk mill that his men had been building for some time. Indeed, just before leaving London he had spent a day with the mill's proprietor, giving assurances that mill work had not been forgotten in the plethora of canal responsibilities. It was a further two days before Brindley returned to Worsley but then he went immediately to Throstle Nest, to supervise the canal's approach to Manchester.[40]

Chapter 9

GROWING FAME

In our century, only a small minority of the population know the discomfort of continuously working outside – and it unlikely that they also travel unsheltered, as did James Brindley. To keep out the cold and rain his pre-Macintosh winter clothes were many-layered and heavy. His leather boots were pre-Wellington and not waterproof, although usually heavy with caked mud. The pre-McAdam surfaces of roads, work-yards and paths were slippery and heavy underfoot where they were not cobbled. The tiring nature of just getting about in the winter, let alone working, in earlier centuries has been mostly lost to us; as has the reliance on the moon to lift the heavy darkness of some long winter nights. The physical effort required to lead Brindley's endless round of outdoor work and travel should be borne in mind as he resumes his canal responsibilities without a day's rest on his return from London.

The spring of 1762 was spent on an endless round of travelling as the daylight hours lengthened. The pattern was a number of days away, then back to Worsley for a week or so, away again, and back. It is unclear how much on-site management Brindley undertook of the Bridgewater Canal's continuing construction at this stage. The periods at Worsley could have been used thus but his notebooks contain no evidence of his activities there. Instead, the visits elsewhere indicate that his responsibilities were still in the forward planning role. Tentative proposals had been made for a canal to link Chester to the planned Trent & Mersey and Brindley is once again the man who does the initial reconnoitring of a new route, stopping at Nantwich to report his findings to the duke's solicitor Henry Tomkinson.[1] Many days were spent in Liverpool, where the duke had purchased land for a transhipment dock, but all we know is that two days were spent pointing a wall, followed by a bathe in salt water. The latter was often recommended as a medicinal measure, so his body may have been complaining about the constant stress of his lifestyle. If it was, he did not listen.

No matter how busy he was, Brindley regularly found time to travel via the silk mill at Congleton. The continuance of his millwright career indicates an innate lack of confidence. No matter how successful he appeared to others, there was still the doubt that it may all end without warning. This unease was amplified by the men around him who were the epitome of establishment England with the security of well-placed families and land ownership. Not only the Duke of Bridgewater and Earl Gower with their aristocratic powerbase but also the Gilberts whose intricate family network managed many great estates, in addition to their own lands. James Brindley, on the other hand, was self-employed, with only his abilities to keep the wolf from the door. He was unmarried, his parents had no influence, and his brother John's presence amongst the potters of Burslem was of little advantage as yet. If anywhere could be called 'home', in the wider sense of where familiarity lends ease to everyday life, then it was by now the Burslem/Newchapel area of Staffordshire, but visits were rare. Later, when the Trent & Mersey Canal would allow him to spend more time there, the settled existence of his friend Josiah Wedgwood would once again accentuate Brindley's precarious situation. With his devoted wife and children Wedgwood was also surrounded by his wider family, a fourth-generation potter who stayed in Staffordshire, although his name would go around the world. A further glowing example was Brindley's engineering contemporary John Smeaton a Royal Academician who moved in circles forever closed to Brindley. By now Smeaton had left London and had returned to the house of his birth near Leeds where he lived and worked for much of the rest of his life, his two daughters helping by finishing his technical drawings in indian ink.[2] This long-rooted stability in a family heartland was the normal pattern of society, at all levels. In contrast James Brindley was always on the move – living in taverns on the road and near worksites. Any personal contacts could only be of a shallow nature. He seldom saw his family, only his brother-in-law, Samuel Simcock, who worked for him on the Bridgewater Canal and later schemes. Brindley was rarely at ease. Those who knew him noted his inability to relax, as after the London theatre visit when he complained it had so disturbed his ideas he had resolved never to see a play again.[3] The cause and effect was a gnawing, deeply felt, sense of insecurity. It would never leave him, instead driving him to take almost every commission offered, the few refusals forced by lack of time, not willingness. Insecurity was the compelling force behind Brindley's career, and it would place his name on almost all of England's early canals. In addition, he would readily agree to give his professional opinion on other waterways – the first manifestation of which was seen in June 1762.

South Yorkshire's river Don descends from the eastern flank of the high Pennines and flows through lessening hills to Doncaster, and beyond to the river Ouse and the Humber estuary. By 1751 boats could reach as far upstream as Tinsley, just beyond Rotherham, but the remaining 55 feet rise in levels to Sheffield had so far prevented them reaching that booming industrial city.

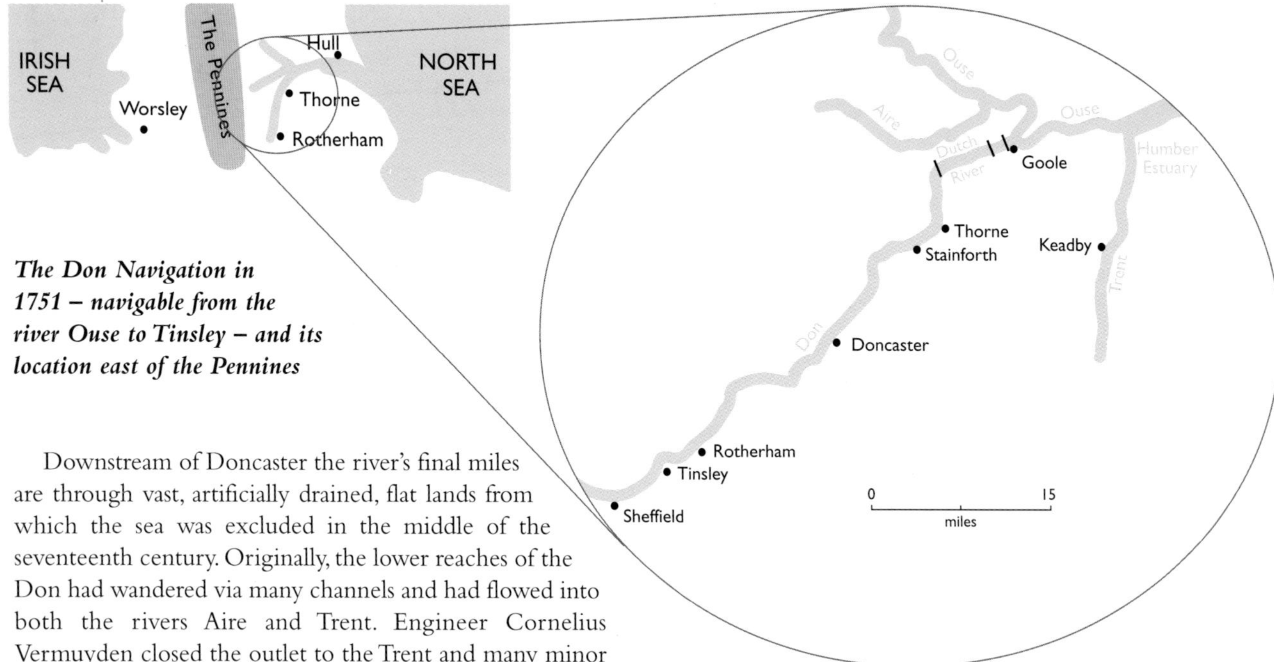

The Don Navigation in 1751 – navigable from the river Ouse to Tinsley – and its location east of the Pennines

Downstream of Doncaster the river's final miles are through vast, artificially drained, flat lands from which the sea was excluded in the middle of the seventeenth century. Originally, the lower reaches of the Don had wandered via many channels and had flowed into both the rivers Aire and Trent. Engineer Cornelius Vermuyden closed the outlet to the Trent and many minor channels, forcing the whole of the Don's waters into the river Aire and reclaiming thousands of acres of land for cultivation. But the Aire could not cope with the Don's floodwaters so Vermuyden cut an artificial channel to the river Ouse at Goole, which became the Don's only outlet. These man-made final miles of the Don are known as the Dutch River, a reference to Vermuyden's nationality. With its piecemeal developments over a long period of time, its fast-running Pennine drainage waters and powerful tidal flows, the Don was an extreme example of the disadvantages of river navigations as cited by the canal lobby. As a leading advocate of that lobby James Brindley was perhaps surprised to receive a missive from the Don Navigation Company seeking his advice on how improvements could be made.[4] He knew nothing of the geography of south Yorkshire and its rivers, had no contacts there and was otherwise very busy with the Bridgewater Canal. Nevertheless, as soon as he received the request the insecure Brindley rode off across the high Pennines to Rotherham. There he inspected the complex of waterways and heard from the representatives of the Navigation Company of a bitter dispute with Messrs Walker, the

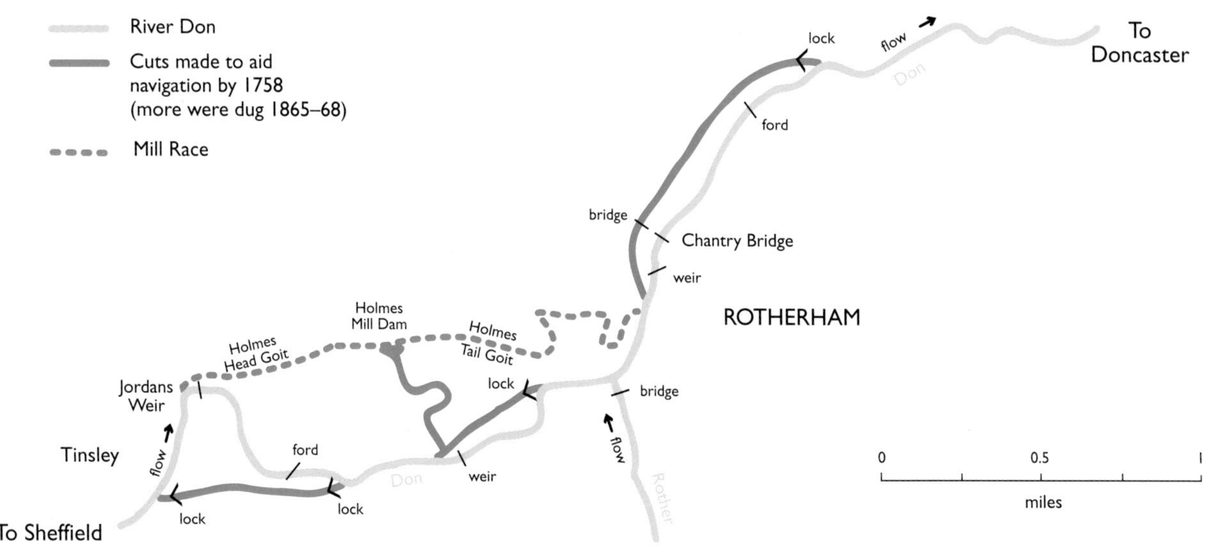

The complexities of the Don Navigation at Rotherham, 1762

proprietors of a fast-developing local ironworks where the machinery that stamped, cut and shaped the iron was powered by water-wheels driven by the river Don. In 1746 Walkers had built Jordans weir to maintain the flow through Holmes goit and into their mill-dam, from where it turned the wheels before being discharged back into the river.[5] This caused disputes when the navigation was extended through the area, with the three adjacent locks starved of water in times of drought. It was hoped that as a millwright/canal engineer Brindley would be able to find a solution acceptable to both camps.

Two days later he rode to Doncaster where he discussed his findings with the Navigation Company and was asked to estimate the costs. Although Brindley was thought 'judicious' by the Navigation Company, it was not in his interests as a consulting engineer to promote a solely arbitrational solution although, in reality, that is what was required.[6] He could, however, help with an improvement downstream on the Dutch River. In normal tidal conditions large keels and coastal sloops could reach Thorne from the Humber, but there were three bridges between the town and the entrance from the river Ouse, each one of which required masts and sails to be lowered. To encourage coastal traffic Brindley was asked to submit an estimate for the construction of three replacement swivel-bridges.[7] Riding out into the vast reclaimed acres beyond Doncaster he saw an unfamiliar landscape – flat, remote, extensive, almost treeless, and criss-crossed by a network of drainage ditches, with the river constrained behind massive earth banks up to 20 feet high.[8] It presented an alien sight to a man who had spent all his years in the high hills of central England – gone was the usual valley-constricted horizon; instead the land stretched for as far as could be seen, topped by an unbelievably large sky. He had known the Cheshire Plain since his apprenticeship, but that natural feature would not have lessened the impact of this land reclaimed from the sea and tidal rivers. However, its alien nature had nothing that would cause an outwardly confident surveyor to refuse a commission. The accompanying gentlemen of the Don Navigation Company also discussed with Brindley the need for a canal to link the Don to the Trent, alleviating the need for boats to take the hazardous and oft-delayed route via the Humber. Having left Worsley a week before with very little notice, there was no time now to undertake any surveying, but Brindley agreed he would return later in the year to design the swivel-bridges and inspect a route for the canal to the Trent.

Rushing off to further his career elsewhere, on projects with no bearing on the developments at Worsley, was the behaviour which caused the most difficulties with John Gilbert. It set Brindley apart in the triumvirate. However, the Bridgewater estate must bear a measure of the blame, gaining as it did from the flexibility inherent in his consultancy status whilst guarding against prolonged absence by paying expenses and fees at lengthy intervals. Arriving back at Worsley on 28th June 1762, with no day

Above: The Dutch River looking downstream from Rawcliffe Bridge. The flat landscape alien to Brindley's hilly area experience

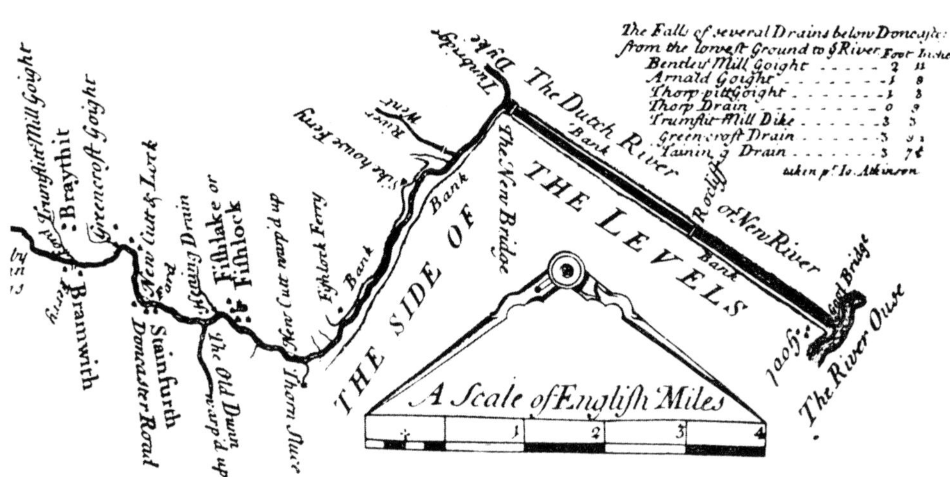

Left: Part of an original map showing the Dutch River section of the Don Navigation, 1722 and the location of the fixed bridges replaced by Brindley-designed swivel bridges, The New Bridge, Rawcliffe Bridge, Goole Bridge

of rest, Brindley immediately set to, using the long hours of summer daylight to advantage.[9] As before, the work was on forward planning and specific structures rather than the 'common cutting' of the canal channel. Remaining through to August was also wise, as an accounting period then ended – expenses for 101 weeks accommodation and stabling alone had added up to £60.12s during the previous three years.[10] But Brindley was conscious of his agreement with the Don Navigation Company and he once again set off across the Pennines in early September. It was a journey to be avoided in the winter and waiting until the spring was not an option as the low-lying lands near Thorne would be waterlogged at that time of year. Pocketing fees for 302 days and the expenses, Brindley went via Staffordshire, calling in at Newchapel to pay Hugh Henshall for his surveying services before going on to Leek for a rare visit to his parents. It was an auspicious time for an eldest son to arrive back at the farm – money in his pocket, new clothes, with tales of his successful canal work and of dukes, earls, the theatre, the teeming port of Liverpool and the machinations of political London. And, furthermore, he was stopping off on his way to the other side of the hills, an area little known by Staffordshire residents.

For over two weeks James Brindley worked without cease near Thorne, reconnoitring and surveying a canal route to the Trent, and making plans for swivel-bridges.[11] Although the commercial need for the canal had been recognised it was another waterway for which the time was not yet right, along with the Trent & Mersey. Later it would form part of the 1790s canal boom, being completed in 1802 between Stainforth on the river Don, and Keadby on the river Trent. But the swivel-bridges at Goole, Rawcliffe, and Newbridge were erected, the work contracted to Martin Worstenholme who was to do the work 'according to the model made by Mr Brindley, Engineer'.[12] A master-carpenter from Eckington, near Chesterfield, Worstenholme would later become one of the professionals at the core of the workforce constructing the Chesterfield Canal, a waterway that Brindley would also plan to take out across the flat carr-lands to the Trent before its route was altered for commercial reasons.[13] The commission from the Don Navigation Company is, therefore, significant as the first awarded to Brindley outside his usual geographical sphere of operations, thus allowing him to gain experience in the practical problems associated with a very different landscape – and the spinning of an early thread in the network of skilled men that would develop around him.

The decision to complete the commission in Yorkshire before the winter set in proved to be well founded. November and December 1762 were blighted by continuous rain, followed by a January of hard frosts – rime left every twig snowy white, the river Severn froze above Worcester, the Thames above London.[14] Elsewhere, Brindley's friend Josiah Wedgwood used the cold months to concentrate on paperwork in his Burslem office. Nearby, there were now 150 separate potteries with a total workforce of nearly 7,000.[15] All continued to suffer the problems inherent in transporting raw materials and finished products via the coast, rivers and un-made roads, but the plans for a canal to pass through the area as it linked the Trent and the Mersey remained dormant. Rather than wait for an doubtful scheme to reach fruition, Wedgwood used his organisational genius to promote turnpike roads. Internationally, the Peace of Paris was signed in February 1763, marking the victorious end of the Seven Years War. Britain had gained many colonies and it was the height of the earliest phase of her empire – augmented by France losing much of North America and influence in India, and Spain having to give up Florida, a previous threat to Britain's ships going to her lucrative West Indies islands.[16] Not only was it the end of a war it was also the start of thirteen years of peace, the longest such period for a generation, during which time the waterways of the first Canal Age would spread across England.

By September 1763 the beacon of that age, the Bridgewater Canal, had reached Cornbrook, one mile from the planned eastern terminus at Castlefield, Manchester.[17] Now that the three Acts of Parliament had been obtained and much of the forward planning completed, James Brindley became involved in the practicalities of canal construction, gaining experience of the day-to-day problems he would delegate to assistants on his later canals. One month, November 1763, will serve as an example.[18]

October ended with a messenger finding Brindley at a nearby work-camp before breakfast. The news was that a bridge had fallen down at Cornbrook, and furthermore it was on George Lloyd's land. This was unfortunate because Mr Lloyd was a vociferous opponent of the scheme, His intransigence would eventually force an exasperated Duke of Bridgewater to purchase Lloyd's Hulme Hall estate for £9,000, to be immediately mortgaged back to Lloyd for £4,500, a debt not discharged for 40 years.[19] But that was to happen in the following year. The priority now was to resolve the bridge problem before it exacerbated an already fraught situation. Brindley rode to Cornbrook and ordered that the bridge over a freshly dug dry section of the canal was to be 'supported again' before noon. The rest of the week was spent on a mix of tasks. Suppliers of construction materials were dealt with before authorising the line past Mr Lloyd's gardens. A deal was struck with a farmer over the location of drainage channels in a wheatfield – business necessarily completed before the afternoon as Brindley thought it prudent to attend the first ingress of water into the new canal up to Mr Lloyd's temporary bridge. At the same time, work was underway on the western arm of the canal at Sale Moor so that merited a morning's attention, before returning to Cornbrook to oversee the felling of a poplar tree. From this he noted that three useful logs could be made – 11 feet, 20 feet, and 14 feet 6 inches – welcome, as timber was already scarce in the area, a map of Worsley manor showing little woodland left.[20] Then the carpenters from the work-site were ordered to Cornbrook to work on Mr Lloyd's bridge, Brindley following them there in the afternoon.

The location was named from the Corne Brook, which flowed down there to the river Irwell. However, its course would be bisected by the new canal and as a tributary of the navigable river, its waters were not to be diverted nor used otherwise. Brindley's solution was to divert the brook through an inverted siphon, the principle he had used with great success at Wet Earth colliery ten years before. Now the Corne Brook was to be fed into a large circular basin, from where it would fall gradually into a smaller basin within it. From there it would flow into a tunnel under the canal, the exit of which was at a lower level than the entrance, thereby forcing the water to find a level and rise into its natural channel for further passage down to the river.[21] Early in the morning of Friday the 4th, work started on damming the brook to take it into the new system – Brindley noting that a collier maimed in digging the tunnel was sent to the infirmary. A mid-day meal at The Bull was followed by a return to the site where work on the dam was suffering from lack of manpower. It was important that the re-channelling be ready to deal with a brook swollen by winter rains. Brindley, therefore, rode to the work-camp and ordered four more men to Cornbrook. The six-day week ended with the measuring of a field opposite Mr Lloyd's house and a work-camp afternoon.

Although Sundays were a day of rest, Brindley often used them to update his accounts, noting how many days to date were to be charged to the Bridgewater estate. He also spent the quiet hours on various calculations, for example, planning the sizes of water-wheels and the pressure of water. On working days he usually shuttled between the canal at Cornbrook and the nearby work-camp, noting anything significant seen or decided. Management was via a number of senior men. Black David's sphere of operations was anything to do with bricks – making, stock-piling, moving, laying. Royle was a general contractor. Busick specialised in excavating the channel, including the cutting of hard rock. Whittle was a carpenter, possibly a millwright. Together they formed a core of experienced professionals, each of whom had a large number of men of his own. Foremost was Thomas Morris who would take a leading role on the Bridgewater Canal's continuing construction when Brindley's national fame took him elsewhere. By then Morris would have advocates of his own in the newspaper letter columns, an arena of battle for engineering fame.

Jopson's Coventry Mercury
28 September 1767

> Your Burslem Correspondent makes Mr Brindley the Sir Isaac Newton of his Age, but seems not to know that the Duke of Bridgewater has another ingenious man, viz Thomas Morris, who has improved on Mr Brindley, and is now raising a Valley to the Level by seven double Water-Locks, which enable him to carry Earth and Stones as if down steps. When each Lock is opened, it admits a loaded Vessel on one Side, and lets out an empty one on the other; by which means Tons of Earth are carried, and the Valley will soon rise to equal the Hills around, and the Navigation keeps its level. [22]

By 11th November Busick had put nineteen men on cutting through the hard rock at Cornbrook, and Black David's men had amassed 186,268 bricks there. At Worsley, masons were cutting stones for the lip of the weir over which the brook would flow into the siphon. Boats for carrying heavy supplies were being caulked. At the mortar-mill, Brindley told Whittle that the pit for the spindle was to be sunk level with the canal. Each week was a sequence of myriad decisions and situation management. Brindley was told by the intransigent Mr Lloyd that the restored bridge on his land was to bear a carriageway 15 feet wide. On the watered sections of canal, the towpath edges were completed by men working from the 20-ton boat, which was large enough to carry them, their tools and materials. In many ways Brindley's role was similar to that of an on-site civil-engineer of our time, but in one respect it was very different. In the eighteenth century engineering was off the land with the basic commodities having to be found nearby – clay for bricks, coal for kilns, timber for scaffolding and numerous other uses, stone for edges and load-bearing. The tools and wheelbarrows were made by on-site blacksmiths, whose forges needed good quality coal which would burn without impurities. All of this was the responsibility of James Brindley.

In the middle of November the weather remained fine, and precious Sundays were added to his working week while the other men rested. There was a smithy at the work-camp near Cornbrook, a new supply of fuel for which Brindley arranged to be tested by the blacksmiths. That involved ordering a boat to Cornbrook to be filled with 'slack', unloading it at the smithy, and washing the cargo to remove detritus before it could be tried by the blacksmiths. As the boat was loaded at Cornbrook the coal would have come from boats on the adjacent river, a cut from which allowed construction materials to be brought to the canal from far afield. The link to the river at Cornbrook, known as the Gut, would be the canal's only outlet until the whole waterway was completed down into the Mersey estuary at Runcorn. The necessity for such a link had long been foreseen and had been agreed between the Mersey & Irwell Navigation and the duke's agent on 14th June 1759, thereafter being incorporated in the first Parliamentary Bill, although the location was changed.[23] The Gut also allowed boats for use on the canal to be built elsewhere, many of which came from Shropshire, via Chester and Liverpool, and up the Mersey and the Irwell to Cornbrook, and onto the canal. This started in 1765 and went on for ten years.[24]

Every day Brindley sent men to various sites as the priorities evolved. He was himself continually riding between the main construction site at Cornbrook, the work-camp, and Worsley – giving advice about the gears of a lime-mill, telling Black David to re-do brickwork and copings, sometimes working until 7pm. The morning of Friday 18th saw further discord between Brindley and John Gilbert, one that was typical of the friction in their relationship as the pressures of the work began to weigh heavily. Meeting at a local inn the two men disagreed about the allocation of work to a group of carpenters. Gilbert wanted them to go to Castlefield to make floors and window-frames for a building there. Brindley had work for them to do at Sale Moor. Gilbert then took it upon himself to issue directions for the drainage of a piece of land adjacent to the canal, voicing his displeasure at the current plans for it. In the afternoon Brindley's mood darkened further when the son of the intransigent land-owner Mr Lloyd annoyed him further. The engineer wiped his hands of the mater by passing it to Mr Tomkinson, the duke's solicitor. Perhaps having had enough of it all, James Brindley ended the day by going to Manchester to purchase a new pair of boots for himself. But there was no escaping it. The next day was again a round of inspections and orders – gravelling towpaths, noting the effect of a strong wind on the waters of the canal.

By Monday 21st the weather had turned very much colder. The carpenters were put on to changing a standard boat into an ice-breaker, meanwhile, the old 20-ton boat was sent to Worsley to break through the ice there. The snow and frost caused the labourers to stop work but the masons and carpenters carried on, as did a gang mending a road. Brindley marked the water levels at various sites so that early signs of snow-melt flooding could be seen, two days later ordering Topping to cut a back drain to let off the excess water. When the weather was very cold tasks requiring a visit to the blacksmiths were always popular – visitors tarried in the comforting, joint-easing warmth of the forge and exchanged gossip and opinions before replacing dried outerwear for a dilatory return to the dark, cold and often damp conditions of outside work. By Thursday 24th the weather allowed a trip to Salford quay to inspect grinding-stones for the mill at Worsley, followed by the selection of timber at a sawpit. More business negotiations followed in the afternoon when Jock agreed to do back-ditching at Sale Moor for 6d per rood, Brindley agreeing to lend him four wheelbarrows until new ones could be made for the job. The following day an inspection of woodwork was followed by orders to the carpenters to incorporate a plank, level with the surface of the water, to walk upon. Too many men were currently employed at the work-camp and Brindley discharged twelve of them. He jotted down the measurements of an area for which gravel, soil and paving-stones were required and was then confronted by Mr Lloyd who said he had the right to take the stones as he wished. As usual, Brindley kept his distance from such matters, only insisting that Mr Lloyd took no more stones or gravel until the matter had been referred to John Gilbert. The morning of Saturday 26th was dry and an order for 20 yards of wheeling-plank was given, and more men discharged. But the afternoon was blighted by great rains and a concerned Brindley noted that the water in the incomplete canal had quickly risen another two inches. Sunday morning he 'lay in bed till noon', listening to the heavy rain and worrying about the resultant floods. In the afternoon of his one day off that week he could bear it no longer and went to check the levels, finding that 'the surface in Longford brook was within six inches of the height of the centre of the weir'.[25]

Such was November 1763 for James Brindley. Cornbrook was only one mile from the planned Manchester terminus at Castlefield, but it would be two years before that relatively

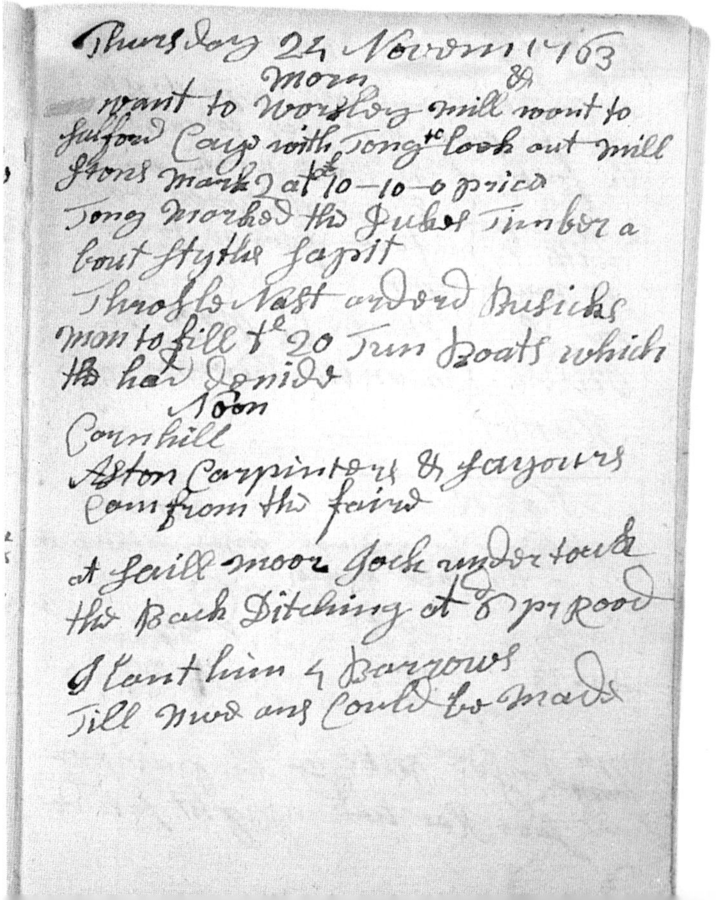
Thursday 24 Novem 1763
Morn
want to Worsley mill went to
Salford Cay with Tong to look out mill
Stones mark at 10-10-0 price
Tong marked the Jubes Timber a
bout Stythe sapit
Throstle Nest ordered Brickes
men to fill the 20 Tun Boats which
the had denide
Noon
Cornhill
Aston Carpinters & Sayours
com from the faire
at Saill moor Jock undertouk
the Back Ditching at 6 pr Rood
I lent him 4 barrows
Till new ons could be made

Brindley's actions on 24 November 1763 when working on the Bridgewater Canal

Courtesy of the Institution of Civil Engineers, Archives

short length of canal was completed, with the whole canal taking another thirteen years. If the Bridgewater Canal had continued in the same vein as those in continental Europe – a one-off scheme backed by private aristocratic finance – that month would probably have been typical of Brindley's career as a canal engineer. But the country was recently victorious in the Seven Years War against France, and resources and capital could be released from war production.[26] The resultant surge in public works – roads, bridges, harbours – would be led by the Trent & Mersey Canal, sloughing off its dormancy to follow the Bridgewater's lead. Perceived as the practical genius behind that example, Brindley's name was already synonymous with engineering success and an ability to overcome all obstacles. Gentlemen throughout the country were reading visitors' accounts such as, 'I have lately been viewing the artificial wonders of London and the natural wonders of the Peak, but none of them gave me so much pleasure as the Duke of Bridgewater's navigation in this country. His projector, the ingenious Mr Brindley, has indeed made such improvements in this way, as are truly astonishing'.[27] Standing in the cold November rain, tormented by what damage might be done by the possible flooding of a brook, Mr Brindley doubtless saw matters in less glowing terms.

Chapter 10

A NATIONAL NETWORK BEGINS

The surge in public works resulted in a growing demand for full-time professional civil engineers, but it was a new field few could enter. As is usual in infant vocations, terminology had not been defined nor methods analysed, although some attempts were being made at doing so. The authors of a reference work found that

> books afford very little assistance here, we have been therefore obliged to have recourse to Workmen themselves, who being often incapable of describing with Precision the Arts they profess, it became necessary for us to clear up and methodize their thoughts; learn the proper Terms of the Art; define them and describe the various Instruments and Machines used in their respective Occupations.[1]

In the light of this, Brindley's use of a round cheese, clay and diagrams to clarify his intentions before parliamentary committees should be viewed as clever expedients. Also taking place was the evolution of the separate roles of consultants and contractors, with Brindley himself increasingly working on the Bridgewater Canal as a consultant.[2] Soon work of a similar nature was also coming from those responsible for other waterways with the trustees of the river Weaver asking him to check their engineer's plan to make Witton Brook navigable by increasing the depth of water.

A more substantial project was offered in December 1764 when Brindley received a letter from the promoters of another river navigation, the Calder & Hebble in the Yorkshire hills. The river Calder had recently been improved up to Brighouse by John Smeaton but there were now disagreements amongst the managing commissioners. One group wanted to extend the navigation even further to Sowerby Bridge, and they won the day. Smeaton was dismissed and the letter to Brindley contained an invitation to become the company's consultant engineer for the extended scheme.[3] That he agreed to do so may appear perplexing – his name being synonymous with the new concept of stillwater canals, and therefore an opponent of traditional river navigations such as the Calder & Hebble. However, the route he was asked to oversee would not enter the river, its height up the valley necessitating a separate canal alongside the unusable small headwaters. Of greater significance to his appointment was the political element caused by a conflict of interests between Yorkshire and Lancashire. The group wanting the extension to Sowerby Bridge was based in Rochdale, Lancashire and, although topographical restraints meant the Calder & Hebble could not reach their town, they at least wanted it to meet with the turnpike road at Sowerby Bridge, which was a major east-west trading link. Powerful support for the Rochdale party came from elsewhere in Lancashire, especially Manchester. Those lobbying against the extension were based in Halifax, Yorkshire, and their influence had appointed Yorkshireman Smeaton to the scheme. The dominant Lancashire group now wanted their own engineer – and Manchester's man was Brindley. He was asked to survey the works as soon as possible, and to prepare

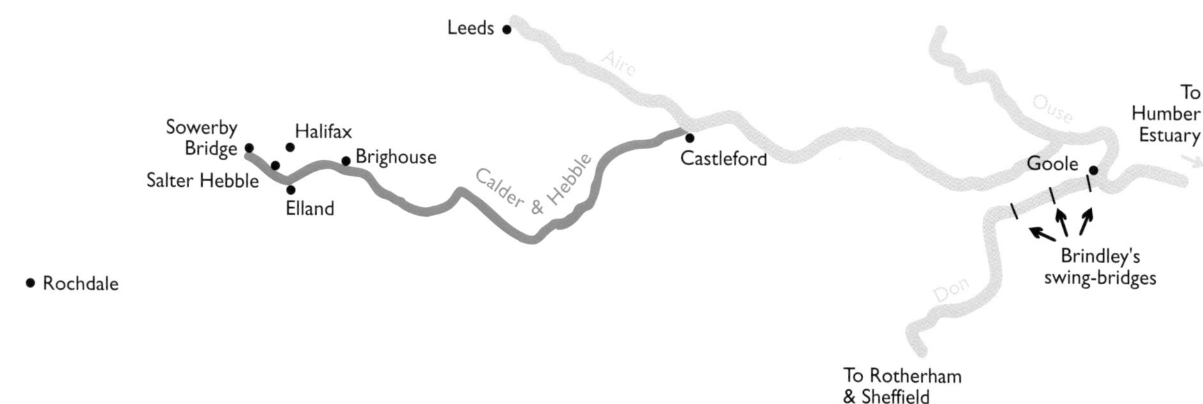

Calder & Hebble Navigation, on the eastern side of the Pennines – and its close proximity to Rochdale on the western side

plans and estimates.[4] As usual, Brindley set off at once and spent some of January 1765 riding through the high, cold Pennine hills, eventually attending a formal meeting on the last day of the month where his plan was accepted, and he was thereupon appointed Surveyor, Manager and Undertaker at £1.11s.6d each day employed, plus expenses.[5] Although driven by his innate insecurity, Brindley also realised it was prudent to accept the commission in the light of Manchester's involvement – currently the location of his main source of employment.

Perhaps that sense of taking the work because it was prudent to do so, rather than it being a project with which he would wish to be identified, explains Brindley's somewhat cursory involvement of less than eighteen months. During that time he was asked to re-survey his cut, taking it on the north side of the Calder instead of the south, which he did. But he left the project before the cut was completed to Salterhebble, although the original configuration of the staircase-pair of locks there is said to have been built to his design. If Brindley had any involvement with the locks on this navigation they would have been his first. The Calder & Hebble suffered from flash floods, as did many river navigations in hilly areas, and much work would be destroyed on the nights of 7th and 8th October 1767, and again in February 1768.[6] The likelihood of such events was another reason why Brindley expediently accepted the commission, but did not tarry – professionally he did not wish his name to be associated with river navigations and all their problems. Perhaps that is why he refused a request in 1765 to survey for improvements to the rivers Chelmer and Blackwater, saying he was too busy.[7] More to the point, Essex was a long way from his area of operations and, far to the east, there was very little chance of his involvement leading to further work. Also, matters would not have been straightforward because he had been approached by a breakaway faction opposed to a survey already done by Thomas Yeoman. Nevertheless, it was a rare refusal, although echoed by Smeaton and Lincolnshire's John Grundy. It is, therefore, surprising that in May of the same year Brindley once again headed across the Pennines to the artificially drained low-lying flat-lands near Doncaster, known as carrs. This time he was asked by the town Corporation to survey the levels in Potteric Carr and to advise on the most effective method of draining the marshy area. His report cannot be found, but it did earn an eight guinea fee even though such work was hardly his forte. The initial survey had been undertaken by Smeaton in 1762 so this is another, although minor, example of the two engineers vying for preferment.

Generally their relationship was one of professional amicability, although Smeaton's acceptance as the establishment's man resulted in a far wider range of engineering commissions whereas Brindley's reputation would forever be linked to canals, with the security of a little mill work. It is, therefore, understandable that matters should become fraught when Smeaton encroached upon Brindley's area of expertise with his appointment as engineer to build the Forth & Clyde Canal in Scotland.

This was a bold scheme to allow shipping to reach the ports of west and east Scotland without long and dangerous voyages around the northern coast. It was also making a strong bid to become the first canal in Britain to cross a watershed, the ultimate test of an artificial river and a challenge to Brindley in the sphere of operations he was making his own. Smeaton, in his initial report of 1st March 1764, had proposed the crossing of the watershed should be made underground, and had described his construction method as digging a deep cutting and then arching it over to form a tunnel.[8] As usual, there were conflicting interests amongst the canal's promoters, with one faction led by a founding partner of the adjacent Carron Ironworks, Samuel Garbett of Birmingham.[9] He was also a business ally of Josiah Wedgwood and on 18th April 1765 he wrote to the potter that Mr Mackenzie, a promoter of the Forth & Clyde, was talking 'of my applying from him to Mr Brindley to review Mr Smeaton's Plan and Estimate of the intended Canal in Scotland'.[10] The two most famous engineers of the period were to be in opposite camps.

It was often the case that routes proposed for canals by engineering luminaries followed courses previously advocated by others. Smeaton's original report contained options first mooted many years before, in January 1707, by John Adair, who himself had gained his knowledge of Scotland's central belt by studying the Roman Antonine Wall, the line of which would be followed by the canal for much of its route. This was not plagiarism, only the dictates of geography and topology.[11]

Nevertheless, Smeaton's report caused years of controversy and political wrangling with very little

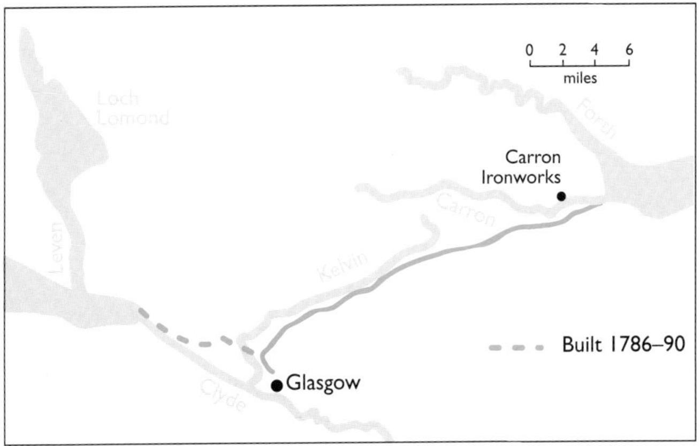

Forth & Clyde Canal in 1777. The final link between the east-coast river Forth and the west-coast river Clyde, was built in 1786–90

agreement on the canal's route or its dimensions, delaying the enabling Act of Parliament until March 1768 – two years after construction of the Trent & Mersey commenced. But the Act did not end the disputes. The owners of the Carron Ironworks were displeased that they would be by-passed by the designated route so they commissioned reports from three engineers (Brindley, Yeoman, and Golborne) which stated the canal should be built to the narrow dimensions chosen for the Trent & Mersey (that is, for boats only 7 feet wide), with a channel 4 feet deep, and re-routed nearer Glasgow. Smeaton's reactions were frustration and anger, both of which he directed at Brindley who had claimed an ability to build the whole canal in only four years.

> As no difficulty is too great for Mr Brindley, I should be glad to see how he would stow a fire-engine cylinder cast at Carron, of 6½ft diameter, in one of his seven feet boats, so as to prevent its breaking the back of the boat, or oversetting ... Mr Brindley recommends to begin at the point of partition [watershed] because, he says, "it is his constant practice to do so ..." but pray, Mr Brindley, is there no way to do a thing right but the way you do? ... do you usually begin at the most difficult part of a work first, with raw hands, before they are trained to business? I have sometimes done so, and repented it.[12]

Smeaton was angry, but Brindley was correct in at least two points – first, that a section of the river Carron should be straightened (done in 1783–5); second that the line should go nearer to Glasgow. Smeaton accused Brindley of only wanting the latter because it would require a large aqueduct over the river Kelvin, along the lines of his great success at Barton,

> That my brother Brindley should prefer the Printfield passage, I can readily comprehend ... every man, how great soever his genius, has a certain hobby-horse he likes to ride; a large aqueduct bridge over a large river does not happen to be mine.[13]

The Kelvin aqueduct would be built, although not until 1786–90, and not by Smeaton, but by Robert Whitworth (Senior) who was trained by Brindley.

The Forth & Clyde Canal was a bold scheme but its geographical position in the north of Britain lessened its strategic importance on a national scale. It did, however, remind influential gentlemen that watersheds could be crossed and that there was the possibility of a canal network in central England. The involvement of Birmingham's Samuel Garbett resulted not only in Brindley's role in Scotland but also in the heightened awareness of Josiah Wedgwood in Staffordshire. Now an independent potter, Wedgwood had his own works at Burslem and he knew the opportunities were great if he could produce the right tableware. He experimented continuously, trying to find the clay mix, the glaze and the kiln techniques that would allow him to create what the market wanted. The middle ranks of an increasingly prosperous society did not want the old, clumsy Dutch delftware, nor the older, dull, pewter plates, nor the fragility of porcelain. What they did want as part of their increasingly comfortable home life was tableware with the simple lines of the neo-classical style that was also tough, durable and reasonably priced. When he found the answer, Wedgwood's cream-coloured earthenware was an immediate success. It could be thrown on a wheel, turned on a lathe or cast in moulds, and as Wedgwood's potters became more skilful, the importation of porcelain from Meissen and Sevres dwindled.[14] London society was the target of Wedgwood's astute marketing, culminating in the creation of a tea and coffee service for Queen Charlotte with which she was so pleased she conferred the right to call it Queen's Ware, later bestowing the title 'Potter to Her Majesty' upon its creator. The royal patronage was cleverly exploited and soon fashionable tables all over the country reflected the court's opinion. As the orders reached Burslem the volume of raw materials, including Cornish china-clay and Devon ball-clay, required increased substantially.[15] The need for regular and safe transportation of raw materials and finished products was now acute – and Josiah Wedgwood was not the kind of man to wring his hands and wait for others to solve his problems, even though his damaged leg still hampered mobility and the pain was sometimes debilitating. One such occasion was in April 1762 when on a visit to Liverpool to arrange shipping for his business, the severity of his disability forced Wedgwood to remain in the port for several tedious weeks.[16] To alleviate his frustration Wedgwood's doctor introduced him to Thomas Bentley, a widely travelled local merchant with a keen intellect. Their immediate companionship soon blossomed into a strong friendship and later to business partnership. Together they would join James Brindley to form the second triumvirate of the engineer's canal career.

Along with his other talents Josiah Wedgwood had a particular genius for organisation, be it factory operations or gathering the support and finance necessary to build a canal. He brought order and method to what could be chaotic. He also realised the importance of cultivating the interest of influential people, doing so by assiduously providing information and guiding the opinions formed.[17] In this he was greatly helped by Thomas Bentley whose background and experience were perfect for the role. An education at the Collegiate Academy in Findern, Derbyshire, had given Bentley classical learning and a knowledge of languages, which was followed by training in business methods and accountancy with a Manchester wholesaler. In 1753 he had toured France and Italy, returning to start a successful warehouse business in

Liverpool. He was well-known in the booming port, within three years helping to found a non-conformist academy, a public library and a chapel. As a result, Bentley knew many people of status in Liverpool, the port that was the objective of the Bridgewater Canal and later the Trent & Mersey. Furthermore, he had all the attributes necessary to mix in the required circles – excellent appearance, courtly manners and the ability to talk on a wide range of literary, scientific and artistic subjects.[18] He gained the ear of those who may perhaps wish to obtain, when they understood the utility of the purchase, a full set of tableware – or a number of canal shares. Bentley also listened to detect those who may oppose either of his commercial interests.

At this time Wedgwood was still actively involved in promoting a number of local turnpike roads, but he had clearly seen that the long-distance answer to his factory's transport needs would be provided by canals. His earlier involvement with the planning of a canal to link the rivers Mersey and Trent had come to nothing, but he had discussed the dormant canal plans with Thomas Bentley from the start of their friendship.[19] Generally, the high-profile success of the Bridgewater Canal had shown that geographical problems could be overcome, and that prospective investors would accept that James Brindley was the man to do so. Added to this, the Duke of Bridgewater's success in guiding three canal construction Acts through Parliament had set a political precedent others could follow. Personally, Wedgwood knew that the leading role in promoting the canal would probably be his if he wished to remain confident that it would resolve the transport problems of the Potteries as well as forming the central strand of a national canal network. Furthermore, the stability provided by his financially successful earthenware had been augmented by his friendship with Thomas Bentley, and his marriage to Sarah, who would be his life-long companion and 'chief helpmate'.[20] At the end of 1764 the time was indeed right for Josiah Wedgwood and for the Trent & Mersey Canal.

James Brindley, on the other hand, had been ready for some time. He was still working on the Bridgewater Canal on a daily payment and expenses basis, and still picking up other commissions where he could, one of which was giving advice to Liverpool Corporation on clearing mud from the docks.[21] The trustees of navigation on the river Weaver also sought his opinion on improvements designed by their own engineer, an assignment he undertook, presenting his estimates at a meeting on 4th October 1764.[22] Hindsight shows that the Bridgewater Canal would not be completed for another twelve years, but even if Brindley had known that fact he could not have confidently expected employment on the project for the whole of the period. As long-term schemes progress, contractors gain practical experience, administrators gain supplier contacts and consultant engineers gain an aura of redundancy. Fortunately, James Brindley's career had a way forward, although he was once again destined to be the insecure elder of a group of three – aged 48, unmarried and nomadic; whereas both Wedgwood and Bentley were 34 years old, the former newly married, the latter a widower (having lost his wife in childbirth eight years before, the infant soon after) whose household was run by his sister-in-law.[23]

In the mid-eighteenth century, the circles of influence in society were very small by modern standards, and quite thinly spread throughout the country. The growing centres of industry and the major ports were hubs of local networks, with strands reaching out to surrounding areas where the owners of large estates delegated their administrative duties to land-agents, who in turn were members of their own brotherhood. Wedgwood and Bentley were members of that circle, James Brindley was not, although known by many and judged to be a man of integrity. Nevertheless, his level of association was one-dimensional when compared with the multi-faceted, family-based, commercially established world of the truly influential. By the end of 1764 Wedgwood had been the source of many informal discussions about the fundamental aspects of the Trent & Mersey Canal. Proposals were filtered through the network and opinions received. Unofficial meetings were held at coaching inns, typical of which was Wedgwood talking with Mr Colquit, a member of Liverpool Corporation, and then asking him to acquaint Thomas Bentley of their agreement when he had returned to the busy port.[24] The suitability of Brindley as the engineering figurehead was quietly ascertained, followed by clarification of his willingness to undertake such a role, on what terms, and his opinions on how the project should be managed. Above all there was the crucial involvement of Earl Gower, who had first commissioned Brindley to survey the route many years before, and his brother-in-law the Duke of Bridgewater, who planned to have his own canal terminate in the same general area as the western end of the Trent & Mersey, although the details of both routes were not yet finalised. Eventually, after many discussions, the matter had to be brought to the attention of the general public – for positive promotional reasons as well as defensively to counter the opposition of those with commercial interests in already established rivers and canals in the North West, such as the Weaver, Irwell, and Sankey.

At the end of 1764 James Brindley was placed on the escalator that would inexorably carry him up to the level of national celebrity. He would not be allowed to fail; instead it was required that his name become synonymous with success – a necessity that would turn the escalator into an ever-faster rotating tread-mill as Britain took the step which would set her apart from continental Europe in the development of inland waterways. Financially and managerially the Bridgewater Canal had followed the pattern set in France during the previous century. It was funded and promoted to serve the relatively narrow interests of an aristocratic figurehead, although economic benefits would also accrue for the general public. However, the Trent & Mersey, its route linking major ports of the west and east coasts while passing through the heartland of English industry and innovation, would be strategically important to the nation, a claim always loudly proclaimed although none the less true for that. The liberal instincts of Josiah Wedgwood and his co-promoters saw that canals should be moved into the realm of ownership by private individuals, each investing by purchasing shares and having a say in how the project would be managed, and subsequently sharing the profits. That the canal would also greatly enhance the commercial prospects of many gentlemen along the route was accepted as right and proper. To give assurance to prospective investors, the still nebulous knowledge of stillwater canals needed to be clarified by two figureheads standing four-square in the swirling mist of opinions. One had to be of the establishment – an aristocratic, land-owning pillar of probity who could not, would not, allow his name to be involved in fraud. Memories of the ruinous financial scam known as the South Sea Bubble were still vivid and painful. For this role Josiah Wedgwood pursued Earl Gower with relentless guile. The second figurehead had to be a man who would not be daunted by the challenge of building the canal, the engineer who would overcome all practical problems, the artisan who would get his own hands dirty, the manager who would not allow himself or others to fail. He did not have to be an intellectual titan, rather someone who would not let the hardest rock stand in his way. Some may have petitioned for John Smeaton, there being little doubt amongst the informed set that he could do the job – his Eddystone lighthouse had proved his dogged determination to complete the most complex of projects in appalling conditions. Even so, he was not a member of the 'canal set', having few contacts in Lancashire and Staffordshire. James Brindley, on the other hand, could be promoted as the driving genius behind the Bridgewater Canal, the embodiment of the beacon to be followed. Commercial necessity dictated that Brindley's name be seen as synonymous with canals. He must have realised the potential of what was before him. Even the dullest of men, and he was certainly not that, would have seen long-term commitments with annual salaries as far preferable to the insecurity of payments per day. Especially when those long-term commitments would not contain exclusivity clauses, thereby allowing him to take on concurrent projects and payments.

The first public manifestation of the plan for a Trent & Mersey Canal was a promotional pamphlet, published in the final months of 1764 and written in Liverpool by Thomas Bentley. It would subsequently be re-issued in various editions incorporating remodelled arguments and maps. Wedgwood's input was substantial, with many letters passing between the friends as they tried to anticipate reactions. Many opposition sheets were circulated but as they also stimulated public debate they too served the interests of the canal's promoters.[25] Battle by pamphlet on many subjects was a widespread activity, so much so that Jonathan Swift complained 'the pamphlets and half-sheets grow so upon our hands it will very well employ a man every day from morning till night to read them'.[26] A further field of conflict was letters planted in the columns of the numerous newspapers now available. Many titles were published in London, some of which had been founded in the previous century, but of more significance to the canal promoters were the 200,000 weekly copies of the 35 provincial newspapers. A typical example was the *Derby Mercury*, filled each week with news local, national and colonial, together with a mosaic of book reviews, features, lost animals, court reports, and the events and announcements columns, many of which in the following years would give advance notice of canal promotional meetings. Print and progress were linked in the public mind: 'One of the improvements of life in which the present age has excelled all that have gone before is the quick circulation of intelligence, by the multitude of newspapers'.[27] There were also books on a wide range of subjects, often of the self-help variety; how to improve your life by digging the garden, cooking exotic meals, taking exercise, or undertaking a little carpentry. The second edition of Johnson's dictionary was available in 165 weekly parts at six pence each; in a similar fashion Smollett's *Complete History of England* sold 10,000 copies, soon the *Encyclopaedia Britannica* would be published likewise.[28]

In 1700 the number of people who could read in Britain was high by European standards but it had not risen substantially since then. More significant, was that reading had become commonplace to a large swathe of the population, with the subsequent marginalisation of the illiterate others – the ability to read was the entrance to the informed society, even for those of little wealth or status. It has been suggested that the main divide in Georgian England was not between rich and poor, nor one class above another, but between those who could tap into the mass of printed information available and those who still had to rely on an essentially oral culture.[29] Echoes of that pretension can be heard in some of the opinions that have survived – 'In appearance and manners, as well as in acquirements, Mr Brindley was a mere peasant …' [30] and 'He remained to the last illiterate, hardly able to write and quite unable to spell …' [31] Both views are repudiated by contemporaries with a broader outlook on life and also by the evidence contained in Brindley's notebooks.

As the pamphlets carried his name into the national awareness, Brindley was involved in a fundamental decision that would set a pattern for future canals. Birmingham industrialist Samuel Garbett had joined forces with Thomas Gilbert to issue a paper strongly suggesting that the proposed Trent & Mersey should be managed by commissioners, who would be a group of influential gentlemen authorised by the future Act of Parliament. This, they argued, would be preferable to control by the shareholders as those proprietors would, for their own benefit, maximise the profits earned at the expense of the public good. Such opinions were directly opposed to Wedgwood's vision and triggered an immediate response. John Gilbert wished his brother had not acted so, and told Wedgwood that Garbett and Thomas Gilbert were meeting Earl Gower at Lichfield where the matter would be decided. His central role in the project under threat, an angry Wedgwood quickly gathered a like-minded group, which included James Brindley, all of whom set off for Lichfield post-haste on 30th December 1764. Their premise was that the commissioners system would give smaller investors scant reward, only a new set of masters, whereas a management committee elected by all investors, one vote per share, would be democratic and well-received.[32] Incredulous that such a basic decision could have been sought without consultation with those who had 'lent their heads, hands, and purses' to the project, the new arrivals were soon involved in heated discussions with Gilbert and Garbett. Eventually all were called to sup with Earl Gower, who listened to presentations by both camps before siding with the Wedgwood–Brindley faction.[33] The management of the infant Canal Age had been settled, an augury of the momentous year to come when a number of decisions would set the pattern for Britain's early waterways.

January 1765 opened with Bentley's promotional pamphlet well received by those at whom it was aimed, with the turn away from traditional river navigations attributed to its sound arguments.[34] One thousand were printed as the Brindley–Bentley–Wedgwood trio also turned its guns onto a rival scheme, the salvoes echoed by the Bridgewater interests.

The drawback with publishing convincing arguments regarding the advantages of transport on canals rather than on rivers is that others may use the approval generated to build a canal of their own. If complementary to one's own project (as the Trent & Mersey would probably be to the Bridgewater Canal) then so much the better, but when a rival project would stymie one's own plans it had to be expunged immediately. When such a proposal would isolate the Bridgewater Canal, blocking any links from the south and also leave only one option for the western end of the Trent & Mersey, then a swift and heavyweight response could be expected. Thus, the plans for a canal to link the river Weaver navigation near Northwich to Manchester melted under the political and financial heat of the combined Bridgewater and Trent & Mersey lobbies, its only legacy a reminder that there was still no clear picture of the canal network to be built.

An impression has been generated that as early as 1765 visionary Brindley saw a 'Grand Cross' joining the ports of Liverpool, Hull, Bristol and London, and almost single-handedly led the canal movement towards such a goal. In truth, although the first three of those ports would quickly have their river hinterlands linked, the routes had been foreseen many years before. For sound business reasons an early title for the Trent & Mersey was the Grand Trunk, its promoters thereby adopting the role of a life-giving tree from which all other branches would sprout – or perhaps not, if the mighty oak thought an off-shoot or nearby stripling would impinge upon its own survival. The fluidity of canals was not only their liquid contents – in the entrepreneurial nature of the time any town or city, if it could raise the money and circumvent the objectors, could build a canal to achieve its own ends. Strategic partnerships with other professional interests could be formed and broken. The proposition that

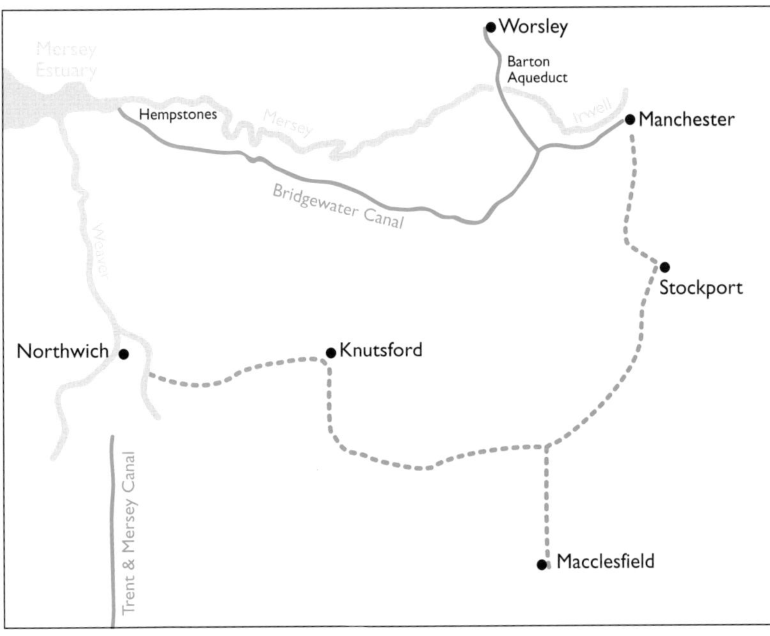

The rival canal proposal to link the river Weaver to Manchester. If built it would restrict the options for the northern terminus of the Trent & Mersey Canal, still undefined as either the river Weaver, the Mersey Estuary, or the Bridgewater Canal

Brindley, or anyone else, could mastermind such an amorphous national situation is untenable. It was in his own interests to maintain his emerging role as the engineer of the Grand Trunk. If he did so, the branches would also sprout under his control, but he could not force those branches to burgeon. It was already evident that canals would be the greatest public works ever undertaken in Britain, requiring planning and finance on a scale previously unknown.[35] The personification of the boundless confidence that would also be required was James Brindley, at least outwardly so.

After the pamphlets the next public indication of the construction of a canal was usually a series of meetings held in various locations, many in the form of one at Burslem on 8th March 1765. Before the event, Wedgwood and Brindley dined together and agreed the latest strategy – then proceeded to address a large group of local potters at The Leopard inn. They met with warm approval and were pressed to undertake the matter further, a similar reaction coming from Hanley, another potteries town, four days later.[36] The canal was now to be 76 miles long, from Wilden Ferry on the Trent, to Frodsham Bridge on the river Weaver, just downstream of the point where the trustees of that river could charge tolls. Also included was a 28-mile branch to Lichfield, Tamworth, and Birmingham, and another of three miles from Stoke-on-Trent to Newcastle-under-Lyme. The dimensions would be those required to carry boats 70 feet long, by 6 feet wide (later increased to near 7 feet wide to increase capacity and aid stability), draught 2 feet 6 inches, capable of carrying 15–20 tons.[37] The boats would not need wider sections in which to turn as they were to be made capable of sailing in both directions by transferring the rudder from one end to the other. The crew would be one man and a boy, and towage would be by horse.[38] The fundamental decision to build the channel, locks and bridges of the innovative Trent & Mersey only wide enough to take narrowboats has been laid at Brindley's door, resulting in his bearing the opprobrium for lacking the foresight to see that if it had been made wider and deeper to take the boats already trading on adjoining rivers, cargo-carrying on Britain's inland waterways would have been better able to deal with competition from the railways a century later, and the roads beyond that. However, on 3rd April 1765 Josiah Wedgwood would write 'a Cut and Vessels on the above Plan have been found to be the most practicable from various Experiments on the Navigations of his Grace the Duke of Bridgewater' – even though they were wide waterways.[39] The other vital consideration was the expense of building the canal. The length was settled by the locations of the termini, but the depth and width were arbitrary. It was difficult enough to retain the faith that a tunnel for narrowboats could be driven through the hill at Harecastle, but to make it capable of taking wide river barges would have presented insurmountable problems. The volume of the excavation would have to increase four-fold, and the thicker walls required would treble the amount of bricks – the effects on costs and completion time becoming inhibiting factors to investors.

Lichfield's ornate and triple-spired cathedral has been a symbol of the city for many centuries

Nothing is known of how they envisaged the boats would be propelled through the towpath-less tunnel. In practice they would be 'legged' through, that is at least two men lying on their backs on the boat, with their legs either up to 'walk' along the tunnel roof and thereby pushing the boat, or one man to each side to 'walk' along the tunnel walls. In the underground waters of the mine at Worsley the boats were moved by the crew pulling on hand-rails in the tunnels, but that does not seem to have been done in the tunnels of the

'Legging' a loaded narrowboat in a tunnel

main canal system. But one thing was clear – however it was done, the boats would have to be moved through Harecastle Tunnel by man-muscle, a vital factor when determining the size and weight of a loaded boat. The average speed a loaded narrowboat could be legged through a tunnel of the length of Harecastle would prove to be no more than one mile per hour, so a wide-boat of double the weight may not have been at all practical. And the tighter the fit of the boat in the tunnel, the more its progress would be impeded by the 'cork in a bottle' effect, although that may not have been realised at this early stage.[40]

A further crucial question was the cost of construction. Even to narrow dimensions, the financing of an unproven project of such magnitude would be onerous. On that subject Brindley's estimate, for a narrowboat canal, was that the section to the west of the Harecastle watershed could be built for £1,000 per mile, even though how it would pass through the hilly country near the river Weaver had not been defined. The tunnel at Harecastle would need £10,000, while the eastern part of the canal could be completed for £700 per mile, its route easier as it followed the Trent valley, although how the river Dove was to be crossed, or the Trent itself at Alrewas, had also not yet been determined.[41] Overall the cost would be £101,000, to be raised by the sale of 505 shares of £200 each, with the safeguard of a 20-share maximum holding to prevent the formation of a powerbase.[42] The cost estimates went unchallenged, not surprising as nobody in Britain had any experience of building a canal of 70-plus miles across a watershed – of course, that also included James Brindley. Nevertheless, if a string of figures is presented with great confidence on a little-known subject, few will publicly demur. In a similar manner, the commercial gentlemen of Birmingham were boldly told that their branch canal would reduce their transport costs to the Trent by £10,000 a year, and that Brindley thought the new waterway would reach their town only three years after construction commenced.[43]

Other meetings, private not public, took place in London spreading the awareness to Westminster and the court of King George III that canals were to progress beyond that of the Duke of Bridgewater. The influence of Earl Gower and his family wisely ensured that those in favour were of a wide spectrum of political opinion. Soon Wedgwood heard a rumour that the Trent & Mersey was the subject of general conversation amongst the nobility, and that Lord Denbigh had shown the plans to the young king who had been impressed by the broad range of support and had therefore indicated his favour.[44]

James Brindley's role was now pivotal. He was the only person involved in the confidential planning of the Trent & Mersey who was also engaged in the ongoing construction of the Bridgewater Canal. Being privy to the aims of both camps his integrity could have been compromised, but he managed the role of intermediary with tact. As a result, when representatives of the two groups met in April 1765 – when Josiah Wedgwood and his party called at the home of John Gilbert on their way to see Earl Gower – the rapport was instantaneous. Wedgwood explained a little of his plans to the Duke of Bridgewater's land manager who immediately asked if the western end of the Trent & Mersey could join the duke's canal rather than the river Weaver. It would give Wedgwood's scheme closer access to Manchester, and would not lose much on the approach to Liverpool, plus the canal would not need a flight of locks to drop it down to the floor of the Weaver valley. In return, Gilbert proposed, perhaps a small toll per boat for the through traffic could be paid to the duke? Meanwhile, he would do what he could to have His Grace look favourably upon the idea.

Continuing their journey to Earl Gower's Trentham estate Wedgwood's group had much to discuss. Samuel Garbett, the arch facilitator in Birmingham, had stressed that Earl Gower's support was of 'extreme consequence', and that 'more depends upon that single point than upon any other'. Wedgwood was advised that if the Earl would also involve his brother-in-law, the Duke of Bridgewater, their joint ministerial weight would obliterate any alarming opposition.[45] On arrival Wedgwood presented a petition from the pottery area of Staffordshire, requesting that the Earl take the intended canal under his protection and patronage. The reply, astutely framed, was that everything possible should be done to promote the scheme of which he was aware, meanwhile if he heard of any difficulties he would advise Wedgwood in order that he should be able to counter them. More than that he would not say, but those present gained the impression that Earl Gower spoke in earnest.[46]

Bridgewater Canal - its construction progress by mid-1765

While the machinations surrounding the Trent & Mersey proposals continued, Brindley still had major challenges to overcome in the construction of the Bridgewater Canal. So far, ten miles had been completed from Worsley to Manchester, where the terminus was still not finished, at an estimated cost of 1,000 guineas per mile. Now, the line towards Hempstones had to pass into Cheshire by crossing over the upper waters of the river Mersey on a second substantial aqueduct.[47] On the far bank an isolated section had already been built across Sale Moor. The greater challenge, however, was to carry the canal, on high approach embankments to maintain its level, across the low, boggy meadows on either side of the Mersey. This many thought impossible according to extracts of letters regarding the Bridgewater Canal in Thomas Bentley's pamphlet, but, of course, to be boldly overcome by James Brindley. A contemporary report stated that the construction of the embankments was underway in 40-yard sections, with massive deal timbers over 30 feet long set vertically, their bases in parallel trenches, backed and supported on the outside with horizontal timbers laid in rows and fastened strongly together. Hundreds of oak piles were then driven into the ground between the rows of uprights and, on the outside of the parallel rows, it was said, clay and earth were compacted to form supporting banks. The end must have been plugged, perhaps with a temporary clay dam, because water from the adjacent completed section of canal was then let into the confined area, filling it to the same level, although over 30 feet deep. A floating coffer-dam may then have been moved to the far end to replace the clay dam. The same source also stated that the flooded section was then gradually filled with spoil, which was carried by special hopper boats. These consisted of a pair of narrow hulls fixed alongside within a few feet of each other. Between them was a large trough that could be filled with soil, clay, rocks, rubble, etc from elsewhere on the completed section of canal. This was then pulled into the flooded section of new embankment and, when in position, a locking pin was pulled from the base of the trough allowing a line of flaps to open, thereby depositing 18 tons of spoil into the water. Gradually, the area between the upright timbers filled, displacing the water as it did so, the channel of the canal and the towpath eventually formed from the top surface. The same was then done for the next 40-yard section.[48] A newspaper correspondent spent two hours in the satisfying contemplation of others working, likening the labours of the swarms of canal men to ants and bees, each man's work depending on, and connected to, his neighbour's. Meanwhile, preparatory work for the adjacent aqueduct also progressed, with nearly 2,000 oak piles already driven to strengthen the foundations. On the Lancashire side of the Mersey, carpenters were making the frame around which the arches would be formed. Their workshops covered the decks of a wide-beam hull, which was pulled along the canal to where the work was taking place. A second hull carried a smith's forge in a similar manner, a third served the masons. On the Cheshire side of the Mersey the river was being used, in true Brindley style, to wash soil down to where men were building up the ground. This was then stamped down, later to be covered in stone, supplies of which lay in barges on the adjacent completed section of canal.[49]

The ingenious means by which he used water to overcome laborious tasks was Brindley's specialisation and

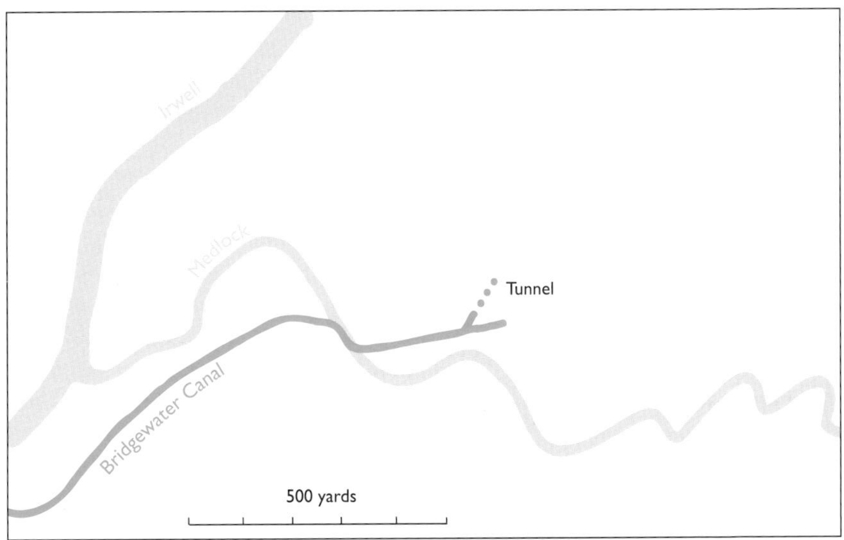

Bridgewater Canal – the eastern end at Castlefield, Manchester

it quickly became a widely admired trait. A further example was at Castlefield, the Manchester terminus, where the first wharf was open by 1st August 1765 for the delivery of the much awaited coal from Worsley. However, as the wharf was at the level of an Irwell tributary, the river Medlock, those coming with their carts to collect the coal had to descend into a small valley before struggling to haul the load back up to the level of the town. This unsatisfactory situation received a typical Brindley solution. A large tunnel was driven into the hill, along this the coal-boats would float, their cargoes already in boxes in an early display of containerisation. A shaft was then sunk to the tunnel from street level and up this the boxes of coal were lifted from the boats moored beneath, the crane powered by a water-wheel. From the top of the shaft a horse could easily pull a ton to any part of town and the waiting customers.[50]

Nearby, a huge clover-leafed weir had already been completed to allow the Medlock to escape and to keep the level in the canal constant. The shape was designed to achieve the largest perimeter possible in a relatively small area. In the centre was a round stone, the outer rim built of squared stones linked together with iron staples flushed in with melted lead. During the weir's construction Brindley diverted most of the Medlock through a side-cut, with the remaining water lifted by a 'spoon'. The spoon was a contraption at the end of a lever with a leather-flapped door that admitted water until full and automatically sealed the door when lifted, the contents eventually running off via a channel at the spoon handle.[51] Fulsome letters appeared in the newspapers, praising Mr Brindley and finding the 'great genius … never at a loss, for if any difficulty arises, he removes it with a facility that appears so much like inspiration, you would think Minerva at his finger tips'.[52]

Eulogies were widespread but it is difficult to know with what justification. For instance, during 1765 – at the time of crucial promotion of the general canal concept and, in particular, the Trent & Mersey – a reciprocal relationship developed between the pamphlets produced by Thomas Bentley, and the *Monthly Review*, a newspaper of some renown. Bentley included a number of laudatory letters previously published in that newspaper, and was rewarded in turn by the majority of his pamphlet being quoted in the *Monthly Review*'s December issue – this after the opinion of Ralph Griffiths, the editor of the *Monthly Review*, had been sought during the compilation of the pamphlet. Hardly independent reporting. Furthermore, prior to publication Thomas Bentley was inundated with letters containing suggestions for improvements to the pamphlet. Josiah Wedgwood in Burslem and Samuel Garbett in Birmingham wrote copiously, as did the astonishing polymath Dr Erasmus Darwin in Lichfield.

Darwin's role in the canal saga was privately to support and advise his great friend Josiah Wedgwood, a public declaration deemed imprudent as many of the physician's

***Erasmus Darwin M.D. An engraving of a painting by Rawlinson. From* The Poetical Works of Erasmus Darwin, MD, FRS, 1789**

patients had business connections hostile to the canal concept.[53] Two years younger than his friend, Darwin was of above average height with an athletic frame inclined towards corpulence. When not smiling, his face lacked animation but his brain was always active.

An advanced advocate of discarding quackery, Darwin introduced new medicines and the practice of giving treatments based on the necessities of a case rather than the stereotyped actions usually thought acceptable. Amongst those who could afford his ministrations, including the Wedgwood family, he was famed for travelling great distances to treat extreme cases, often with success.[54] As a result, Darwin knew a wide circle of influential people, not only as a physician but also as a botanist, poet, and materialist with enlightened views on slavery, agriculture, alcohol, insanity and evolution, all well grounded in the science of his day. On the latter he wrote, 'would it be too bold to imagine, that all warm-blooded animals have arisen from one living filament … ?' [55] A tenet to be developed further by his grandson, Charles. However, the politics of Erasmus Darwin were never revolutionary. His framework of free-market capitalism and industrialisation contained the essential factors of law, order and property.[56] All of these influenced his advice to Wedgwood that the idea of canals should be further promoted to the general public by degrees because if it was perceived that 'instruction is offered them, without asking for it, they are sure to be refractory'.[57]

Darwin's views on the contents of the crucial pamphlets were always sought. Facts and figures on the current costs, the savings anticipated, the movement of raw materials and the increased volume of trade that would ensue, were assiduously culled from all possible sources – but how the personnel involved should be described was a matter of political expediency. In one draft Bentley wrote some sycophantic paragraphs about Thomas Gilbert but Wedgwood would have none of it, describing the words as 'a little flummery cooked up for Mr Gilbert … but I do not like it, as he hath … rendered himself obnoxious to many in the House of Lords …' [58] That the Brindley-flattering letters, purporting to be from un-biased commentators and reproduced in the pamphlet, were actually the clandestine work of the canal cabal is evident from Darwin's comment that nothing more than 'ingenious' should be attached to Brindley's name – the very wording used in a quoted letter, the authorship of which was hidden by the initials 'T.L.' [59] In the understated style favoured by Darwin, individual references to Brindley on other pages are likewise relatively subdued, but surreptitiously a compelling image is still created of the Duke of Bridgewater's 'excellent engineer', the sole 'projector' of the 'extraordinary' ducal waterway. The readers were left to form their own opinion that he could easily build a canal from the Trent to the Mersey. First published in Liverpool and then by London booksellers in the Strand and Paternoster Row, and elsewhere as the demand grew, the pamphlet was a major source of Brindley's national fame and celebrity.[60]

Behind the scenes the major practical area of uncertainty was still the unresolved question of where the western end of the Trent & Mersey should terminate. Seeking to keep options open until it was clear which would be the most advantageous solution, Wedgwood promised all things to all men when he met the Trustees of the Weaver Navigation and intimated that the proposed canal would form a junction with their river. As a result the trustees undertook the expense of having two new surveys made of the land between Harecastle and the Weaver, one for the canal to go to Winsford, the other to go to Northwich, via Middlewich.[61] But, a week or so later, Wedgwood wrote to Liverpool Corporation stating the Trent & Mersey's western terminus would be with the Bridgewater Canal, with only a side branch to the Weaver.[62] Subsequently the Corporation increased its donation to the canal's funds by 300 per cent.[63] The matter was further complicated by the Duke of Bridgewater refusing to state whether or not his canal would end at the Mersey estuary (and if so, where) or cross on an aqueduct more spectacular than anything else yet built to continue the route into Liverpool docks. He was also keeping all options open, including the scenario that if he should advocate a meeting of the two canals, would it be advantageous to alter the route of his waterway to form such a junction? Only Brindley knew the thinking of both camps. It was therefore with him that Josiah Wedgwood met in early December. The potter said he must ask the engineer some serious questions, although he recognised Brindley's involvement in the on-going Bridgewater project and did not wish him to do anything inconsistent with his professional and moral responsibilities. But he must ask, as nationally many were depending on Brindley's well-known abilities and integrity to prevent their being deceived – by any party. First, was there a practical route for the Trent & Mersey to run parallel with the Weaver allowing it to make its way further north to reach the duke's canal? If so, could it be done at not too great an expense? Brindley's answer to both was a categorical, yes, there was such a route. Second, did the duke mean to allow the Trent & Mersey to pass into his area of operations without either taking it over or blocking its progress? The answer was again definite – yes, they may depend upon it. Third, the major obstacle on the Trent & Mersey's route in that area would be crossing the river Dane on an aqueduct. Would the duke allow a certain engineer to plan and build such an aqueduct, or perhaps he, Brindley, as a self-employed man, may choose to do it himself? This time Brindley was more circumspect – he would not answer for the duke, but he would consider the subject himself.

The activity was now frantic and wearing, often at the cost of other commercial interests. Wedgwood wrote to his friend Darwin 'if I should furnish a name to the list of

Bankrupts through neglect of business you must not be astonished at it, for I assure you this, Navigating & Pottery do not by any means agree together.'[64] Furthermore, those involved had the extra pressures of knowing that success was not guaranteed. Nor was there comfort to be derived from proven schemes elsewhere. Although it was lauded as the example to follow, the Bridgewater Canal was only half completed and currently hindered by dire financial problems – to many it looked like an open watery drain down which the duke's vast wealth was flowing with ever-increasing rapidity. It was also evident that amending its route to form a junction with the Trent & Mersey would seriously aggravate the financial situation.[65] In addition, the general justification for stillwater canals continued to be viewed as unproven by a substantial lobby of influential opinion. The status quo always has many advocates with the claimed ability to discern the truly innovative from change-for-changes-sake – a clarity of vision given to few, but in many honed to perfection by hindsight. The duke's plans were, therefore, still beset by the powerful owners of land on the proposed route to the Mersey estuary, many of whom were energetically fermenting opposition, their efforts bolstered by the fact that although a canal's enabling Act of Parliament gave authority for land to be purchased, it did not stipulate the price to be paid – and haggling can be an endless process, especially if one party is content for it to be so. For the Duke of Bridgewater mollification was not an option; instead his opponents would have to be out manoeuvred if possible, and attacked head-on if necessary – all at a great expense of sparse finances and even more valuable time. His enormous workforce would not be retainable if unemployed and would drift away, their collective expertise eventually diluted to extinction.

The baton of canal-herald had not yet been passed to the Trent & Mersey and it was vital to the national interest in this interim period that the duke's waterway maintain its progress. It can therefore be argued that if, even at this late stage, the intransigence of landowners had halted the Bridgewater Canal then the subsequent Canal Age would have been seriously delayed, along with its coal-starved sibling, the infant Industrial Revolution. A successful protest would have been noted by others elsewhere who would have gained confidence in what they saw as their God-given duty to expunge the canal blight from the estates of future family generations. And if the canals had failed, the railways in their turn would have had no successful pattern to follow.

There was little that others could do to smooth the progress of the privately projected Bridgewater Canal. They could, however, do everything in their power to hasten the birth of a protégé that would have the sturdiness of mass-support. Hundreds of horse-back miles were ridden by canal activists as they sought to persuade others to their cause. In the dark days of December 1765 Brindley could scarce see to do any engineering work outside and was, therefore, free to accompany Josiah Wedgwood on a visit to an estate on the Bridgewater Canal's route at Dunham to dine with Lord Grey and Sir Harry Mainwaring to solicit support for the Trent & Mersey. Lord Grey was one of two MPs for Staffordshire, and was inclined to give his backing, but could perhaps waver. On the other hand, during what must have been an irascible meal, Sir Harry could not keep his temper when canals were discussed, a fact Brindley duly reported to John Gilbert to add to the pool of intelligence. Elsewhere John Sparrow, a hard-headed Newcastle-under-Lyme solicitor, was leading a team endeavouring to obtain the consent of landowners on the possible routes west of the Harecastle watershed, and trying to ascertain the financial costs involved.[66] Meanwhile, Thomas Bentley was organising presentations to Liverpool Corporation and, thereby, gaining a pledge of support – but only if he would arrange for letters of recommendation to be sent to all the Members of Parliament in Lancashire and adjacent counties.[67] Dr Erasmus Darwin's role was to listen to opinions in politically and financially important Lichfield. The amorphous complexities of the scheme eventually led to a decision to simplify matters by deleting the branch canals that had been planned to sprout from the 'Grand Trunk' – even though that removed Birmingham and Lichfield from the towns to be included. The complementary route to the river Severn, foreseen by Thomas Congreve 60 years before, would be delegated to a separate band of promoters.[68]

Therefore, as 1765 drew to a close, James Brindley was in a finely balanced situation – using his contacts with the Duke of Bridgewater to promote a junction between the two canals while endeavouring not to betray the trust of either party. The pressure was now intense as Wedgwood's associates were pressing to have their canal introduced at Westminster in the approaching session of Parliament.[69] Before that could be done, plans had to be made to counter the opposing arguments that would be powerfully voiced but it was not yet clear who would mount the most organised attack. It was not only the 'Old Navigators' who would again stand against a canal, there would also be vehement hostility from those who would miss out in the general growth of trade that would result from traffic carried on the future Trent & Mersey.

Brindley's concealed advocacy of the Bridgewater Canal and the Trent & Mersey forming a junction, and excluding of the old-style river Weaver navigation, was undertaken with tact and an eye to the future. His career depended on his relationship with Wedgwood, and thereby his involvement in the possible expansion of a canal network to all parts of the country. That he could successfully reconcile his role as intermediary with such overwhelming personal prospects indicates a character of immense probity. His triumph became evident when the suggestion that the two canals should meet was formally aired by Wedgwood when he met the Duke of Bridgewater and John Gilbert at Earl Gower's Trentham home. The suggestion evoked a reaction noted by Wedgwood, 'they looked at each other as though some secret design of their own had been discovered by another before the time they thought proper to avow it, and therefore were shy in saying anything about it'.[70] Just three days later the duke sent John Gilbert to Burslem personally to advise Josiah Wedgwood on how matters should be progressed. Gilbert counselled that nothing was yet to be mentioned elsewhere, but with a significant nod it was made clear that 'great things might be done at a proper time' and that Wedgwood's objective of having Earl Gower publicly state his approval of the Trent & Mersey would also be achieved in the near future. Meanwhile, nothing of consequence was to be trusted to the post, instead Wedgwood was to keep four or five running footmen at his elbow at all times ready to deliver any important intelligence directly into the hands of the duke at Worsley, or to John Gilbert if they knew him to be near Burslem.[71]

Eventually, and with much relief, a major public meeting was convened, at which Wedgwood achieved the main objective of his campaign when Earl Gower took the chair and publicly gave a clear commitment to support the Trent & Mersey Canal. The scheme now had the two figureheads it required to gain the confidence of investors – Earl Gower and James Brindley – one an aristocrat of ancient lineage, the other an ingenious millwright of Quaker stock. Those at the meeting, at an inn at Wolseley Bridge, Staffordshire, on 30th December 1765, witnessed the birth of the first Canal Age when it became evident that the Bridgewater Canal's lead would be followed on a national scale. The baton had been passed, and James's Brindley's personification of an epoch was assured.

Crowded into that room were men who had considered it worthwhile to ride out on a cold, short December day – community stalwarts who were also ambitious to achieve more: landowners, traders, gentlemen and manufacturers. Also present were the Members of Parliament for all the local constituencies, as well as a great number of people from neighbouring counties. Earl Gower addressed the meeting from the chair. He spoke of his certainty that a stillwater canal linking the west and east coasts of the country, and passing through Staffordshire, would be extremely advantageous to manufacturing, both locally and in the kingdom in general. He admitted that since hearing of the scheme he had wished to lend it his support, both provincially and politically, for it was evident that landowners and traders would gain mutual advantage. It must have been music to Wedgwood's ears. His Lordship concluded by hoping that every gentleman present would join him in carrying so noble a design into execution. Brindley was then called forward to explain what was proposed and how he would carry it out.[72] He did so with such extraordinary clarity that Wedgwood's judgement was that even the dullest intellect present understood. Brindley also presented a physical image of great confidence as he assuaged any doubts that he could construct the amazing proposition – a canal 93½ miles long and 3 feet deep, with 76 locks and a near 2½ mile tunnel at Harecastle from which soughs would be extended into the hill to extract coal and mineral deposits. All at an estimated cost of £101,000. To erase any lingering confusion maps and plans were produced and closely studied before agreement on the route was reached with very little alteration.[73] Triumphantly, a number of votes were carried unanimously by which it was agreed that an Act of Parliament should be obtained as soon as possible, the funding of which would be separately raised. Construction finance would be via 505 shares sold at various locations, with each subscriber having controlling votes according to his shareholding. Finally, to engender wider support, it was agreed that the resolutions would be published in the public newspapers.[74] Thus the country's first canal of national significance was launched, its sturdy constitution a tribute to the untiring efforts and moral fortitude of Josiah Wedgwood.

That evening a huge celebratory bonfire was lit in Burslem market-place as the potters and workmen drank the health of Earl Gower and Josiah Wedgwood. Everyone was convinced that the new canal would bring great opportunities to all.[75] It was indeed the start of a new chapter, for no one more so than for James Brindley. He

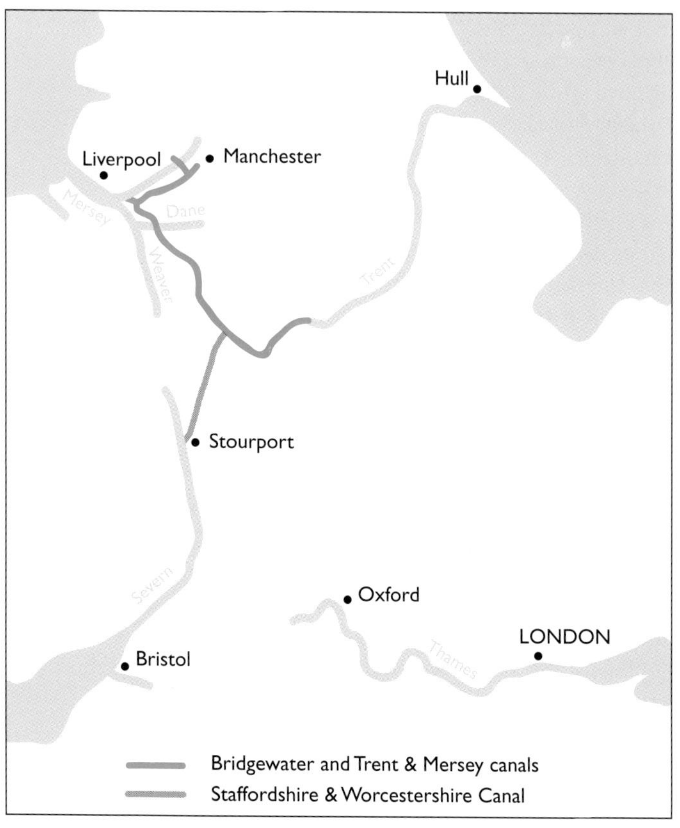

The ports of Liverpool, Hull and Bristol to be linked – Brindley canals planned or under construction, 1766

would now have a senior contracted position not only with the Trent & Mersey company, but also with the group that was to build the complementary waterway to the river Severn, now known as the Staffordshire & Worcestershire Canal. Gone were the uncertainties of daily pay-rates and employment at the whim of one man, instead he would have legal entitlements to annual salaries from both canal companies. He would also be able to delegate the daily engineering tasks to a hierarchy of assistants. Already a man of comfortable wealth from his work for the Duke of Bridgewater, James Brindley had recently decided that his forthcoming responsibilities in Staffordshire would give him the opportunity to settle in that familiar county – and to marry.

Three weeks earlier, on 8th December 1765, James Brindley had married Anne Henshall, at St Margaret's church, Wolstanton, Staffordshire. The ceremony perhaps prudently arranged for the day following the receipt of £175.7s.0d for 250 days work on the Bridgewater Canal.[76] Described in the church register as 'of the parish of Leek, Engineer', the groom was 49, his bride nineteen.[77] Such disparate ages were not uncommon in the middling classes – generally a woman had no independence and stayed in her family home until a husband could be found. If she was unmarried at the death of her father she had to rely on brothers or other male relatives to provide a home or financial support. Therefore, acquiring a husband of means was an uppermost ambition. He would provide security for life and a comfortable home with household servants in which she could ensure any future daughters would in turn be found prospective husbands. Similarly, a responsible father saw it as his duty to ensure all of his daughters were settled in a secure future. To all concerned, the ages of those marrying were irrelevant.

Brindley would have met Anne, the sister of Hugh Henshall his surveyor-assistant, at The Bent, their family home less than three miles north of Burslem. Under a mile away was Turnhurst Hall, a very large residence with many rooms – parlours, chambers, stables, extensive gardens, many cellars, brewhouses and barns – which was let for multi-occupancy by its owner. The Hall's close proximity to Harecastle Tunnel, Burslem and Anne Henshall's family, lends credibility to the claims that it became the home of the Brindley's, although it seems they lived in only a portion of it. There is also some evidence that James had lived there, informally without a lease, since 1760. Further claims that his office was in a little summer-house at the corner of an outer courtyard cannot be substantiated, and the strong local tradition that he built 'a model lock' in the garden could not be proved by assiduous research and excavations undertaken in the 1990s.[78] Nevertheless, the sparse facts do seem to indicate residence at Turnhurst Hall.

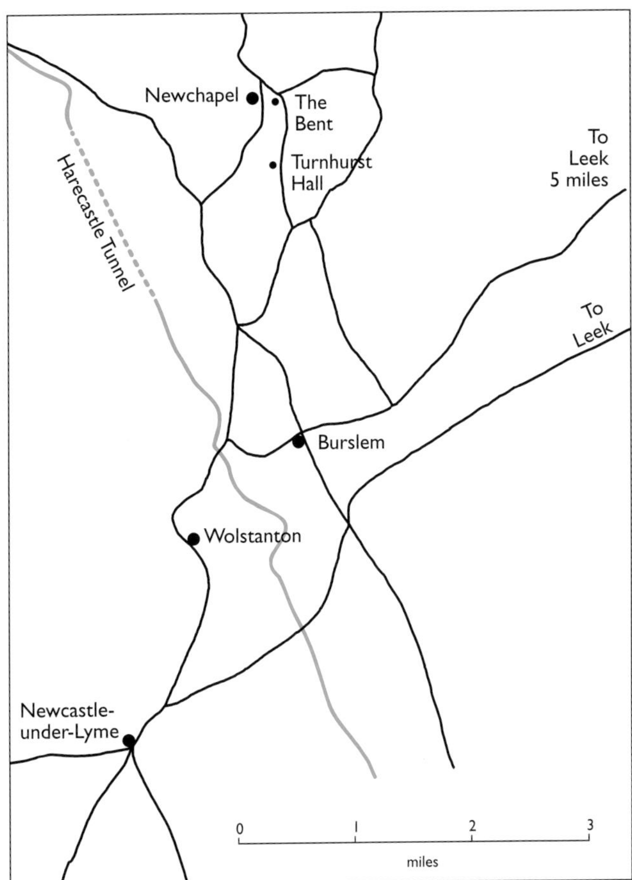

The close proximity of Brindley's home at Turnhurst Hall and Harecastle Tunnel

No time was wasted after the momentous meeting at Wolseley Bridge. A pamphlet was rapidly published, not only promoting the canal but also making the case for it joining the river Mersey and/or the Bridgewater Canal in the north, and the free-navigation sections of the Trent beyond Burton in the south.[79] A petition to Parliament for leave to bring in a Bill was despatched from the area only twelve days after the meeting, swiftly followed, or as swiftly as could be achieved in mid-winter, by Brindley, Wedgwood, Bentley and their coterie.[80] As usual, the Commons delegated investigation of the matter to a committee of the House, evidence before which commenced on Wednesday, 15th January 1766. Over the next few days the canal's promoters faced the massed opposition of those with interests in river navigations or packhorse trains, as well as the waggoners, coastal traders, and corporations of cities that would still be dependent on road transport.[81] Furthermore, the concept of stillwater canals remained unacceptable to a large swathe of the influential, with their numbers swollen by those who simply doubted that such things were possible. James Brindley, therefore, had the responsibility of arguing the general case as well as the specific. The famous engineers who would tread the same path in later years – Telford,

Rennie, Jessop, etc. – would have the benefit of canals being proven. Now, the opponents expressed amazement that gentlemen of fortune and understanding could be borne along by a fanciful torrent, even submitting their estates to being cut into pieces while claiming the public good. How, they asked, could the canal lobby contemplate such actions when the damage done would far outweigh any advantage gained from a small reduction in freight rates when canals and rivers were compared. It was agreed that it was more efficient to pull boats by horses instead of men – so why not build towpaths along already navigable rivers and save £1,000 a mile?[82] Others doubted that a canal could be carried across the river Dane and the swampy land on both of its banks, even though the Bridgewater Canal's aqueducts over the rivers Irwell and Mersey were there to be seen – but Lancashire is a long way from the restricted circle of London administrators.[83] Of all the arguments voiced, the opposition of the River Weaver Navigation worried Wedgwood most, as he confided to his friend Bentley 'the Weaver will die hardest'. The majority of the trade along that river was to and from the canal's target, Liverpool, and to prepare a convincing case Bentley had been busy in the port collecting facts to undermine the impression that transport using the river Weaver was already efficient. He now quoted figures on the delays suffered by merchandise, especially the salt vital in a non-refrigerated society, and stated that management by commissioners was incapable of improving matters, although it was very good at spending money and enlarging company debts.[84]

Such assiduous preparation eventually won the day and the House committee recommended that permission to bring in a Bill be given, an action duly taken by the Commons on 7th February. When mentally picturing the scene at Westminster it should be remembered that the building entered by Brindley and the others would be almost completely destroyed by fire in 1834. However, the chamber of the House of Commons in 1766 would have looked familiar to us – the current design of opposing benches facing each other having followed the traditional layout. On those benches sat MPs who dressed in their normal attire, in the winter entering in great-coats, and with boots and spurs. Visitors often saw one or more of them stretched out asleep as others were debating. Some cracked nuts, others enjoyed oranges or whatever else was in season. And there was no end to the coming and going.[85] MPs did not belong to political parties on modern lines. About half were country gentlemen who had no political ambitions and who guarded their right to form their own opinions on all matters. For traditional reasons many tended to support the government ministers appointed by the king, but others voted with the opposition. Nothing could be relied upon. The other half of the Commons consisted of men intent on making a career in politics and who were, therefore, more predictable in their actions. Each of them tended to give his allegiance to a leader, usually a titled grandee, who was probably responsible for the MP being in parliament. This group usually voted as their sponsor wished and this is the basis of the power wielded in the Commons by the family-linked Earl Gower, Duke of Bridgewater and Duke of Bedford. When legislation reached the House of Lords they could also speak personally to aid its passage.

It took only three weeks for the first and second readings to clear the Commons, but a further anxious two months before the crucial third reading was completed and the Bill was sent to the Lords for their approval. The news was received with great rejoicing in the Potteries area of Staffordshire, everyone knowing that the canal's representation in the Lords would ensure its acceptance, after which there would be only the ceremonial of Royal Assent needed to convert the Bill into an Act – which was duly given on 14th May 1766.

James Brindley's future was assured. In the first of many such appointments he was now Surveyor-General of the company of proprietors of the Trent & Mersey Canal, at £200 per annum. On the same day he also gained the office of Surveyor for the company of the Staffordshire & Worcestershire Canal, at a further £200 per annum – that waterway's legislative passage through Westminster having been speeded by hanging on to the coat-tails of the other.

Chapter 11

PERSONIFICATION

By 1766 Britain was growing used to the novelty of being at peace. Able to concentrate on internal matters, the inherent need for nationally celebrated heroes shifted its focus from the naval and military ranks to the leaders of technological progress. Influential free-thinkers had created an environment where entrepreneurs could flourish and produce a culture of practical erudition, within which science was widely viewed as the way forward. Observation, recording and experimentation were becoming widespread passions among many levels of society from the august members of the Royal Society to individual country gentlemen, many of whom would eventually leave notebooks full of their deductions, the accuracy of which would surprise later centuries. The second half of the eighteenth century would be an era of promise and potential, with innovation advancing on many fronts. Optimism thrived with the natural vigour of a plant in a congenial climate.

Manufacturers received the warmest praise. Their output was acclaimed as central to the good of the nation, not only in the creation of items of use in everyday life, but also in expanding civilisation to the lower levels of society by making products available at lower prices. Entrepreneurs were likewise feted. Capital for industrial processes was easily obtainable and good profits continued to be made, much of which were reinvested to continuously improve productivity. By the end of the 1750s there were manufacturing sites throughout the country within a pattern of regional specialisations. The towns were full of bustling activity. Nottingham rang to the thumping and squeaking of stocking frames producing 20,000 pairs of hosiery a week. There were fifteen glass-furnaces in Bristol, as well as factories making pipes, turpentine, lamp-black; nearby were many brass and zinc works and lead smelters. Salisbury had factories making excellent scissors from Newcastle steel, works for carriage-springs; there were and looms for flannel and light cloth. Liverpool had many sites producing glass, tobacco pipes, earthenware; there were anchor forges and salt pans; shoemakers and saddlers made goods for export. Before the advance of inland waterways the domestic production of bar iron had already burgeoned but still could not keep pace with demand. An average of 38,000 tons was imported every year, mainly from Sweden and Russia, almost all of which was distributed to forges around the country by coastal shipping and rivers.[1] The volume of manufacturing achieved by a relatively small population had already gained the attention of other nations and industrial spies were despatched to report on how it was achieved. Already, England was Europe's leading exponent of the application of technology. The image of Britain as a rural society waiting for the canals to make possible the transition to industrialisation is erroneous. More accurately, the waterway revolution allowed an already widespread process to burst forth without the hindrance of constrictive transport methods.

A perfect example of a mid-eighteenth century industrialist is Josiah Wedgwood. His pottery in Burslem was rapidly creating items with the three attributes most prized – beauty, singularity and utility – and his wares carried his name into influential households where he swiftly attained national notability. Furthermore, he was obeying the gospel of continual progress by planning extensive new premises alongside the embryonic Trent & Mersey Canal, premises that could be described as a factory rather than a pottery. His high-profile involvement in the development of waterways also placed him in the much-favoured role of the practical visionary – a man not content with improving his own lot but also striving to create something that would enable further developments for the good of the nation.

In 1766 Wedgwood and his friend and colleague Thomas Bentley were both 36, Erasmus Darwin 34, and the Duke of Bridgewater was still a young man of 30. Canals were the enterprise of young men, which was understandable, but nevertheless disconcerting to those not quite so sure of the great way forward. Such contemporaries instinctively looked towards James Brindley who, at the age of 50, did not project the image of a young firebrand of commerce: they were reassured by his age and his Quaker-like ethics and simplicity of dress, all of which made him very much the father-figure of canal construction. Furthermore, his ingenious methods of using water-power to ease the muscles of labourers also placed him as an exemplar of the much sought-after doctrine of profits with humanity. For these reasons, when disparate groups of proprietors began to promote the construction of canals throughout the country it was his name with which they wished to be associated. This rapidly led to the perception of Brindley as the personification of a sparkling new transport system, pulling together the regions of a socially still-fragmented island. Of course glory was also gained from his association with the Duke of Bridgewater, Wedgwood and Darwin, with strands of contact also spreading to the latent giants of industrialisation – James Watt, Matthew Boulton and the Quaker-led mass-production ironworks at Coalbrookdale. It was against this background that Brindley's achievements were lauded at all levels of society.

It was, therefore, at a highly favourable time that Brindley added official responsibility for two more canals to his on-going duties on the Bridgewater but nothing had prepared him for the role he was about to undertake. What were Brindley's duties to be? He had two job-titles and two salaries, but there were no precedents to define the relationship between the shareholders of the canal companies and their engineer or how he should approach the organisation and management of the canals' construction. If his duties were clarified, how was he to carry them out on a daily basis?

It was generally accepted that the shareholders of each canal company would vote a Management Committee into being amongst their number, and that this committee would meet to decide all matters relevant to the canal's construction, becoming the channel of communication with the engineers. Twice a year there would be General Meetings of all the shareholders, with progress reports and committee re-elections. Written minutes would be kept. But which decisions should be made by the committee, and which by Brindley? It would now be impossible for him to spend as much time on-site as he had done on the Bridgewater where he worried about individual weirs, dealt with difficult land-owners, allocated numbers of men to each phase, measured trees for timber, ordered work-boats to where needed. That level of involvement could not be undertaken on three canals building at the same time. And, on a personal level, he was now a married man with a home, not a workaholic single man lodging at an inn. How much time would each committee expect to be allocated to their project? Nobody would know the answers to most of those questions until work was underway, on the Trent & Mersey from the Harecastle summit eastwards towards the Trent, and on the Staffordshire & Worcestershire from its summit near Wolverhampton south-westwards towards the Severn. As the canals progressed, the work-sites would become further and further apart, further from the Bridgewater's construction in Cheshire and also more remote from Brindley's home at Turnhurst Hall. The difficulties of travelling by horse, especially in bad weather, would dictate that visits to each site would be infrequent.

James Brindley would also face personal challenges. Until now he had always been self-employed, and had flourished in that direct mode of working. Now the security of fixed salaries would bring the frustrations inherent in operating through committees. Diplomacy would be required. It must also have been evident to him that within his spheres of responsibility he would have to acquire the skill of delegation – but delegation to whom? In the past – as a well-established craftsman – he had designed steam-engines and had left others to do the basic building work while still being involved in the technicalities. Later he allocated the task of running the machine to teams of his men. The construction phases of his mills and colliery tunnels had followed similar patterns. But now he would be at an altogether more lofty level of management – those getting their hands dirty would be at least three steps further down the ladder. That being so, through what channels would he give his instructions, and how would he ensure compliance? It soon became evident that the key would be a small group of trusted men, the role of whom would set the pattern for all the canal

Turnhurst Hall 1862. Described in an auction leaflet as 'well and substantially built, having all requisite and suitable outbuildings and offices, fish pond, gardens, walled round and well stocked with fruit trees, conservatory and summer house, making the whole a very desirable family residence.' Demolished in 1929

schemes for which Brindley would be responsible, and whose names appear throughout their master's triumphs.

The first of that small group was Hugh Henshall, the brother of Brindley's wife Anne. He had been involved in the surveying of the Trent & Mersey's route since the waterway was first proposed and had been present at the meetings with John Smeaton. With his family links and living near Harecastle Tunnel he was the obvious man to be Brindley's senior on-site representative during the construction of that canal, with the usual title of Clerk of the Works. The situation on the Staffordshire & Worcestershire was not so clear. There, politics ordained that John Baker should be the Clerk of the Works to represent that canal's Wolverhampton powerbase, although he was not an engineer. Brindley, therefore, found it necessary to allocate one of his group to that project to balance matters. He chose Samuel Simcock, a senior carpenter and engineer who was married to one of Brindley's sisters and had worked on the Bridgewater Canal since its inception. Alongside Simcock was Thomas Dadford, a man of vast practical experience.[2]

On both canals the next level of management was the contractors who entered bids for specific structures or lengths of channel, and who employed the men doing the actual work. Eventually, some of their number would become trusted men on subsequent projects as Brindley's core of professionals grew. The senior craftsmen – the master brickmakers, masons, blacksmiths, and carpenters – did not need instruction on how their trades should be carried out, only how the volume of their work should be organised in accordance with the whole scheme. The logistics of finding, purchasing and moving bulk raw materials usually fell to the Clerk of the Works – clay, stone, timber, limestone for mortar, coal for kilns, iron for making bolts and tools. Adjuncts were the timber-valuers who negotiated with nearby landowners for stands of trees, or even a copse, before referring the final purchase decisions to the Management Committee. Stone, if it was locally available, would be obtained from outcrops or by the purchase and development of existing quarries. Clay for bricks was vital, with the surveyors working ahead of the construction gangs always looking for, or seeking local advice on, the location of large deposits. Negotiations for the purchase of land on the route was often an on-going duty for a team headed by the clerk to the Management Committee, who usually had a legal background. Coal, iron, limestone, gunpowder, paper, tiles, oakum, tallow oil for lamps, bedding, cordage, lead and pitch, were some of the items bought from an army of suppliers, the cost of which the Treasurer and his book-keepers tried to monitor. And the navvies? At this stage of the first canal age they were mostly men local to each project, many of them farm workers used to labouring in all weathers. One aspect of employing manpower from that source was that Clerks of the Works often had to organise matters around the harvest periods when many of the men went back to the farms, as did many of the horses and carts. It is relevant here to remember that the large and infamously rowdy navvy gangs, with many Irishmen, were a product of the second canal age, c1790–1810, the period of 'canal mania', and subsequently the construction of the railways.

James Brindley's role, at the top of the pyramid, was not to define the minutiae of how the work should be done. 'Brindley canals' were, and are, labelled thus in the same way that modern buildings bear the name of their architect. Similarly, Brindley did not always specify how a shaft should be sunk, nor how a lock-gate should be hung, anymore than he would tell a brick-maker how to do his job, although in an age when hand-made bricks came from the kilns in various states of perfection he did specify the standards to be achieved and expected a trusted subordinate to ensure such was done. Most importantly, Brindley defined the methodology of an entire project. It was central to his whole being that water should be used as a tool. An all too often heard cliché of modern condescension is 'how wonderful that they did all that work without JCBs' whereas Brindley would think it dire that we squander resources to create, power and maintain complex yellow machines when water can carry, lift, turn, mix, and clean at very little cost before being discharged for re-cycling by the natural environment. Nor would he understand the 'efficiency' of the hidden workforce behind the solitary JCB driver; those who make the steel and the machine's other components, obtain its oil and transport it half way around the world, manufacture the paint and glass, tap the rubber and make the tyres and produce the energy to make it all possible. In comparison, an army of work-hardened men with shovels, picks and wheelbarrows made on-site could create earthworks of magnitude with an independence and flexibility of purpose long lost to modern engineering.

One matter ordained by Brindley's use of water was the order in which his canals would be built. The Duke of Bridgewater's decision to have his canal maintain one level had allowed it to extend as a conduit between the water-sources and the work-camps. However, Brindley's latest projects were canals that climbed across watersheds before descending to river valleys. Therefore, water to aid the construction could only be made available if the work commenced at the highest point, the summit pound, and extended downhill in two directions from there, allowing water to flow down to where it was required as the work progressed. A second consideration, although no less important, was that in the same way canal lengths could be filled with water and made usable as the canals extended to their destinations, allowing construction materials to be moved easily by boat and also for income to be generated by carrying goods. Also, if the summit pound was complicated by a tunnel having to be built in its length, as at Harecastle, then subterranean water oozing into the works could be pumped away along the canal that would be extending from one of the portals.

Within this basic concept Brindley's level of involvement would evolve and lessen through the forthcoming years as he and his core of skilled men gained experience and as more commissions were undertaken concurrently. Initially his orders were verbal but that proved unsatisfactory and from March 1767 it was resolved that when visiting the workings on the Staffordshire & Worcestershire Canal his instructions would be noted by an assistant in a book, which Brindley would then sign. The book was then lodged with John Baker, the Clerk of the Works, where it could be referred to 'by every inferior Officer whom it might concern'.[3] This may have been viewed as insurance by one party, or both, and is perhaps indicative of a lack of trust between Brindley and a Clerk of the Works not of his choosing. Baker, always described as a 'gentleman', was not involved in engineering aspects, instead confining himself to administrative tasks such as discussions with landowners to ascertain where bridges should be built, and what type they should be for the traffic anticipated.[4] Overall, Baker was a figurehead. The duties normally inherent in Baker's title carried out by an Under Clerk of the Works, John Green, to whom Brindley did delegate supervisory tasks. Visits to the work-sites were made approximately once a month and Brindley's observations and orders covered a variety of subjects. Rock to be cut through was first to have bore holes drilled every 40 yards to ascertain its depth – a task to be overseen by John Green – and subsequently, when cut through, the sides were to be sloped 1 in 2 except where the rock was very strong. The carpenters were to create gutters of specific diameters by hollowing-out tree boughs which, when joined together, were used to drain water from cuttings and fields and to divert flows around work-sites. Much attention was given to the dimensions to which weirs, culverts and channels were to be built, and the depths and volumes of water to be accommodated. For safety reasons, lock chambers were not to be dug to their full depth and width until the materials to finish the job were at hand. Only a trench was to be sunk along the central length of a planned chamber, to full depth and to be a yard wide at the bottom, along which timber drainage trunking would be laid. In other areas, test borings were done to ascertain the presence of quicksand, which, when found, gained Brindley's personal attention, after which he gave his orders on how the work was to proceed and agreed extra payments for the contractors who were to tackle the problem.[5]

It was not always geographical difficulties that warranted special attention. Sometimes it was political – with plans and elevations of bridges to important estates ordered to be drawn up for Brindley's personal attention on his next visit. The construction of bridges of all sorts, many of them swivel types, was delegated to Mr Pyatt, who specialised in such work, whilst Thomas Dadford's role was supervising the building of the locks. Throughout, Brindley was not a man to be defied. When he noticed poor quality bricks being used to build a lock he confronted the brickmaker. When told that John Baker had ordered the bricks to be used, on threat of dismissal, he immediately issued written directions defining 'who shall be the Judges of what Bricks are to be used and where'. The tone clearly indicates that John Baker's name was not on the list, even though he was Clerk of the Works. On another occasion he saw bricklayer Gabriel Featherstone incorrectly keying an arch, and dismissed him on the spot. But Brindley's humanity and his affinity with working men mellowed his mood, and he allowed Featherstone to remain after a pledge of good behaviour, given in writing and signed by both parties.[6]

Without a team of support engineers Brindley could not have undertaken the number of schemes he did. When considering the construction of a canal it is important to remember that the entire package was rather more than a channel, locks, and bridges. On the Staffordshire & Worcestershire it also included wharfs, warehouses, bridges over brooks, a water-bridge to carry a brook over the canal, aqueducts over rivers, subterranean passages through hard rock, roads, embankments, the taking down of houses to be rebuilt elsewhere, loading basins, flood prevention measures and diversions to the courses of local rivers. And when thinking of the planning one should not image modern-style reports, engineering diagrams and detailed dimensions. At one point there was doubt about whether a lock was long enough for the workboats to pass through – a matter clarified by measuring two boats nearby and then the lock. None of the factors proved to be of the imagined 'standard' size, a concept unknown when boats were made by their builder's 'eye' from the timbers to hand. Nor was the whole canal surveyed, with locks and bridges precisely located, when work commenced. By February 1770 the Staffordshire & Worcestershire was very nearly completed south-west from its summit-level near Wolverhampton down to the river Severn near Kidderminster. But in the other direction, from the summit north-east to a junction with the Trent & Mersey, the route was still undefined in anything other than general terms. The required length of the summit was judged to be 'somewhat more than ten miles' before the canal would have to drop down into the Trent valley – a descent estimated at a suspiciously round-figured 100 feet, and vaguely requiring 'at least twelve locks'. Nor would details be known of the two aqueducts needed to cross the rivers Sow and Trent. All of which is not surprising when Green admitted that 'not a third part of the way is set out'. But when it was, the route from the summit-level to the Trent & Mersey would be estimated at 'about sixteen miles', in fact it would prove to be 22 miles.[7] By modern standards such planning appears lackadaisical, but we worship exactitude with a fervour often devoid of practical justification.

Construction of the Trent & Mersey also began at its most elevated point with the excavation of Harecastle Tunnel through the watershed, from where the canal was simultaneously built south-eastwards, keeping to the valley of the river Trent. Although meandering and convoluted routes are said to be attributes of Brindley's canals, following the natural contours of the land to negate the need for expensive and time-consuming locks, his earliest works did not markedly do so. Before work began, Wedgwood noticed that in his local area the posts marking the route to be followed went in a straight line through the fields. Berating Hugh Henshall for surveying it so and not taking a more aesthetic way he received the reply that the canal must go the 'nearest and best way or Mr Brindley would go mad'.[8] However, any aspersions cast on the route by outsiders, and by association on Brindley himself, met with robust and instant rebuttals. There had to be no doubts about the engineer in charge. Construction work was about to start but it was still a precarious situation both politically and financially, and would remain so until the canal was almost completed, many years in the future. Wedgwood railed against slanderous reports on Brindley's character – industrially spread, he maintained, by a certain party – and privately feared that such aspersions if not challenged would 'retard our progress, if not defeat the whole undertaking'.[9] Rather more to the liking of the promoters of Brindley's canals had been the description of him in the *Gentleman's Magazine* in January 1766 as 'one of those great geniuses which nature sometimes rears by her own force, and brings to maturity without the necessity of cultivation'.[10] Published in London, the magazine was an intellectual journal with an increasingly influential readership in the capital, its coverage of developments in the country fundamental to reputations. Fundamental, also, to investments. The Midlands and the North fought for the creation of canals as part of an improved national infrastructure but a sizeable proportion of the share and loan capital behind the Trent & Mersey came from London. It was accepted that the manufacturers who would gain the most direct benefit from a canal would only directly invest in its creation if money could be spared from their commercial enterprises. No one expected them to starve their businesses in order to create a transport system. Therefore, only five per cent of the Trent & Mersey's funding came from the Staffordshire potters. Instead the largest groups were landowners (£141,000), London (£56,000), and Lichfield (£46,500). London investors were mostly traders and professional men with no direct contact with the scheme but attracted by the promotional activities – a crucial part of which was Brindley's role as the engineering figurehead.[11]

Further strands of the Brindley image continued to be formed at Worsley where the completed sections of the Duke of Bridgewater's canal still rated as a not-to-be-missed feature of the extensive tours so popular with gentlemen of means. Joseph Banks, an amateur scientist of wealth soon to accompany Captain Cook to the Pacific, noted in his journal that full credit for the ingenious use of water as power for the many machines on site was unequivocally given to Brindley. Also that he had done most of the engineering work on the canal itself. The rumblings of disquiet from Worsley that would later indicate annoyance at the perceived picture of Brindley as the progenitor of the entire scheme were not yet evident. Conversely, it very much suited the duke to promote the abilities of the Trent & Mersey's engineer; the proposal for that waterway to form a junction with the Bridgewater was of vital importance to his own future. Yet, human nature being what it is, it was also explained that Brindley's success was the result of John Gilbert's perspicacity – he having found Brindley in Staffordshire where he was famous only for being 'the best millwright in the country' but whom he had nevertheless recommended to the duke as the man to build a canal. This was said to be an act of much discernment as the engineer was a man of 'no education but of extremely strong natural parts'.[12]

Meanwhile, in keeping with his high profile, James Brindley attended the ceremonial cutting of the Trent & Mersey's first spadeful of soil on 26th July 1766, at Brownhills, Burslem. A general holiday had been granted in the area and nearly all the potteries closed down. At noon a large crowd gathered, including noblemen, gentry, ladies, masters and workmen all in the best clothes they possessed. In their midst stood a dignified group of gentlemen who had been involved in the scheme to date. Speeches told of the many hours of toil, the battles fought and won, and the gains to be made by everyone in the area. Amidst loud cheers Josiah Wedgwood limped forward to push the first spade into the soil, lifting its contents and placing them in a wheelbarrow, which was then wheeled away by Brindley. More speeches were endured before a cask of Staffordshire ale was opened and tankards filled to toast the health of Earl Gower and everybody else of official status who had given their backing to the project. After which the throng dispersed to the local inns for lunches and dinners, whilst the master potters entertained various members of the official party at their homes. Outside, a sheep was roasted for the poorer potters. At sunset bonfires were lit throughout Burslem, culminating in a sumptuous feast in front of Wedgwood's house.[13]

By 1766 public perception was that all canal schemes involved James Brindley. There still persists an image of him as a pied-piper figure going throughout the land

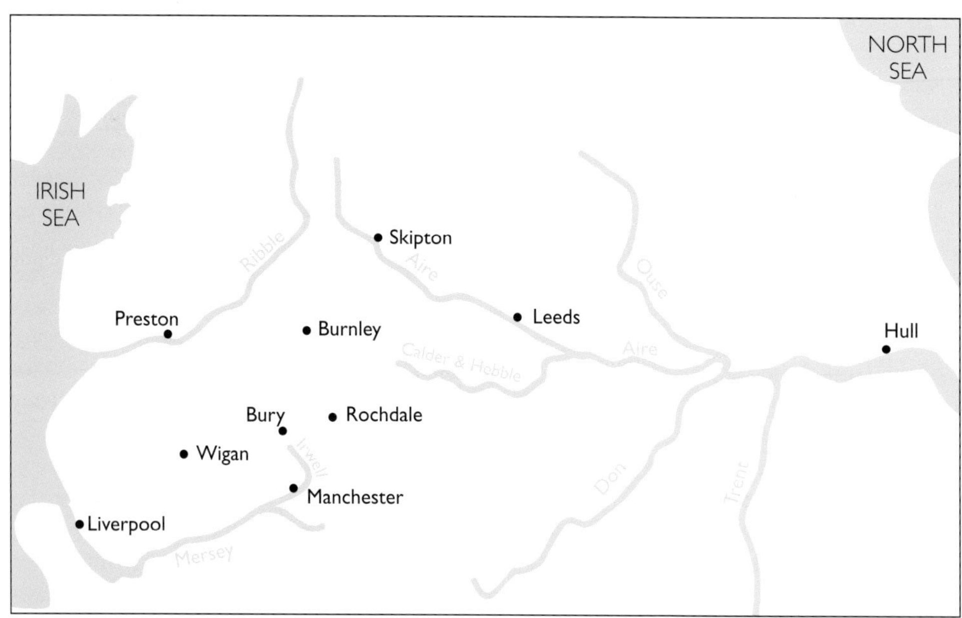

The rivers Aire and Ribble – their valleys providing a route for a canal across the high Pennines. The Calder & Hebble Navigation is also approaching the river Irwell

calling the canal tune to a growing band of followers. It was, however, far more than the cult of celebrity. He was very much a safe pair of hands whose opinions were often sought publicly to assuage the doubts of investors, and privately to bolster the confidence of those delegated to carry matters out. It was this role that linked his name to many canal schemes outside his main area of operations. One example is in Yorkshire as early as 1758: here others had independently planned another canal to connect the west and east coasts, this time to serve the north of England rather than the midlands. Now known as the Leeds & Liverpool Canal, it was a bold plan to join these two cities by crossing the high Pennines along the valleys of the rivers Aire and Ribble, linking them through a low watershed, a wild and sparsely populated area just north of Skipton. But it was another scheme that needed the impetus generated by the Duke of Bridgewater's success to gain the required volume of public support.[14] At this early stage Brindley was not publicly involved, but the strong influence of Quaker wool merchants in Yorkshire was later to lead to his opinion being sought when route disputes threatened to disrupt the whole scheme. Similarly, others were already actively promoting the Rochdale Canal, again to link rivers of the west and east coasts. Brindley had been the engineer of the traditional Calder & Hebble Navigation the previous year and therefore knew John Royds the treasurer. Now Royds was a leading promoter of this canal which was to go from the upper limit of the Calder & Hebble across to the river Irwell and Manchester, via Rochdale or Bury.[15] Unsurprisingly, Brindley was asked to survey two routes and give costings.[16] Nearer to his core business, a group of commissioners was seeking to make the river Soar navigable from its confluence with the Trent up to Loughborough. Although river improvements were anathema to him, the Soar would bring more traffic to the Trent & Mersey so the scheme was aided by Wedgwood and others, with Brindley doing a survey.[17] He recommended a canal for part of the route but the commissioners had no power to do so. Consequently the scheme failed and was not revived until 1775.[18]

Nearer to home, only two miles from Turnhurst Hall, work had already commenced on Harecastle Tunnel, another canal feature that visitors viewed with varying degrees of knowledge. It was eight years since the line had been set out over the watershed and the decision made to tunnel through the hills rather than have the Trent & Mersey climb higher to cross above ground with a reduction in the water catchment area available.[19] Eventually 2,880 yards long Harecastle Tunnel was cut straight with no towpath, a task which would take approximately nine years. It was brick-lined with the excavation work done from each portal and from shafts sunk along its length. From the bottom of these shafts workfaces were extended in both directions, all joining up to form one tunnel – rather like cutting along a dotted line. Almost nothing is known of the men who did the work but such a specialised task must have required mining knowledge and there was no shortage of that in the area. In the nearby Pennines many soughs had been excavated to drain lead-mines and some of them were of great length with accurately measured inclines. For example, 1766 also saw the start of work on Hillcarr Sough in Derbyshire most of which would be 6 feet wide and 7–8 feet high, and many thousands of yards longer than Harecastle.[20] Despite this, as work progressed visitors were encouraged to come and see the canal tunnel by strident publicity couched in a roll-up, roll-up, magical-mystery-tour style.

Gentlemen, come to view our Eighth Wonder of the

World – the subterraneous Navigation which is cutting by the great Mr Brindley who handles Rocks as easily as you would Plumb-Pyes and makes the four elements subservient to his will. He is as plain a looking man as one of his own Carters, but when he speaks all Ears listen, and every Mind is filled with Wonder at the things he pronounces to be practicable. He has cut a mile through Bogs, which he binds up, embanking them with Stones which he gets out of other Parts of the Navigation, besides about a quarter of a Mile into the Hill, on the side of which he has a pump, which is worked by Water, and a Stove, the Fire of which sucks through a Pipe the Damps that would annoy the Men who are cutting toward the Centre of the Hill. The clay he cuts out, serves for bricks to arch the subterranean Part, which we heartily wish to see finished to Wilden Ferry, when we shall be able to send Coals and Pots to London and to different parts of the Globe. [21]

Those who did accept the invitation had some comments on the construction standards. Joseph Banks, still on his tour through Wales and the Midlands, thought very little care was taken with making the mortar, its resultant softness giving rise to fears of accidents when the brickwork reached the sections with the greatest weight of ground above.[22] Over 50 years later this opinion would be borne out by John Rennie who would inspect the tunnel at the request of the canal company. He found that wherever the mortar was underwater, or had otherwise been kept damp, it was as soft as clay, and the bricks in those places could be pulled out with very little labour.[23] Unfortunately that is a feature of mortar made from crushed and burnt limestone, which is all that was available in the Brindley era. Such mortar has the advantage of making a flexible bond, so if there is any movement it does not pull away from the bricks, but it takes about ten days to cure. It is also corrosive to the touch.[24] Such mortars were not really good enough for canal work as their efficiency depended on their being applied to dry surfaces. Smeaton had a similar problem when he was building Eddystone lighthouse on its rock base well out to sea. After months of patient experimentation he found that if he mixed volcanic ash into the crushed limestone before burning, the mortar produced would set in damp conditions.[25] Brindley had also experimented but he found a much cheaper alternative by heating limestone that had a high clay content. This limestone, however, had been found many miles away near the Bridgewater Canal and was not available for Harecastle Tunnel.[26] There were no standard formulations to follow. They had to make the best of what was at hand, while keeping costs to a minimum at the start of a many-years canal project, a completed example of which was unknown in Britain.

Brindley was still involved in the continuing construction of the Bridgewater Canal. He did enough work to warrant £283 expenses being paid in October 1766 for the previous twelve months, £105 of which was for surveying a branch canal to Stockport which was never built.[27] The horse-back travelling between his three major canal responsibilities under construction – the Bridgewater, the Trent & Mersey, and the Staffordshire & Worcestershire – must have been exhausting, and of course that did not include journeys for the schemes on the periphery. There would be much more work and travel in the future, but already his friends were worried about his health. Wedgwood wrote to Bentley in March 1767 telling of his fears for their mutual friend and complaining that Brindley was incessantly harassed on every side and had little time to rest his body or his mind. Those around him constantly advised that he should take more care of himself, but to no avail. Unheeded they implored him to do less, otherwise he may fatally go beyond the limits of prudent behaviour. Was the fame and the wealth worth such a price? In the opinion of all, no. But still the feeling of insecurity, the fear that his good fortune would end, would slip from his grasp if he relaxed, drove Brindley to take almost all of the work offered to him. Wedgwood thought him an object of pity. 'He may get a few thousands, but what does he give in exchange? His health, & I fear his life too'.

What Brindley's friends and family could probably see were the symptoms of his diabetes, present for two years. The classic signs, which gradually increase in intensity, are a raging thirst, frequent urination and loss of energy, with the tiredness becoming very profound. Perhaps also blurred vision from time to time and pain in the legs. Brindley may have inherited a tendency towards diabetes although environmental factors could have triggered it. In middle-age the exact time of onset can never be clearly defined but it is sometimes associated with changes in diet or lifestyle. The amount of insulin produced may be able to cope if the intake of food is not excessive. However, too much starchy food exacerbates the situation and eventually the supply of insulin slowly fades away.[28] It may be coincidence, but later others would look back and judge the time of the first perceived symptoms to be just after Brindley's marriage. After his years of bachelor existence the provision of a comfortable home, the close proximity of friends to visit, and a wife and servants to ensure his table was well-stocked, may well have combined to overwhelm his diabetes-prone system. But that is diagnosis with hindsight – it would the next century before the causes of diabetes were ascertained, and the 1920s before insulin was isolated and effective treatments developed.[29] So if Dr Erasmus Darwin had investigated matters he would not have had the knowledge to improve Brindley's health, although a change of diet may have worked wonders. Unfortunately, his illness coincided with circumstances in 1767, which would dictate that the leadership and support in canal matters, reliably supplied by Josiah Wedgwood would become intermittent.

The politics behind the Trent & Mersey had not abated when construction began. Wedgwood was tired of the unending stream of bothersome duties and fervently wished that the bustle could soon be over, allowing him to resume the life of a potter once again.[30] Nothing was straightforward, certainly not the task of planning his new factory on land destined to be alongside the Trent & Mersey Canal. To be called Etruria, after the current fashion for anything Etruscan, it would be the main production site of his company until 1936. Negotiations for the purchase of the land had dragged on since the previous year. The vendor Mrs Ashenhurst complaining of ill-usage, made shrill threats to sell to others, who, she huffed and puffed, were willing to pay the price Wedgwood deemed extortionate. Seemingly Mrs Ashenhurst was one of the first landowners to become astutely aware that an adjacent transport system can double the value of 350 acres, and Wedgwood was guileless in expecting otherwise.[31] If naive in some matters he was a visionary in many others. A visit to Matthew Boulton's celebrated Soho Ironworks in Birmingham had shown Wedgwood the levels of production that could be achieved – methods he was now busily incorporating into his planned layout.[32] Outside there were rumblings of discontent. It had been noticed by other potters in Burslem that the Etruria site was a valuable canal-side location. Was it coincidence that the marked route would so well serve the interests of the waterway's leading promoter? Collusion? Conspiracy? Embarrassingly, the group making the ugly insinuations was led by Brindley's brother John. They informed the fledgling canal company's management committee that the route should take a shorter course along the meadows instead of veering off through Etruria. The matter was resolved in a manner which again indicates the perceived integrity of James Brindley. Although his brother was a leading complainant, and it could be argued that he himself had colluded in defining the route to Wedgwood's advantage, the subject was referred to the canal's engineer and when he reported that the planned route was still the best that could be achieved, all things being considered, the committee accepted his opinion without demur.[33]

Wedgwood's Etruria works, on its strategic canalside site, 1777, having been officially opened on 13th June 1769

If professionally Wedgwood was under pressure it was as nothing to the traumas within his beloved family. The joy of his life was his first child Susannah, known affectionately as Sukey. It was, therefore, a decision of great courage to have the two-year-old and her baby brother John, inoculated against smallpox. This hazardous action can only have been prompted by Josiah's own experience – scarcely cheating death in 1741 at the price of great damage to his right leg, which still gave debilitating pain.[34] In the 1760s and 1770s smallpox mainly killed young children but it was realised that the body built an immunity after an attack, so inoculation was newly recommended. It was, however, risky as the shallow scratch actually delivered a mild strain of smallpox itself, rather than the safe cowpox later introduced by Jenner.[35] By early March 1767 Wedgwood could report to Bentley that

> they are now past the worst, and I hope out of danger... They both had convulsions at the first appearance of the eruption, and have had a pretty smart pox as our Doctor terms it. I believe they have had no dangerous symptoms but have been so very ill that I confess I repented what we had done … however I am very thankful that all is well with them …[36]

He could not have been more thankful if he had known of the impact on scientific thinking that would be made by Charles Darwin, one of Sukey's future children after her marriage to a son of her father's lifelong friend Erasmus Darwin.

Three months later Wedgwood received the news that his brother John had drowned in the Thames, an accident while walking in the dark near Westminster Bridge after an evening visit to the famous pleasure gardens at Ranelagh to see the fireworks. This was a dire blow and Josiah's spirits sank, resulting in a bilious complaint and leaving him disheartened in the prosecution of his canal work. In the midst of this came the worry, and thankfully the joy, of the birth of his third child, Richard. During this long period the ailing Brindley could not call on Wedgwood's otherwise continual support. It must have been with some relief that Brindley saw the potter's naturally resilient character begin to re-assert itself, augmented by an exercise regime of riding on horse-back from 10 to 20 miles a day, and eating whey and the yolks of eggs in abundance, together with rhubarb.[37]

Wedgwood's recovery was essential, as 1767 would be a vital year of consolidation for the new canal era, with an immense increase in pressure on James Brindley. Birmingham, which had lost its proposed branch from the Trent & Mersey, now wanted a canal westwards to the planned route of the Staffordshire & Worcestershire waterway. Enthusiasts led by Samuel Garbett asked Brindley to do a survey and by March the project was well underway. At the same time Coventry also asked for his help with a canal from the Trent & Mersey, with a further scheme projected to go from that city to Oxford and ultimately the river Thames. The money for these surveys was raised by subscriptions, but when Brindley was approached he replied that they were too precipitate, and that he would 'look over the country in a year or two if he could'.[38] His failing health was now preventing the immediate acceptance of every job offered. But he was not relaxing, having just returned from visiting the Loughborough project he had promised to accompany Samuel Garbett to Scotland and Ireland to inspect proposed waterways there.[39] It was all too much, and by April the Garbett trip was abandoned because Brindley's health was too bad even to attend a local General Meeting of the Trent & Mersey's proprietors. The lack of rest, both physically and mentally, was exacerbating the effects of his still-undiagnosed diabetes. In a rare acknowledgement of his failing capabilities, Brindley told his friends that he would make a constitutional visit to Buxton, a spa town high in Derbyshire's Peak District and only a handful of miles from his birthplace. Wedgwood endeavoured to persuade him that he should extend his holiday for the whole of the summer, but without success. James and Anne Brindley's visit to Buxton was delayed by work again and again until they eventually left in August.[40]

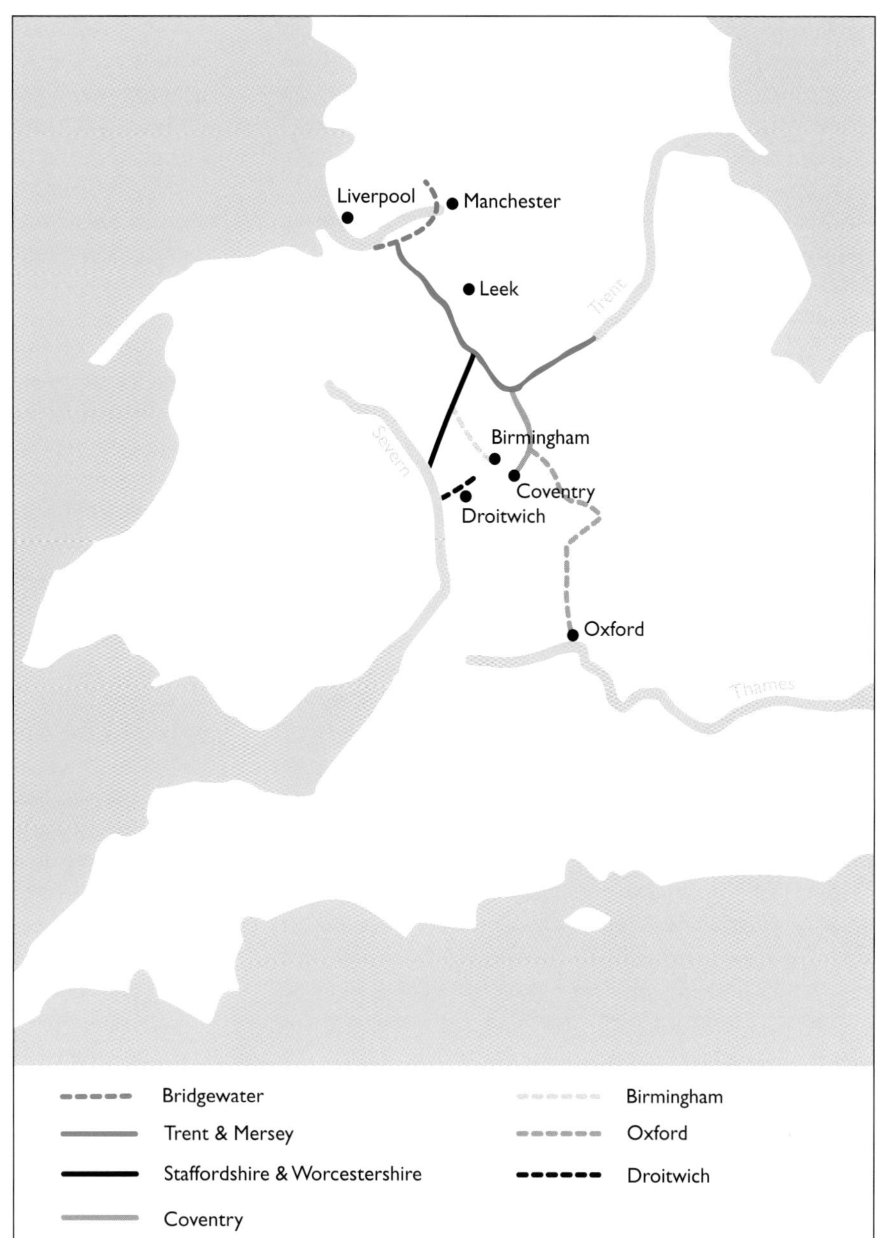

The heart of a future network – the first seven of Brindley's eight canals

In the intervening period the development of canals continued at a frantic pace, with Brindley continuing his regular inspections of work underway on the Staffordshire & Worcestershire. By June the first survey and estimates for the connected Birmingham Canal had been completed, although they had been delegated to Robert Whitworth, a very capable surveyor who would become Brindley's senior assistant. Two routes were put forward, but Brindley put his name to the one via Smethwick and Bilston, with branches to various coal pits. Only one month later £35,400 had been subscribed, with the whole £50,000 available soon after.[41] In the neighbouring areas around Coventry there was too much momentum to accept Brindley's advice to delay matters. Some of the leading promoters were colliery owners with experience of using drainage soughs as navigable channels and they were confident the undertaking was viable.[42] In mid-August a public meeting was held to consider a canal from the Trent & Mersey. Less than three weeks later £17,000 had been subscribed, but only for the route to Coventry, an extension to the Thames at Oxford being deferred.[43]

Even if he had wanted to, and by now he may have, Brindley could not refuse a leading role in the canals to Birmingham and Coventry because they would bring additional traffic to his principal waterway, the Trent & Mersey. His name was still the most influential factor behind the subscriptions flooding into the coffers of the new canal companies, his success a treadmill from which he could not escape. Friends and associates had major involvements in his work, their prosperity dependent on the enlargement of the new-born canal network, which widespread opinion said needed Brindley's active involvement as both engineer and figurehead. Even at social events the company was commercial. Josiah and Sarah Wedgwood often hosted amiable gatherings at their home, especially when Thomas Bentley was visiting from Liverpool.[44] They were enlightened meetings of erudite people and Brindley's attendance disproves later descriptions of him as dour and illiterate. Dr Erasmus Darwin was usually present and he had a common interest with Brindley in the development of steam power. James Watt had recently visited him. His improvements to the steam-engine were still undeveloped, but he had revealed the details. Over the years Watt would continue to look to Darwin for encouragement, ideas and medical advice. Another guest of the Wedgwoods was James Keir, a mutual friend of many present. Keir helped to launch the chemical industry by discovering at his Tipton works how to make caustic soda from salt on a large scale. Also often present was John Whitehurst, who made special clocking-in devices for the Etruria works, but whose speciality was geology, an obvious subject of interest to a canal engineer. These social gatherings set the pattern for the acclaimed Lunar Society, at which Wedgwood, Boulton, Darwin and other far-seeing commercial gentlemen met once a month, when the moon was full to light them home, to discuss technological advances.[45]

Erasmus Darwin's home in Lichfield, 1756–81

With canal matters progressing at such a rapid pace Brindley's ill health demanded that the delayed holiday be taken now. Relaxing in the genteel town of Buxton should have been restorative, but the properties of the thermal springs brought people there from a wide area many of whom now took the opportunity to meet the famous Mr Brindley and his wife. After only two weeks they returned to Turnhurst Hall having rested only a little more than if they had stayed at home. The only positive thing to come from the fortnight was Brindley's report to Wedgwood that he had noticed that brooks in the area contained the refuse from adjacent lead mines and were therefore abundant in a great variety of minerals and fossils, both of which the potter needed for experiments to improve his products.[46]

To exacerbate matters the weather in the autumn of 1767 was destructively bad.[47] Very heavy rain, often lasting for many days at a time, was widespread over the Pennines. On the eastern flank of the hills great damage was caused in Sheffield, and further north many of the works on the Calder & Hebble Navigation were washed away, making stretches of it impassable by any vessel.[48] On the western side the river Bollin roared with floodwaters and smashed into the piers of Brindley's aqueduct, still under construction to carry the Bridgewater Canal across its valley. When it was obstructed by the central arch, the river broke up the foundations until the whole structure gave way. John Gilbert immediately sent for Brindley, meanwhile ordering major repair work to begin. No blame for the failure was attached to Brindley, nor was he accused of bad workmanship, only that, in hindsight, it was thought that a deep hole dug in the river-bed upstream of the aqueduct would have stilled the storm waters. Gilbert's response was instead relief that the accident had taken place before the Bollin aqueduct and the Bridgewater Canal were both completed, he and the duke consoling themselves that otherwise the inconvenience and the expense would have been far greater.[49]

Such mishaps did not quell the fever for canal investments amongst those who were at the forefront of the movement, such as the gentlemen of the Trent & Mersey's management committee who discussed

John Gilbert

opening a second share subscription offer. Brindley counselled restraint until the future was a little clearer, not for parsimonious reasons but because those present might discover a wish to buy more shares themselves before offering them to others. He gave confidence by boldly stating that he would give a further £2,000, the legal limit, when a second subscription opened, which would double his investment. Why not, he continued, when shares in the Staffordshire & Worcestershire were already 30 per cent above their purchase price? The Trent & Mersey, as the 'Grand Trunk' from which all others would branch, must therefore be a more substantial security than any other canal. Wedgwood remembered Brindley's words as: 'everything which communicates with must benefit us, and no parallel can ever be made to injure ours'. The next day he wrote to Bentley who had a friend in Liverpool who wished to buy some shares, 'What effect these assurances from a man of Mr Brindley's known integrity may have upon our stocks, I do not know …' Shares were still at their original price, but Wedgwood would not promise to get them at that for Bentley's friend.[50]

Elsewhere, the town of Droitwich decided a canal would be the thing to provide more efficient transportation of its vast salt exports down to the river Severn, for onward carriage to all parts of the country. A simple affair, the canal would follow the route of the river Salwarpe and be built to wide dimensions, but it was still to Brindley that they turned. He delegated the initial investigations to Robert Whitworth, although acting in his master's name.

By December 1767 all but one of the canals Brindley would build were either under construction or at the initial planning and surveying stage. More than 600 men were constantly employed on the Trent & Mersey alone. Work on Harecastle Tunnel was on-going and 10 miles of open canal was also completed.[51] What would later be referred to as the 'Grand Cross' had been organised, with the commencement of the Coventry Canal imminent and an extension to the Thames via the Oxford Canal all but finalised. If only on paper, the rivers Mersey, Humber, Severn and Thames had been linked by Brindley canals. In reality very little had been built, with even the first canal to get underway, the Bridgewater, far from completion. The year ended with terrible weather – snow drifts, freezing temperatures, the Thames un-navigable in the centre of London, and generally the worst conditions for nearly thirty years.[52] In Derbyshire a group of Quaker businessmen, one of whom knew Brindley, was almost ready to approach the engineer to ask him to build a canal from their town, Chesterfield, to the river Trent.[53] The last and most boldly engineered of Brindley's canals was about to be announced.

Chapter 12
BRINDLEY & CO

James Brindley was now at the head of a canal construction company, possibly with group interests in the installation of mill machinery and steam-powered engines. The geographical spread of the waterways for which he was responsible, and their varying progress, necessitated delegation through many levels of subordinates. Hugh Henshall continued his responsibilities for the day-to-day engineering on the nationally strategic Trent & Mersey, his assistants reporting back by letter. One such was Edmund Lingard who spent January 1768 looking for brick-making clay at the eastern end of the route, with uncertain success. The navvies had fixed upon a supply at Findern but Lingard judged it to be unsuitable. Instead he looked by the canal and found some good 'water clay', augmented by some 'red' a hundred yards away. He thought the two clays mixed together would make good bricks but the men thought otherwise, insisting on making a brick or two from the water-clay, which they wanted to send back to Staffordshire for firing. The on-site manager was obviously having trouble with his workforce, suggesting to Henshall that the men should report to him at the first opportunity.[1] Training in Brindley methodology was undertaken as each new canal project joined the network, even down to the style of the hundreds of wheelbarrows to be made to order.[2] The Coventry Canal's Clerk of the Works, Joseph Parker, was sent to Henshall for a month's training and, soon afterwards, John Bushel, the contractor for the locks on the Droitwich Canal, arrived for the same purpose.[3] Elsewhere, the senior men were moved around to maximise the benefit of their expertise. Samuel Simcock, Brindley's brother-in-law, had been involved in the Staffordshire & Worcestershire since its inception. Now he was at the eastern end of the Trent & Mersey, before being allocated to the Birmingham Canal, as senior engineer, later in the year.[4] On the Staffordshire & Worcestershire Thomas Dadford was promoted to Simcock's previous role.[5]

Robert Whitworth was the itinerant member of the team. A masterly surveyor, it was to him that Brindley delegated the numerous requests received for canals throughout the country. In the south-west Whitworth surveyed a line for the abortive Exeter & Uphill, in the south the Salisbury & Southampton and the Andover canals, in the north he wrote a report on the practicalities of a canal from Stockton to Darlington and beyond.[6] The 'Brindley' surveys of the Leeds & Liverpool, and the Lancaster, were Whitworth's work, as was the initial definition of the route for the Birmingham, Coventry and Oxford canals.[7] In exchange Whitworth, as well as Brindley's other young men, had his approval to take on the independent work that came along because of their association with him. This was, of course, a stratagem that spread Brindley's influence wider than he could personally have sustained. For instance, Whitworth's first individual report was on the Lagan Navigation in Northern Ireland, which was well received, with one of his options eventually implemented.[8]

For much of their time Brindley's middle managers were involved in lengthy negotiations with landowners. There was still a great deal of mistrust between the parties. The Earl of Uxbridge had an estate at the eastern end of the Trent & Mersey's proposed route, near Burton-on-Trent. His agent, William Wyatt, kept a keen eye on proceedings because the exact course had still not been marked out across the Earl's land. He estimated it would be less than a mile if a straight line were taken. However, it would be the approach to the river Dove and no one had yet decided where the canal would cross that tributary of the Trent.[9] Brindley's men needed to display diplomacy of a high order when dealing with titled estate owners, tinged with just the right amount of obsequious deference. At the end of February 1768 the line had been defined but the Earl's permission to enter his land was not forthcoming. The navvies were at a standstill while Brindley's surveyors repeatedly called on Wyatt, whom they asked to write to the Earl, 'begging' his permission. If it was a problem with the money for the land then they would 'endeavour to make those payments more agreeable to your Lordship'.[10] And when work did get underway there would be complaints stating that more than half the vegetation of the pastures had been arbitrarily destroyed.[11] Disputes of this nature were a common and on-going factor of canal construction. Brindley's involvement would have been unproductive, not only because his engineering capabilities could be better utilised, but also because he had little time for pretension.

The surveyors and land-valuers were the pathfinders of a canal, both literally and figuratively. Behind them the navvies created a not always continuous channel. Lengths blighted by political or geographical problems were left to a later date, as was the completion of complex engineering structures, such as a flight of locks. The order of progress was also dependent on the availability of water supplies at any one point, and courses into which a surplus could be discharged. Progress was publicised by press releases, thus we know that October 1768 saw 22 miles of the Trent & Mersey completed, together with fourteen locks, and 26 bridges over and through which floated six construction boats. At Harecastle 409 yards of the tunnel had been cut and vaulted, with vast openings at each portal.[12] Ever a magnet for visitors, the opportunity was usually taken to associate the wonders with Mr Brindley's name. There were fifteen shafts along the tunnel's line, with horse-gins at the top to draw up the earth, rock and coal excavated. Small volumes of subterranean water were removed by wind-pumps but if vast quantities were encountered, enough to hinder or endanger the miners, then Brindley had a steam-engine at the top of the hill to drain the works as undertaken at collieries, an echo of his past with steam-pumps for the Broad family.[13]

The success of this canal construction company is due in no small measure to Brindley's ability to choose reliable and capable men to assist him. He did not suffer fools gladly and had little patience with those who did not work to his standards, but he was also a staunch representative of his men and did not curry favour with the powerful at their expense. Financially, the rewards were substantial for all. An insight from an outsider's point of view was given by engineer Davis Dukart when negotiating salaries with Lord Abercorn for a canal in Northern Ireland.[14] At least £100 a year would have to be paid for a capable Clerk of the Works who could work for more than one week in Dukart's absence. In his experience, paying less only wasted more than it saved, especially if the work was difficult – cutting through high rock, building locks in low marshy ground, or embanking across valleys. If the project was to be free of such challenges then £150 for himself, and only £40 for an assistant would suffice. Otherwise he, Dukart, would need £200 per annum. He justified his claims by quoting the salaries currently being paid elsewhere.

> Brindley has £500 per year for the Staffordshire work only, his Overseer has £300, & many under overseers 40, 50 & some 60 pounds per annum. Brindley does not attend one month in twelve; he has besides this, the Duke's work, the river Calder in Yorkshire, & many others. Smeaton has £500 per annum for the Scotch canal, and his Overseer £300, & his attendance, I mean Smeaton's, is but one month in twelve. What this work is & how executed I can only guess …[15]

Smiles would have us believe that Brindley was not adequately paid for his work, but that was obviously not the opinion of his contemporaries.

Further income came with Brindley's appointment as Engineer and Surveyor of the newly authorised Coventry Canal in February 1768, another £150 per annum, for which he undertook to give at least two months attendance in each year. A week later a claim for £225.10s.0d landed on the Treasurer's desk for the planning stage of the canal, including attendance in London giving supportive evidence before yet another committee of the House. It was paid in full.[16]

It is easy to create an image of Brindley doing very little work on each of the projects for which he was responsible, but that was not the case. At management committee meetings he gave detailed instructions defining the construction standards to be achieved, some of which were for specific locations and indicate a lengthy on-site presence. They also show Brindley's use of local raw materials whenever possible, to save both time and money – only specifying otherwise when a specialised product was required (Appendix F). In this frugality he differed from Smeaton who was now responsible for the canal to link the Forth & the Clyde, which had eventually made progress. For the Coventry Canal Brindley specified timber piles of oak or elm. Smeaton wanted beech from Sussex taken all the way to his Scottish canal, stating that it was the 'best and cheapest' (a rare combination in life). Brindley ordered a small sample of the specialised Barrow limestone to be obtained from Leicestershire, to experiment with its capability for making lime mortar which would set underwater. For the same purpose, Smeaton recommended 50 to 100 tons of pozzuolana cement be purchased from Italy.[17] Brindley's thrift was perceptive. He knew the ramifications of six canals requiring public finance being built in a relatively constricted area of central England, where only a low percentage of a small population was able to invest. The London involvement in the Trent & Mersey was not replicated in the branches of the 'Grand Trunk'. The Birmingham Canal had only 66 shares purchased outside of its area. Financially, the Coventry was one of the weakest of the canals of this era with only 22 shares (5 per cent) from other than along its route. In 1771 it would exhaust its authorised share capital and work would stop until extra finance could be raised.[18] Its administration was the least influenced by Brindley. Three different surveyors worked on the line, and the management committee even took it upon itself to negotiate terms fundamental to the order in which construction would take place.[19] When first consulted, Brindley had advised them to wait a year or two before proceeding – that they did not do so seems to have been detrimental to their working relationship. The Coventry Canal was to be a branch of the Trent & Mersey, therefore Brindley took the appointment of Engineer and Surveyor to protect his wider interests but matters would deteriorate the following year.

By early March 1768 the private income of James Brindley had been augmented by two more appointments as each of his canals progressed to receiving parliamentary approval and financial support. The Birmingham gave him the title of Engineer and £200 per annum, with John Meredith as his on-site Clerk of the Works. For the Droitwich, a canal to be as little as 6 miles long, Brindley only took the more remote role of Inspector of the Works at £60 a year, meagre indeed when compared with his 'assistant' John Priddey who was Resident Engineer at an annual £90.[20] It was evident that Brindley would have little to do with the actual construction of the Droitwich Canal, simply giving it the support of his company organisation with further advice as necessary.

Mr and Mrs Brindley could, therefore, live in comfort and some considerable style. Nearby friends added to the amiability and, when her husband's work took him away for prolonged periods, Anne Brindley frequently stayed with the Wedgwoods at their welcoming Burslem home. It was a friendship of reciprocity as Josiah often had to visit his pottery's new showroom in the most fashionable quarter of London, returning on one occasion with a handsome carved mahogany tea-tray as a gift for Anne Brindley.[21]

The relationship between the two couples was marked by Josiah Wedgwood's deep respect for James Brindley who, at the age of 52, was his senior by fourteen years. Wedgwood himself was a man of high moral standards treating his employees with benevolence and later vigorously campaigning for the abolition of slavery.[22] As an adherent of the Unitarian form of Christianity he took personal integrity to be a staple requirement of life. It is, therefore, of great significance that Brindley was held in high esteem by such a man. Although not a practising Quaker, it is obvious that the engineer continued to take the fundamental ethos of his family's sect as his model. Wedgwood declared that he improved morally and intellectually whenever he spent time with Brindley and concluded that with such company he would be a 'blockhead of grain' if he were not wise before the age of fifty.[23] Furthermore, he thought 'Brindley the Great to be an honest man, and that he will give in a true state of the case, let the event be what it may'.[24] And it is evident that Brindley was considered so by all his contemporaries, a factor of supreme importance in the context of the political, commercial and financial uncertainties of the early canal age.

On a personal level, Brindley still valued the continued support of his friend in the complex area of canal promotion because many decisions were yet to be made. The Duke of Bridgewater had acquired the legal right to divert his canal to Preston Brook on its way to the Mersey estuary thereby allowing for a junction with the Trent & Mersey.[25] However, Wedgwood and his partners had still not agreed upon the western terminus of their canal and were keeping their options open. One option was to build a canal from Chester to the 'Grand Trunk', or even making that city the terminus, instead of Liverpool. Plans and surveys were done, but still the promoters of the Trent & Mersey would not make a definite commitment. They were still discussing taking their canal to the Mersey, without meeting with the Bridgewater, from where it would cross the estuary on a vast aqueduct before independently proceeding to Liverpool, with Brindley asked to survey and estimate the costs.[26] The situation was further confused by ideas promoted by independent gentlemen – such as George Marchant's letter to the Mayor of Liverpool advocating a barrage across the Mersey with entrances to the city's docks above and below it, thereby creating a freshwater river navigation unhindered by tidal variations. Marchant asked that the scheme be referred to Brindley as 'from his character I have no doubt of his acquiissence [sic] … his candour will no doubt allow it possible for others to be as successfull under water as he has been above'.[27] The scheme was not progressed and it may have been a step too far for eighteenth century engineering, but the concept was sound, as any visitor to the Cardiff Bay barrage can now see.

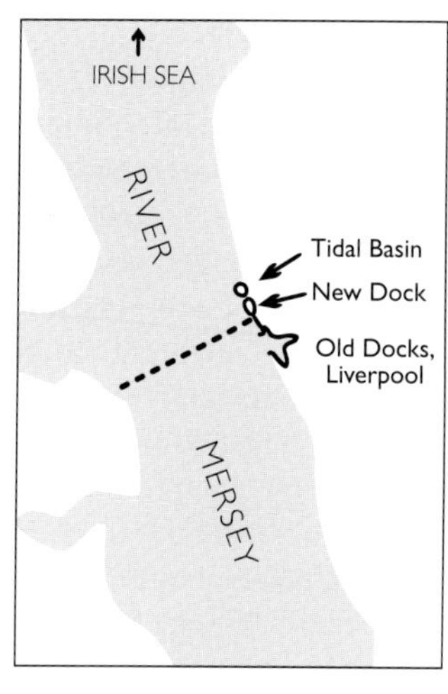

George Marchant's proposal for a barrage across the Mersey estuary

Added to the engineering uncertainties was the knowledge that any canal scheme could run into trouble, no matter how advanced its construction may be, as would soon be evinced by the Bridgewater's progress being halted across the Norton Priory estate. The dispute here would rage for six years, almost bringing financial ruin upon the duke before it was resolved.[28] It was always possible that a similar altercation could yet stop the advance of the strategically important Trent & Mersey. As today, a scheme of magnitude needs one or two people who will drive it and single-mindedly make it happen – and more so if it is unproven technology, as the canal concept continued to be in the eighteenth century. It, therefore, remained significant to Brindley's advance that he retained the active support of Wedgwood's political and organisational skills. He did, however, lose the advocacy of his friend for a second short period.

Josiah Wedgwood's right leg had been painful and of little use since a childhood attack of smallpox had damaged the muscles. In mid-May 1768, he was debilitated to such an extent that he could not even write the influential letters he normally produced to good effect. Ten days later, at his suggestion, the leg was amputated. For the next three weeks the pain was relieved with laudanum, during which time, unbelievably, his baby son Richard suddenly died.[29] It was a time of appalling anxiety and grief for Sarah Wedgwood. Thankfully her husband's recovery was remarkably speedy and, less than a month after the operation, he could dress the wound himself, even taking delight in measuring its length with a compass. Later he would have a false leg fitted but would evermore be nervous about going out in frosty weather in case a fall harmed his remaining leg and laid him up 'for good and all'.[30]

Although Wedgwood's health was bad, Brindley's had improved enough for him to travel to Scotland where disgruntled parties had sought his opinion on aspects of the Forth & Clyde Canal, even though the project was the responsibility of John Smeaton. While he was there the Glasgow city authorities seized the opportunity of Brindley's presence to ask his advice on the problems affecting navigation on the river Clyde, as well as the silted-up harbour at Port Glasgow. He declined the work, but did make cursory surveys, together with engineer John Golborne. Nevertheless, Glasgow still wished to honour a distinguished visitor and on 9th September 1768 he was made a Burgess of the city in a ceremony before assembled dignitaries. On giving the Oath of Fidelity, 'James Brindley Esquire Engineer' was honoured with the 'Privileges and Immunities' of a guild-brother.[31] That Glasgow should honour him so, indicates that in his lifetime Brindley's renown had spread far wider than the English Midlands.

It had certainly reached the county of Oxford where moves were underway to build a canal from a junction with the Coventry to the river Thames, thus forming the fourth arm of what would later become known as the Grand Cross. As had become normal practice, his name was used promotionally at public meetings, resulting in the usual success . It took less than three weeks to raise over £50,000 and the Oxford Canal was born. There followed the repeated rigmaroles of discussions with promoters and visits to Westminster for an Act of Parliament.[32] By now it was routine, even the House of Commons had come to accept that canals were viable, although to many members they remained an aberration of the northern counties. It is evident that with three of his projects Brindley's involvement was almost perfunctory, necessary for financial, political and engineering reasons but without personal interest. His relationships with the management committees of the Birmingham, Coventry, and Oxford canals displayed a lack of patience culminating in only a cursory interest in their schemes. Those waterways were very much the product of Brindley & Co, rather than of the man himself. This could be seen as an understandable consequence of his growing commercial empire, added to which were the sometimes debilitating effects of the diabetes. That this was not so is clearly shown by Brindley's involvement in his final project, the Chesterfield Canal, which in 1768 had merely reached the initial planning stage.

As the only one of his canals built on the eastern side of the Pennines his greater interest and involvement was obviously not due to the convenience of little travelling nor (other than in the long term) because it would be an extension to the central system. Instead, there was a personal affinity with its promoters that was missing elsewhere. For them he would plan his boldest canal, one that would have all the features displayed on his other schemes, and more: a tunnel as long as the one at Harecastle, great flights of staircase locks, embankments, aqueducts, loading basins, and a lock into a viciously tidal river.

It was Chesterfield's misfortune to be situated half way between the navigable waters of the Don and the Trent, leaving the thriving market-town with no easy outlet for its goods despite the improvements made to the nation's rivers. By 1768, the rivers had become extensive trade routes reaching far inland but not as far as north

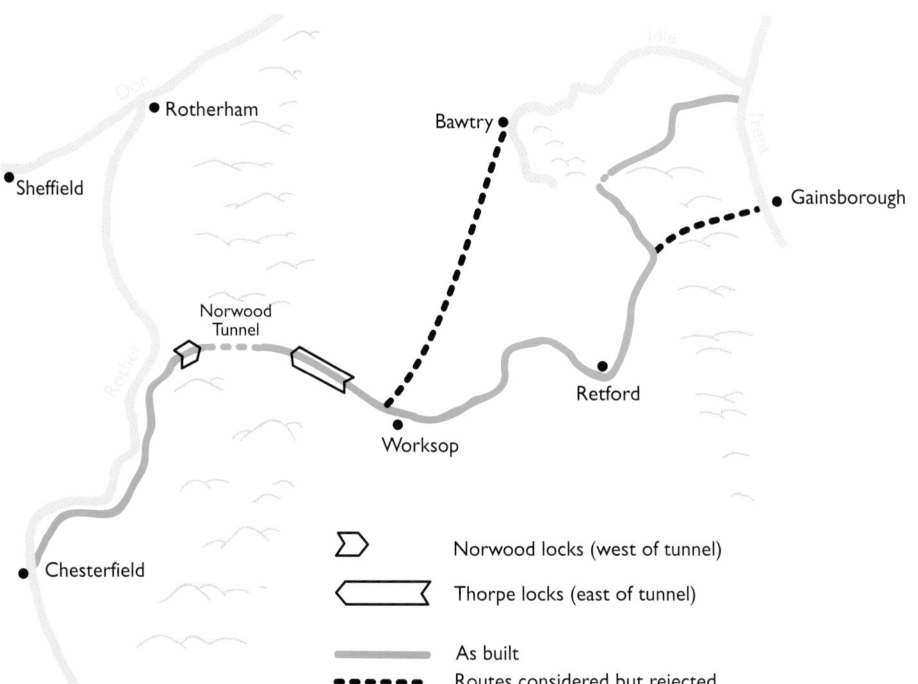

The Chesterfield Canal – with multi-staircase flights of locks on both sides of the 2,880-yard Norwood Tunnel – to the west, the Norwood flight with thirteen locks grouped as 4, 3, 3, 3, in one-third of a mile – to the east, the Thorpe flight with fifteen locks, 3, 1, 1, 1, 3, 1, 2, 1, 2 in half a mile

Derbyshire. Midway between the east and west coasts, and hemmed in by the Pennines, Chesterfield was the outlet for substantial volumes of heavy raw materials extracted from the surrounding area – coal, stone, marble, as well as smelted lead. Much of this had, for many centuries, been laboriously hauled by road almost 30 miles to the inland port of Bawtry, from where it was shipped down the river Idle to the Trent, and national markets. It was obvious to the businessmen of Chesterfield that their town required the transport solution currently underway in Staffordshire on the other side of the hills.

The impetus came from the London Lead Company, a national conglomerate operating mines in the Derbyshire Peaks and elsewhere. It had strong business links to the Duke of Devonshire and his Chatsworth estate. The most influential landowner in the area, his approval of a canal would be fundamental. Brindley's early career had expanded from that of a millwright as a result of his contacts with mine owners in the area, and it would now come full-circle to help those gentlemen again. However, the most important factor to Brindley agreeing so fulsomely to take on the project was that the London Lead Company was a Quaker organisation and the sect had a strong presence in Chesterfield. Locally the Company's chief agent was Joseph Whitfield who had, for many years, travelled to Coalbrookdale to order engineering equipment and had dined at Abiah Darby's table, as had another customer, James Brindley.[33] Abiah, wife of ironmaster Abraham Darby, always stopped overnight at Chesterfield when travelling in the area, dining with senior Quaker Joseph Storrs, who was about to undertake a leading role in the promotion of the Chesterfield Canal.[34] Furthermore, the Darby family had mutual contacts with Brindley's Quaker relatives.[35]

This strong involvement reveals the fundamental veracity of James Brindley and his business projects. Before any Quaker could enter into a trading venture, he had to formally convince fellow members of the sect that it would not impinge upon their overall responsibility for solvency and honest dealing. Also, that it would be within the limits allowed by their sense of social and spiritual truth, and would not involve anyone of dubious integrity. After which he could rely on the brotherly support of the widespread Quaker business network.[36] There is no doubt that Brindley felt at home in such company – there was a mutual distrust of worldly amusements, especially the theatre, with an aversion to unproductive actions designed solely to fill idle time. They shared a simplicity of dress, feelings of equality and brotherhood, frugality, and a willingness to make commercial progress by initially undertaking considerable periods of patient experimentation with little return.[37] Such an affinity would be required to build a canal across difficult terrain at some distance from Brindley's other responsibilities.

The obvious route for Chesterfield's canal was to follow the valley of the river Rother to Rotherham, to a junction with the Don Navigation, a straightforward and inexpensive option. But that would make the cargoes liable to the high tolls charged by that well-established navigation company. Instead, Derbyshire wanted to undercut the price of the Yorkshire coal shipped down the Don by creating an independent route of its own. The difficulty was that Bawtry, the intended destination, was the other side of a limestone ridge that would have to be crossed. At its narrowest point, at Norwood, there would have to be a steep flight of locks up the western side, then a long tunnel through the summit, and another great set of locks down the eastern flank. The provision of an adequate water supply to feed so many locks would be difficult. After that the route would cross the flat, artificially drained, carr-lands Brindley had seen many years before when designing swing-bridges for the Don Navigation Company. This man of the hills had no experience of building a canal across such an area, where any change to the complex inter-connected drainage could easily result in the flooding of adjacent land, but saw it as another challenge to be overcome. There is no evidence that Brindley was aware of what he would face in taking a canal across the carr-lands to Bawtry, the complexities not apparent to one who was ill-versed in the sluggish nature of water at such places. It was, perhaps, fortunate that later developments would see a change of route away from Bawtry.

By 1769 James Brindley was responsible for canals in all stages of construction, and, in hindsight, he had reached his highest level of achievement. The Bridgewater was still the most illustrious of the waterways associated with his name, much to the chagrin of those working full-time, but virtually anonymously, to achieve its completion. Although it was then known as 'the Duke of Bridgewater's Canal' its eponymous nobleman was already showing signs of a festering resentment of the widespread public perception of Brindley as the scheme's sole genius, although in practice he now held only a consultancy role. The duke was under considerable pressure; the financial weight of completing the canal was proving to be almost beyond his means. Furthermore, an objecting landowner was blocking the route, and still the gentlemen of the Trent & Mersey prevaricated about which mutual route, or routes, should be chosen for the two canals to approach their destination of Liverpool. To add to his frustration, the man he had plucked from obscurity was now the nation's sole arbiter on what should, or should not, be done on any waterways matter including possible junctions with his own precious canal.

The young duke's rancour is understandable but misguided. Certainly, Brindley did not underplay his role as England's canal supremo, but neither did he actively seek the plaudits for the Bridgewater's success. He had no need to – the other canals for which he was responsible would spread the stillwater message throughout the nation and with it their engineer's fame. Centrally the Trent & Mersey and its junior sibling the Staffordshire & Worcestershire continued to receive the majority of Brindley's personal attention – a result of their early conception, their strategic importance to the network, the on-going challenge of excavating Harecastle Tunnel and their relatively close proximity to Brindley's home. Brindley's involvement tended to be with anything out of the ordinary and therefore requiring definitive rulings, such as Dunstall Water Bridge which, unusually, was to carry a brook, the Smestow, over a canal, the Staffordshire & Worcestershire. As well as the engineering aspects, which Brindley defined and ordered to be drawn up for his next visit, there was also the political importance of a nearby hall which may have been the reason for the design having to allow room for a gentleman to ride his horse under the bridge.[38] Finally, there was the legal consideration of the brook driving more than 30 mills and forges, including a carpet works, the owners of all of which would have a right to compensation from the canal company if their supply of water was abated.[39]

Conversely, out to the west the six-mile Droitwich was a project of Brindley & Co where the surveying had been done by company man Robert Whitworth before his local colleague John Priddey took over. Intriguingly, Brindley had jotted 'salt work at Droitwich' in his notebook seven years before, whilst in London, but there is no indication of who approached him to become involved in the project, nor why matters were not actively pursued at the time.[40] Now, in 1769, an estimate of the costs bore Brindley's name, as did a progress report, but they are not in his handwriting[41] and it is unclear how much direct involvement he had in the scheme, with his name only twice mentioned in the Company's minutes.[42] Nevertheless, the Droitwich was constructed to Brindley's overall standard, the contractor for the eight locks, John Bushel, having received the training to augment his knowledge of building docks and harbours in the Liverpool area.[43] That being so it did not preclude cost cutting, the main impact of which was suffered by the men doing the work. Twelve of them rebelled and put their signatures to a written protest

> Com posol of the Bricklars at Lady Wood at the lock to be all in one mine. We af Bin yoused Very ill for Thy Will not pay for Wat we work for. If you don't pay for watt Time as Bind We Will not Work and wee will not Work for under 11s a wick and to be yusde well.[44]

Five of Brindley's canals were to remain fully navigable throughout the intervening centuries, with only the Droitwich and the western section of the Chesterfield falling out of use. The restoration of the latter two were, therefore, rare opportunities to investigate the original construction methods. In the case of the Droitwich it would appear that the bricklayers of 1770 had cause for complaint. The materials used to construct their lock were poor, with badly made and damaged bricks, although the cosmetic surface courses were acceptable.[45] We know Brindley did not allow such lax standards on the Staffordshire & Worcestershire, so it reflects badly on Priddey and Bushel that such practices, let alone the bad staff management, were evident on a canal where his presence was minimal.

The salt-enriched waters of the area have preserved many of the original timber features of the Droitwich, although it is difficult to know if they are Brindley's designs or Priddey's. To guard against leakage from an embankment that would have flooded adjacent farmland, wooden gates were installed in the bed of the canal which, when raised, would isolate the relevant section. Unfortunately, the panels of the gates filled with mud making them impossible to move. In the locks, massive elm timbers were laid along the floor of the chamber, with other timbers forming a frame that was infilled with bricks to create the walls. The beams pushed to open or close the lock-gates were 'sway poles' made from unsawn tree-trunks, presenting a different sight to the uniform and machine-smoothed items of today. Swing-bridges were more numerous on all Brindley canals than is now evident. On the Droitwich they swivelled on roller-bearing turntables, the iron-castings for which were ordered from near Coalbrookdale. Craft entered the canal by a lock from the tidal river Severn which, at that point, regularly rose and fell by 5 feet, which made construction of the lock difficult. The site was protected from the river by a coffer-dam but labourers still had to operate wood and leather pumps 24-hours a day to remove the water leaking through it.[46] Bushel's experience in harbour construction, where similar methods must have been used, indicates that this work could have been done with little Brindley involvement, and his hallmark would surely have been an ingenious pumping method, rather than laborious muscle-power.

To the east, interest in the Chesterfield's route had been shown in Retford, more specifically by the Reverend Seth Ellis Stevenson who realised the benefits it would bring to his town if the canal was re-routed through it instead of Bawtry, the original destination. His campaign was successful, although it still left open the question of which way the canal should go beyond Retford on its way to the Trent. The now discarded Bawtry destination had ordained that cargoes would be transhipped onto the long-established Idle Navigation, eventually arriving at the small port at its Trent confluence, West Stockwith. However, with Bawtry out of the picture, the fundamental question of where the canal should meet the Trent was open to discussion.

Brindley, with his awareness of the national picture, said he favoured tunnelling through a second hilly ridge to arrive on the bank opposite Gainsborough.[47] His stated reason was the town's strategic importance as the point where cargoes were transhipped between small inland craft coming down the Trent and coastal shipping coming up from the Humber; huge warehouses and busy quays lined the river. Unrevealed, at this stage, was his wider aim to make the Chesterfield Canal the northern part of a longer route, the southern section of which would go from the Trent & Mersey at Swarkestone, via the valleys of the rivers Derwent and Amber, across the watershed via a long tunnel near Clay Cross and through to Chesterfield from the south. This would not only bring water transport to a number of towns in central Derbyshire but the entire route would form the Trent & Mersey's link to the Humber, bypassing the troublesome sections of the river Trent navigation, its shallows irksome. Downstream of Gainsborough there were no such problems, although opposition from by-passed Nottingham and Newark would be vociferous.

The river Trent, and the planned Trent & Mersey and Chesterfield canals – a canal link between them could be via the river valleys between Clay Cross and Swarkestone

Initially, it was said that taking the Chesterfield Canal to Gainsborough was an option favoured by its promoters. The booming inland port would be a good market for their Derbyshire coal, the temptation of which caused a number of Gainsborough traders to contribute substantial amounts towards the surveying costs.[48] However, it is difficult to ascertain the underlying politics of the situation although there are striking similarities to a previous decision elsewhere in which Brindley was involved.

When the Staffordshire & Worcestershire Canal had been planned it was strongly indicated that its destination on the river Severn would be the established port of Bewdley – although that would mean a long tunnel, and many locks, to eliminate the intervening high ground. Nevertheless, investors could identify with such a destination, as could the traders of Bewdley, and, as a concept, it would mollify potential political doubters at Westminster. In reality, after the financial and political aims had been achieved, Brindley's route would take the prudent option of keeping to the valley of the Stour as it made its way to become a tributary of the Severn, four miles downstream of Bewdley. The often repeated story that the residents of Bewdley did not want Brindley's 'stinking ditch' in their town was probably a petulant response to the disappointment of losing the obvious trading benefits previously promised.

Now Gainsborough was being treated in a similar way. The promoters of an approaching canal wooed the port's traders when expedient only to eventually decide that a second long tunnel in addition to the unavoidable one at Norwood would be unacceptable. Instead, it was announced that the canal would go further north to Drakeholes. Here a very short tunnel could go through a narrow section of the hills with the canal ending, once again, at West Stockwith, which is the mouth of a navigable tributary of the Trent, four miles downstream of Gainsborough. This time the ire of the port's merchants would not manifest itself in derogatory public outbursts but in strong, and successful, demands to the newly formed Chesterfield Canal Company for reimbursement of the whole of the sum invested by various Gainsborough gentlemen towards the surveying costs.

Brindley's role in the Bewdley and Gainsborough stratagems cannot be judged as that of an innocent bystander, he was always aware of the national implications of the routes for his canals, and by now he had unequalled experience of what was involved in pushing through such contentious concepts, with their often undeclared further agendas. For example, the route of the Chesterfield Canal now to be built did not harm the integrity of Brindley's undisclosed wider plan (of an extension to the south to meet the Trent & Mersey at Swarkestone) and he embarked upon a programme of public meetings throughout the area using his status and fame to give confidence to the local gentlemen considering involvement in the undertaking. This role was still vitally important as, although the canal concept had already been established, neither the Bridgewater nor any of Brindley's other waterways had been completed and they were, therefore, only earning meagre incomes for their investors, if anything at all. The scale of the decision for each individual must also be considered in the light of the price of the shares, in this case £100 each (the equivalent of £5,870 today) and that they would be purchased in instalments, thereby locking investors in for the long-term. The targets covered a wide spectrum of society, from the Retford saddler who bought one share, to the Duke of Newcastle who had 30.

If everyone in the country had by now been smitten with canal-investment fever, Brindley's promotional role at the crowded meetings could be seen as that of a mere figurehead, but this was not the case. There was still a large anti-canal lobby vociferously stating that such schemes were pointless when rivers already served an area with transport, and that canals were built at the price of ruining many a good estate. Pamphlets proliferated. Seth Ellis Stevenson himself wrote and paid for the printing of 1,000 copies of one.[49] He concentrated on making a financial picture, but others ranged wider promising advantages to every sector of society, especially the poor and disadvantaged, but also the landed classes, the manufacturers, the farmers. No one would be omitted from the largesse. And the man to make it all possible was James Brindley

> so justly famed for his amazing Skill in teaching the watery Element to flow in new Channels, and over sandy Soils, distributing the Bounties of Nature more equally among the Inhabitants of our Island ... if then Mr Brindley has confirmed the Practicability of the Scheme, let that rest upon the Pillar of his Reputation ...[50]

Still no mention was made of the extended plan to Swarkestone. That was eventually launched publicly one month after the Act for the Chesterfield Canal had been obtained, and after a substantial number of investors had committed their funds.[51] In May 1771 notices were placed in local newspapers, announcing that James Brindley would be present at the George Inn in Derby on the 27th of June and giving an outline of the proposal there to be announced. It was a naive move. Opponents were given more than a month's notice and they did not waste it. Soon, the same newspapers contained inflammatory calls to action – those with land on the projected route should rise up less their estates be 'cut through and destroyed ... under the specious pretence of public Utility'.[52] Subsequently the meeting must have been a very uncomfortable experience for James Brindley, its outcome the only instance of his not winning the day, and by a great majority. He and his supporters from Chesterfield and Retford had arrived in the area without any political preparations, devoid of the local influence that Brindley's experience proved was always a vital component of success. Nobody had carried out the crucial roles undertaken on the Bridgewater by the duke and John Gilbert; on behalf of the Trent & Mersey by Thomas Bentley in Liverpool and Josiah Wedgwood in Staffordshire; and recently by the Quakers in Chesterfield and Seth Ellis Stevenson in Retford. The quiet conversations, the political manoeuvrings, the favours called in, the individually crafted appeals to each man of influence on the route, the artful timing of public announcements – all were missing. As a result Brindley was faced by a crowd of gentlemen aggressively stating their opposition to his 'pompous accounts'. They spoke of the lands through which the Trent & Mersey had already passed where 'the great Inconvenience and Damage appear to every Spectator too plain and too great to require proof'. Where 'some gentlemen ... were persuaded ... to consent to their Estates being cut in Pieces, but they now find they have been impos'd on, their Estates greatly injured, and the Community not benefited. It were to be wished that Gentlemen would wait to see the Canals now making finish'd, and their Utility prov'd, and not cut the Country in Pieces for notional Advantages.'[53]

It was a clear message that in the promotion of a stillwater canal, Brindley's name alone was not enough to carry the day.

Seal of the Chesterfield Canal Company. The two towns involved in the project are represented – the diamonds were from the centre of Chesterfield's town arms, and the birds are choughs, an ancient symbol of Retford

Nor did matters always go smoothly elsewhere. In January 1769 Samuel Garbett angrily resigned from the management committee of the Birmingham Canal, sold most of his shares, and embarked on a campaign of opposition. He had known Brindley from the earliest canal days and the dispute placed the engineer in a difficult situation. Garbett's accusation was that the committee was steering the canal project to increase the profits of the local colliery owners and, thereby, ignoring their public promises to supply coal as cheaply as possible. The dispute raged hotly, with Garbett threatening to go to Parliament with petitions hostile to the canal company's interests.[54] Brindley had never been close to the remaining members of the committee and now indicated his support of Garbett's opinions by judiciously avoiding involvement. When he came to inspect the works he did not notify the committee that he was doing so, nor did he visit them when passing through Birmingham on other business, much to their dissatisfaction.[55]

Relationships with a management committee were even worse on the nearby Coventry Canal, where Brindley was actually dismissed in September 1769 and his Clerk of the Works, Joseph Parker, warned for disregarding the orders given.[56] Superficial reasons were given, but the root cause was the disquiet caused by Brindley also being the engineer of the Oxford Canal, which was to join with the Coventry to form the link between the Trent & Mersey and the river Thames. Fundamentally, the two companies disagreed about where their two waterways should meet, a subject fraught with complications for water supplies for both and the charging of tolls, the two subjects closest to the heart of all canal administrators.[57] A typical flash point was the Coventry, writing to the Oxford's Clerk of the Works, James King, ordering him not to cut into their canal at a certain point to form a junction, a matter swiftly referred to Brindley.[58] Having sacked their illustrious engineer, the Coventry initially replaced him with Thomas Yeoman, then one month later with Edmund Lingard, last noted on the Trent & Mersey writing to Hugh Henshall about clay for bricks. Promotion can be rapid in a new field of endeavour.[59]

The pace of progress had been so rapid that by 1770 experienced men were spread very thinly throughout the Brindley empire, although Hugh Henshall continued as the steadying hand on the senior waterway, the Trent & Mersey. Elsewhere the Coventry had unproven Lingard at its helm, the Oxford's James King needed considerable support having produced a survey for his management committee whilst expressing 'a doubt of the exactness of his Plan from his Inexperience hitherto in the Business of Canals'. One can almost hear the frustration of the committee chairman as he orders his clerk to write at once to 'Mr Brindley and desire his attendance ... in order to revise Mr King's survey'.[60] James Brindley was aware of King's limitations and had allocated the trusted Samuel Simcock to the Oxford. Also transferred there was John Priddey when he had completed the Droitwich.[61] The surveying of the Chesterfield Canal was allocated to John Varley, for whom it would be the first great challenge, with the role of Clerk of the Works almost certainly his when the enabling Act was obtained. All of these men relied on the salaries allocated when a canal company was officially formed, after all the legalities had been completed. Until then, they were not paid by Brindley & Co. In Varley's case he had been all over the countryside surveying routes to Bawtry, Gainsborough and West Stockwith as the gentlemen argued about the canal's terminus. At this early stage of a project, money was gathered from the promoters to pay for surveys, but that often took some time to materialise. In the meantime, Varley took some private work nearby, surveying what would become the Greasbrough Canal, but other than that he found himself borrowing money from Seth Ellis Stevenson with promises of repayment when he was salaried.[62]

***For security reasons the bridge at the entrance to Coventry canal basin was built without a towpath, and from August 1769 it was blocked each night with a large tree trunk 19 feet long and 13 inches square.* (Coventry Canal Company *Journal*, 10th September 1769)**

Brindley and his senior men formed the links between the various canal schemes but it soon became evident that each undertaking would benefit from national standards, for both engineering and administration. John Sparrow of the Trent & Mersey wrote to five of the 'Brindley Seven', asking that two representatives of each waterway should meet in Lichfield on the 14th of December 1769. The Droitwich was not included as it was a non-standard wide canal, and the Chesterfield was omitted possibly because the central powerbase knew little, if anything, of the plans for it. However, it was at that meeting that the dimensions of what we now know as narrow canals were set, although it was only official confirmation of what was already happening in practice. Nevertheless, it was an important standardisation of a national transport network and Brindley was minuted to inspect the works already done to see if any structures varied from that agreed.[63]

Three days later Brindley also reached a landmark in his personal life with the birth of his first daughter, given her mother's name, Anne. The baby was not very strong at birth but she survived, an addition to what was now a wealthy household at Turnhurst Hall.[64] Her 54 year old father was probably absent as he had been inspecting the works on the Oxford Canal the previous day.[65] Baby Anne would see little of her father, his work schedule remaining full with many horseback journeys in all weathers. More travelling was accepted when he was honoured with a request to report on how a section of the river Thames could be improved for navigation. Having based his reputation on building alternatives to unruly rivers, it is perhaps surprising that he accepted the commission but he and his fellow canal enthusiasts could not risk offending the suppliers of finance in London. Furthermore, he was due to give evidence to Parliament at the end of February 1770, in support of a petition for authority to raise more public capital for the Trent & Mersey. It was, therefore, an opportunity to look at the length of the Thames in question, that between Sonning and Monkey Island (2 miles below Maidenhead).[66] Brindley probably spent the whole of March in the area, during which time he was asked to extend his inspection from Monkey Island to Isleworth.

It was also an opportunity to have his portrait painted. Brindley's character does not indicate a personal need for such an action, bordering perhaps on the Quakers' attitude of spurning portraiture as vanity, but as the figurehead of the canal movement it was professionally adroit. Portraits in the pre-photographic age were used to project an image, a status, a standing in society, and showed how the subject wished to be seen by his contemporaries and future generations. It is, therefore, significant that Brindley chose to be depicted standing under a tree with Barton aqueduct in the background, an indication that nothing in the intervening years had surpassed that structure in the public perception of Brindley's achievements, nor in his own view. At the height of his fame his appearance is of a genteel country professional, his brown suit with brass buttons plain but not cheap. Beneath a fashionable, grey, powdered bob-wig his blue eyes look out from a ruddy-cheeked face. Wigs were almost always worn by middle-class men appearing in public and Brindley's demeanour and attire reflect the hearty masculinity that was in vogue to counteract the continental mannerisms of the aristocracy. The painting is also another example of his individuality – the artisan engineer confident enough not to bother too much about his social standing. The dominant convention was for professional people to be depicted as if in their private homes, presenting the genius at work in a semi-relaxed manner. Brindley, however, is shown as very much the outdoor man, 'more like a proud land or horse owner with his prize'.[67] The painting, by Francis Parsons, was displayed in London at the 1771 exhibition of the Society of Artists and is now in the National Portrait Gallery, and the judgement is that all other depictions are based upon it. Whatever the reason for the portrait, it did not over-ride Brindley's morality, indicated by his refusal to pay the 60 guineas charged by the artist because he deemed it exorbitant.[68]

Claims have been made that two earlier portraits of Brindley are in private ownership, both said to have been painted by Johann Zoffany. Such portraits would indicate events of some social stature as Zoffany was a fashionable London artist charging high fees, far in excess of Brindley's ability, or willingness, to pay. But much depends on the date of the portraits; if they were done in the early part of 1762, when Brindley was in London for two months playing a major role in supporting the crucial third Act for the Bridgewater Canal, they would predate Zoffany's fame. The fact that Brindley does not mention them in the budget entries in his personal notebook is of minimal relevance as at that time the painting could have been sponsored by the Duke of Bridgewater for political reasons. However,it must be borne in mind that the provenance and style of both portraits – and even the identity of the gentleman shown – have been discounted by the National Portrait Gallery in London, and in the nineteenth century many works came to be falsely attributed to Zoffany in order to bask in his fashionable light.

The visit to London lasted until the beginning of April 1770 when Brindley rode north and, as was his habit after a prolonged absence, went straight to the works of one of his local canals, this time the Staffordshire & Worcestershire.[69] An indication of how busy he was came in May 1770 when he refused of the post of Chief Engineer for the construction of the Leeds & Liverpool Canal, at an annual salary of £400.[70] His health was still bad, resulting in an almost perfunctory approach to new schemes.

A tunnel as long as the Trent & Mersey's Harecastle would be needed on the Chesterfield at Norwood, that was unavoidable, but Brindley had championed the Gainsborough option, which would have required another just as long on the same canal. Added to that his rejected through-route to Swarkestone would have meant yet another tunnel, perhaps even longer than the others. When one considers that only 944 yards of Harecastle Tunnel had been completed after four years effort, and that it would take a further five years to finish its 2,880 yards, his willingness, if he had been allowed, to take on four simultaneously was bordering on the reckless.[71] The cutting of Norwood Tunnel would suffer from a lack of men with the necessary skills, most of whom were still working at Harecastle. We shall never know where Brindley thought he could find the men to excavate two more tunnels of similar magnitude. Nor where the finance could have been found for that most expensive of canal features – he already knew his estimates for both the Trent & Mersey and the Staffordshire & Worcestershire had fallen short, with both canals needing considerably more capital if they were to be completed.[72] The Coventry was also in a dire financial situation. Furthermore, he had recently told the promoters of the Chesterfield Canal that as a result of past experience, his estimate was based on amounts one-third higher than he had used before.[73]

Of course, as the figurehead of the canal movement, Brindley needed to present a bold, confident image as George Stephenson would later do in the promotion of railway construction. People had invested not only substantial amounts of money in canals, as yet unproven ventures, but also their more valuable time, reputations and the potential of their commercial interests – and they did not need a Chief Engineer who prevaricated, nor one who played safe. However, by 1770 Brindley sometimes crossed the thin line between boldness and imprudence. His patience was sorely strained, especially so by administrators with their endless committees and, in some cases, their affectations. Relationships with the scholastic gentlemen of Oxford had never been warm but now the ailing Brindley found tolerance a rare commodity. There were many matters on which he disagreed with the management committee but a boiling point was reached in July when they had the temerity to write in the Minute Book that Brindley and his senior men were not to 'associate or drink with any of the Inferior Officers or Workmen employed by this Company under any Pretence whatsoever'.[74] The embargo against drink was one thing, but to command Brindley to have no association with the type of men he had always respected and understood was untenable. The final straw was when, only two months later, the Clerk of the Works, James King – he who had timidly presented a survey saying it might be wrong because he was new to canal building – formally complained to the committee that the experienced, trusted Samuel Simcock was interfering with his work. The committee, of course, backed King.[75]

James Brindley had never suffered fools gladly. His resignation letter thumped on to the committee's table in less than two weeks. The consternation of the Oxford gentlemen was great, as actual work on building the canal had been underway only for a year.[76] No reason had been given in the letter, which was answered in a tone indicative of capitulation,

> We are very sorry that anything has happened that has given you Offence and shall always be ready to place the greatest Confidence in you, as we consider the Assistance of your Abilities and Experience essential to carrying this Navigation effectually into Execution.[77]

Brindley had made his point and subsequently continued in his post with more influence than before, even to the extent of taking a seat on the committee.[78]

Many things were contriving to add to his frustrations. His report on the Thames scheme was rejected, although it should not have surprised the London gentlemen that rather than improving the river, Brindley proposed to build a canal capable of taking 200-ton craft parallel to it, with branches down to Windsor and Staines. Asked to think again about using the river, Robert Whitworth was delegated to do the work and, surely with his master's blessing, designed a complex scheme allowing Brindley to hope that it would be rejected – which it ultimately was after a Parliamentary Bill was presented.[79] The situation had been handled in a masterly fashion. Brindley had extricated himself from a major scheme that was far from his centre of operations and which would, by improving a river, have impinged upon his professional identity as the man who built canals and would have nothing to do with naturally flowing waters. Furthermore, he had, by ostensibly doing as they had asked, avoided antagonising the London financial markets.

As Brindley's health deteriorated further such victories became rare; instead a lackadaisical approach, induced by his overwhelming tiredness, became evident in the administrative and political aspects of his work. He had no patience for the type of local disputes that were still delaying the completion of the city end of the Birmingham Canal. There the construction was dogged by its effect on well-established commercial interests, the most famous of which was Matthew Boulton's engineering works. He had invested £20,000 in machinery, buildings and tools, and already employed a work-force of over 700. Now, the streams that powered his 'manufactory' were often diverted to re-fill the badly leaking canal. In February Boulton vent his frustration in a letter to Thomas Gilbert

> let Mr Smeaton or Brindley or all the Engineers upon Earth give what evidence they will before Parliament, I am convinced from last summer's experience that if the proprietors of the canal continue to take the two streams on which my mill depends, it is ruined … think of my summer situation, when I have no water, my work people standing-still murmuring. My orders

> not executed, my foreign friends complaining & countermanding their orders. Think what a distressing situation, what reward is this for my labours and hazards? ... As a Member of Parliament – as an old aquaintance – as a friend of your country – as a good man, I beg you will save me from destruction. [80]

Ten days later Boulton wrote to Samuel Garbett of Birmingham, that supreme manipulator who had been involved in canal promotion since its earliest days.

> I have seen the questioning of ... engineers Smeaton and Yeoman and I value the opinions neither of them nor Brindley nor Simcox, in this case, nor of the whole tribe of jobbing ditchers, who are retained as evidence on any side which first applies for them ... A mischievous man, or unlucky boy, or a water rat, or a boat pole, carelessly used, may at any time in a few hours ruin any canal upon the side of a sand hill. How easy it is to pin down a stop-gate, or how probable it is that bungling contrivance should not rise if the canal should break down is very obvious. [81]

Such stop-gates, or 'doors' had also been installed on the Bridgewater and Droitwich canals and were meant to rise automatically from the bed of the waterway when flowing water indicated that the channel was leaking.[82] They have the hallmark of Brindley resourcefulness, but were not a success as their tendency to stick in the mud meant they could not be relied upon.

The unwell Brindley could not cope with Birmingham's convoluted problems, instead he reverted to what he knew best and what he could do automatically – riding through the countryside using his millwright eyes to see not only the actual route of a canal, but also how it could be supplied with water and how the channel could be made level.[83] After which he could leave the accurate surveying and the infernal dealing with landowners to a number of his assistants. The initial construction work on a canal was also fundamental and, therefore, devoid of the frustrations which developed after the first few months when the committees made complex the most simple of tasks. The Chesterfield Canal was at that early stage and it must have been with some relief that Brindley travelled many times to ensure the integrity of its crucial summit pound, taking its level down the ridge with a resultant increase in the length of Norwood Tunnel to equal that of Harecastle.[84] He valued the congenial company of Seth Ellis Stevenson and his associates but elsewhere he displayed indifference to problematical situations in the face of the double disincentives of travel and bothersome relationships.

During this period two canals became mainly responsible for the widespread assertion that Brindley's routes followed the contours and are, therefore, extremely convoluted, winding through the countryside for miles to avoid the insertion of a cutting or an embankment. The Birmingham ended up longer and far more intricate than had been planned, mainly due to problems encountered during construction.[85] It gave rise to accusations that the winding course had been so designed to increase the mileage boats would travel and therefore the tolls that could be charged. Brindley, as ever, sided with his assistant, Samuel Simcock, saying the course chosen would benefit many more people than if it had been straight.[86] The other culprit was the Oxford where the route wandered off up every little valley and back down again after crossing insubstantial brooks. The original survey by Whitworth in 1768 had not produced a route markedly complex, so it is

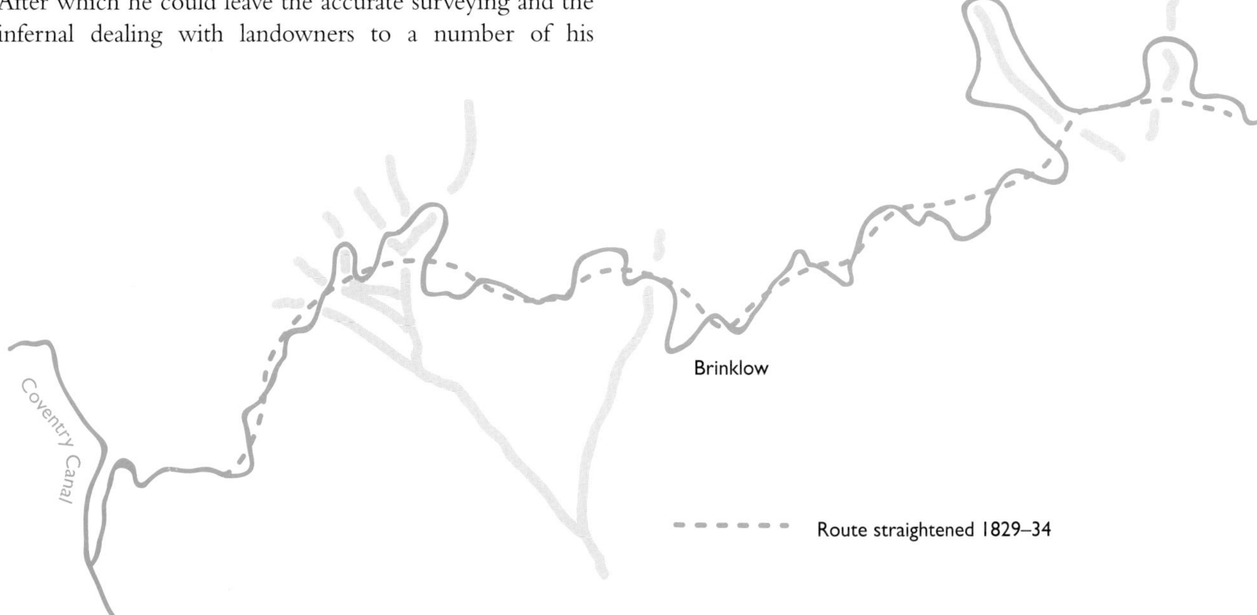

The Oxford Canal – the winding northern end as originally built and the route as straightened in 1829–34

difficult to find any justification. Work had commenced at the northern end, from the junction with the Coventry and, by the middle of 1772, had reached the vicinity of Brinklow. Again Simcock is the man on site and he would continue to build the canal in the same eccentric manner when he took overall control in September of that year.[87] Both canals would later be straightened resulting in the phenomena of 'lost loops' for enthusiasts to discover.

There are many reasons why the construction of Brindley's canals did not match the original surveys and not all can be laid at the engineer's door. The political machinations of trade, cargoes and existing river navigations led to the western end of the Trent & Mersey being built to dimensions wider than used for the central section of the canal. The prize to be gained was the transport of salt from Cheshire to Liverpool, vast quantities of which were needed for food preservation. The key was a tunnel at Preston Brook, the decisions about its dimensions devoid of engineering input. To take the salt trade from the Weaver Navigation costs, would have to be minimised by loading it just once into boats capable of taking it all the way to Liverpool. In 1769 the option of an aqueduct across a restricted section of the Mersey estuary was still open, with Brindley's opinion that it could be built if it carried a narrow channel, but not if it had to accommodate larger craft.[88] Either way, Wedgwood and his associates, in opposition to Brindley's plans, decided that Preston Brook tunnel would have to be wide so as not to preclude any later developments as they could not 'think of giving up the salt trade'.[89] A further, obscure, reason for the eventual configuration was Thomas Bentley's move in 1770 from Liverpool to Chelsea at the behest of Wedgwood to be the London agent for his tableware at a new showroom.[90] In an age without instant communications, it had repeatedly been shown that a canal scheme would founder without local

Trent & Mersey Canal – built to wide dimensions between Middlewich and its junction with the Bridgewater Canal

enthusiasts to champion its cause. Without Bentley's continuous interactions with Liverpool Corporation on behalf of the Trent & Mersey, the way was left clear for the Duke of Bridgewater to advance his own case.[91] For this reason, the idea of the Trent & Mersey crossing the estuary on an aqueduct was dropped, and instead it was agreed that it would simply form a junction with the Bridgewater, to facilitate which the duke diverted his canal south before taking it onto Runcorn instead of the original terminus at Hempstones. Both waterways are 'Brindley canals' but he had little to do with the approach of either to the Mersey, nor with the locks to the river at Runcorn (Appendix G).

When judging Brindley's engineering achievements it is important to bear in mind that his canals reflect many conflicting eighteenth-century interests, as well as his personal well-being, or otherwise, at various stages of their construction. When studying the subject it is easy to concentrate on the actions of those involved and enthusiastic and thereby miss the contrary opinions and doubts that remained widespread. From our perspective it appears that as each subsequent canal proved the efficacy of the concept, the work would become more straightforward. However, that does not allow for the experience also gained by opponents which expanded with each scheme undertaken. By 1771, when the Chesterfield Canal was getting underway, the Duke of Leeds, a local landowner, had the benefit of advice from the other side of the country to aid his negotiations with Brindley's representatives. A correspondent with an estate at Dunham, by the Bridgewater Canal, told him, 'The experience I have had of this kind of work gives me a very great dislike to Navigations …' going on to give detailed advice such as forcing the engineers to state where bridges, roads and fords will require extra breadths of land otherwise they will 'cut the ground to serve their present purpose, and afterwards turn a deaf ear to your applications for money'. The duke was also urged to include in the price of the land a premium for the vexation of having a canal through his estate, for 'be assured that inconveniences of this sort are found very great, and no relief will easily be got afterwards, if not included in the value of the land first'.[92]

All of which shows that Brindley's responsibilities did not lessen with time, instead the wealth of raw materials in Britain's central areas meant that more schemes continued to come to the fore. When requested to make a survey for a canal to Lancaster, in November 1771, the task was delegated to Robert Whitworth as was usual with distance work, but perhaps the birth of Brindley's second daughter, Susanna, less than two months later, may also have had an influence on his decision to stay near home.[93] Professionally 1772 was a good year with a number of his canal schemes coming to fruition. The Droitwich had been open since March the previous year; now the Staffordshire & Worcestershire was completed at the end of May, and the

Birmingham in September. The eastern end of the Trent & Mersey was almost concluded from the river Trent to Stoke, which was a personal triumph as it had been the subject of Brindley's first canal survey in February 1758. Work was still underway on Harecastle Tunnel and the geographically difficult route from Middlewich to the western terminus was still to be finalised, but the work was in Hugh Henshall's capable hands.[94] Of the others the Coventry was stalled for many reasons but that was no longer his responsibility. Only the Oxford and the Chesterfield still required long-distance travelling, with the latter's bold flights of staircase locks at both ends of the summit pound planned, and initial work on Thorpe top-treble and other locks underway by mid-summer 1772.[95] As recently as 2nd September he had enjoyed a convivial meal with Seth Ellis Stevenson and other promoters of the Chesterfield at a Retford coaching inn.[96]

The White Hart, Retford. The coaching inn where Brindley and the Chesterfield Canal promoters dined 3rd September 1772

Only a fortnight later Brindley was at Froghall, at the far end of the route being surveyed for the proposed Caldon Canal, which would carry stone from quarries to the summit level of the Trent & Mersey. After all his travelling he was back on familiar ground not far from his current home at Turnhurst Hall, even nearer to Burslem where as a millwright he had opened a workshop in 1750. In that vicinity his steam-engines pumped water from flooded collieries. The Caldon Canal would pass near Leek, where he had first started as an independent millwright in 1742, and where his widowed mother still lived on the family farm. Beyond was Macclesfield where he had commenced his millwright apprenticeship in 1734. Above, in Derbyshire's High Peak, was Tunstead, his birthplace in 1716 and where, during his first ten years, the love and understanding of high hills had forged his character.

Now, aged 56, the country's most famous canal engineer was riding in the Staffordshire moorland when it started to rain. It is said that he rapidly caught a chill and was taken to an inn at Ipstones where he was put into a damp bed. He quickly became very ill. The following day, 17th September 1772, he was carried home to Turnhurst Hall where his

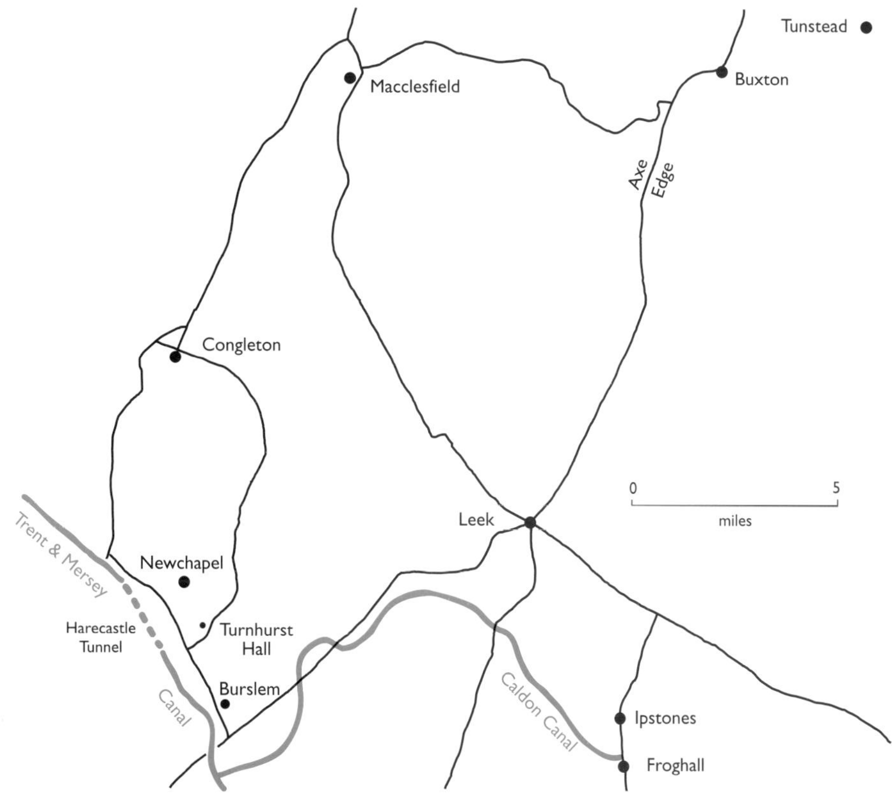

Caldon Canal and its close vicinity to locations personally important to Brindley throughout his lifetime

friend Josiah Wedgwood came to see him. The seriousness of the situation was evident to all, including James Brindley. His wife was fraught with worry, hardly listening to advice that she should take time to eat and rest although she acknowledged she must look after herself for the sake of her two young children.[97] Wedgwood visited almost every day. By the 26th the potter feared that there was little hope, writing to Thomas Bentley that they may soon be deprived 'of a valuable friend'.[98] The doctors could do little, although they did diagnose diabetes, even though they knew nothing of its cause or treatment. For the last seven years Brindley had suffered from a constant thirst, which may have been caused by the diabetes or may have been the result of his also constant fever. If the insidious onset of the diabetes had plagued him for as long as seven years its symptoms could have included complications to his eyes, kidneys and circulation. However, the cause of his present illness was probably pneumonia.[99]

From his bed Brindley whispered to Wedgwood that he did not expect to live. Thoughtfully he gave his wife permission to purchase the portrait painted two years before in London but rejected after a payment dispute, knowing that she had 'set her heart upon having it'.[100] During the early hours of 27th September 1772 James Brindley woke and was given a drink, then he said 'enough, I shall need no more', shutting his eyes for the last time. After a further nine hours sleep James Brindley died peacefully at midday.[101]

Ann Brindley was inconsolable at the loss of 'a sensible friend and affectionate Husband' who had faced his final illness with the 'fortitude and strength of mind which characterised all his actions'.[102] Dr Erasmus Darwin had not been present and was frustrated that his colleagues had not told him of the seriousness of the situation, saying that otherwise nothing would have hindered him from going to Brindley's bedside.[103] When news filtered through to Retford the Reverend Seth Ellis Stevenson did not immediately think of the uncertain future of the Chesterfield Canal, only that he had lost a 'worthy and much respected friend'.[104] Josiah Wedgwood asked Thomas Bentley to write eulogies for their mutual friend for inclusion in the nation's newspapers. He was also politician enough to know that the words should include phrases to protect the future of the canal movement, mobilising John Sparrow, solicitor to Brindley and the Trent & Mersey Canal Company, to ensure that published accounts of the engineer's death were accurate. For the same reason, Wedgwood ensured that the obituaries also looked to the future with phrases such as 'Mr Brindley had long been sensible of the precarious situation of his health, and wished to be succeeded in his profession by his brother-in-law Mr Henshall … he spared no pains to qualify him for that important trust … '[105] It was also arranged that Hugh Henshall would be the estate administrator as the wealthy Brindley had died intestate, and take on the legal guardianship of his two, now fatherless, nieces.[106] No inventory of Brindley's affairs has been found but his estate has been calculated as £7,000, based on the sum which 'bound' Henshall and the solicitors.[107]

The funeral took place on 30th September at the church at Newchapel, near Turnhurst Hall.

In the 1950s a descendent wrote that a few items inherited from James Brindley were in his possession. They included a bound copy of four religious books presented by the Duke of Bridgewater and passed from Brindley's widow to their eldest daughter, and a miniature of the engineer, painted near the end of his life, at the back of which was an oval panel containing a lock of hair.[108] A number of items were described as bearing the family arms, but unless the design was used without authority, the only heraldic device in the family was awarded to the descendent of John Brindley, the engineer's brother.[109]

No matter. James Brindley led the construction of the central strands of the national canal network we have today. Of the eight waterways only three were completed routes at the time of his death – the Staffordshire & Worcestershire, the Birmingham, and the Droitwich canals. His two long tunnels, Harecastle and Norwood, would not be finished until another three years had passed. However, the men he had trained, and who had flourished with the responsibilities he gave them, would take the canal movement forward, and thereafter form the basis for the nationwide resources which would build the railways and the roads.

The canals are James Brindley's memorial. His epitaph is that men of education, integrity and high moral values such as Josiah Wedgwood, Thomas Bentley, Erasmus Darwin and Seth Ellis Stevenson considered him worthy of respect, trust and friendship.

Chapter 13
ENDURING FAME

By the end of the eighteenth century Brindley had been eulogised in many national publications, and the myths were starting to flourish.

A biographical dictionary published in 1778 allocated fourteen pages to James Brindley, the facts for which were claimed to have been provided by Hugh Henshall, Josiah Wedgwood and Thomas Bentley. The editor also gave space for a transcript of an article from the *Morning Post*, August 1776, which he thought 'may serve to amuse our readers', but without guarantee of authenticity:

> Employment in many considerable works, had made him [Brindley] think there was nothing impossible to him. He had always a favourite scheme of joining the two islands [Britain and Ireland] from Port Patrick to Donnaghdee, by a floating road and canal, which he was confident he could execute in such a manner as to stand the most violent attacks of the waves.[1]

This in turn led to a war of words in the widely-read *Gentleman's Magazine* in 1780, where two correspondents disagreed about the practicality of joining Scotland and Ireland in some way. One justified his views with, 'the deference I have for so great a genius [Brindley] would induce me to rely upon his judgement ... one [should be] cautious of charging such a man with forming chimerical plans.' So, an unproven anecdote had already become 'fact' in the national press.

Later Dr Erasmus Darwin wrote a poem about his friend in his book *The Botanic Garden*, published in 1794.[2] And in the 1830s Brindley's name was still being eulogised, and rated alongside that of James Watt in the league of famous engineers.[3]

Memorial tablet on the gravestone of James Brindley in the churchyard of St James, Newchapel. The flowers were placed by the Brindley International Historical Foundation in July 2002

In the intervening centuries a number of memorials and statues have been created, and there is a full list in Appendix B. They include Brindley's gravestone which was restored by public subscription in 1958 when a memorial tablet was also installed. However, visitors to Brindley's grave should take the time to go past the church to the back of the churchyard. Looking at the expansive view over the hills and valleys where he made his name is the best place to appreciate James Brindley's nationally significant achievements.

Brindley Memorial Well at Wormhill, Derbyshire installed in 1875. The inscription reads 'In memory of James Brindley Civil Engineer, born this parish, AD 1716'

Brindley Mill Museum, Leek, Staffordshire. This view of the back of the mill shows the water-wheel

Statue by James Butler R.A. at Coventry Basin, Coventry

'James Brindley' pub, Gas Street Basin, Birmingham

***Right:* Memorial stone on the site of the cottage where James Brindley was born** Christopher Lewis

***Below:* Proposed statue for Droitwich by John McKenna** Courtesy of The Droitwich Canals Trust

***Bottom right:* Statue by Colin Melbourn unveiled on 20th July 1990 beside the Caldon Canal near its junction with the Trent & Mersey Canal in Stoke-on-Trent**

APPENDIX A

FAMILY TREES

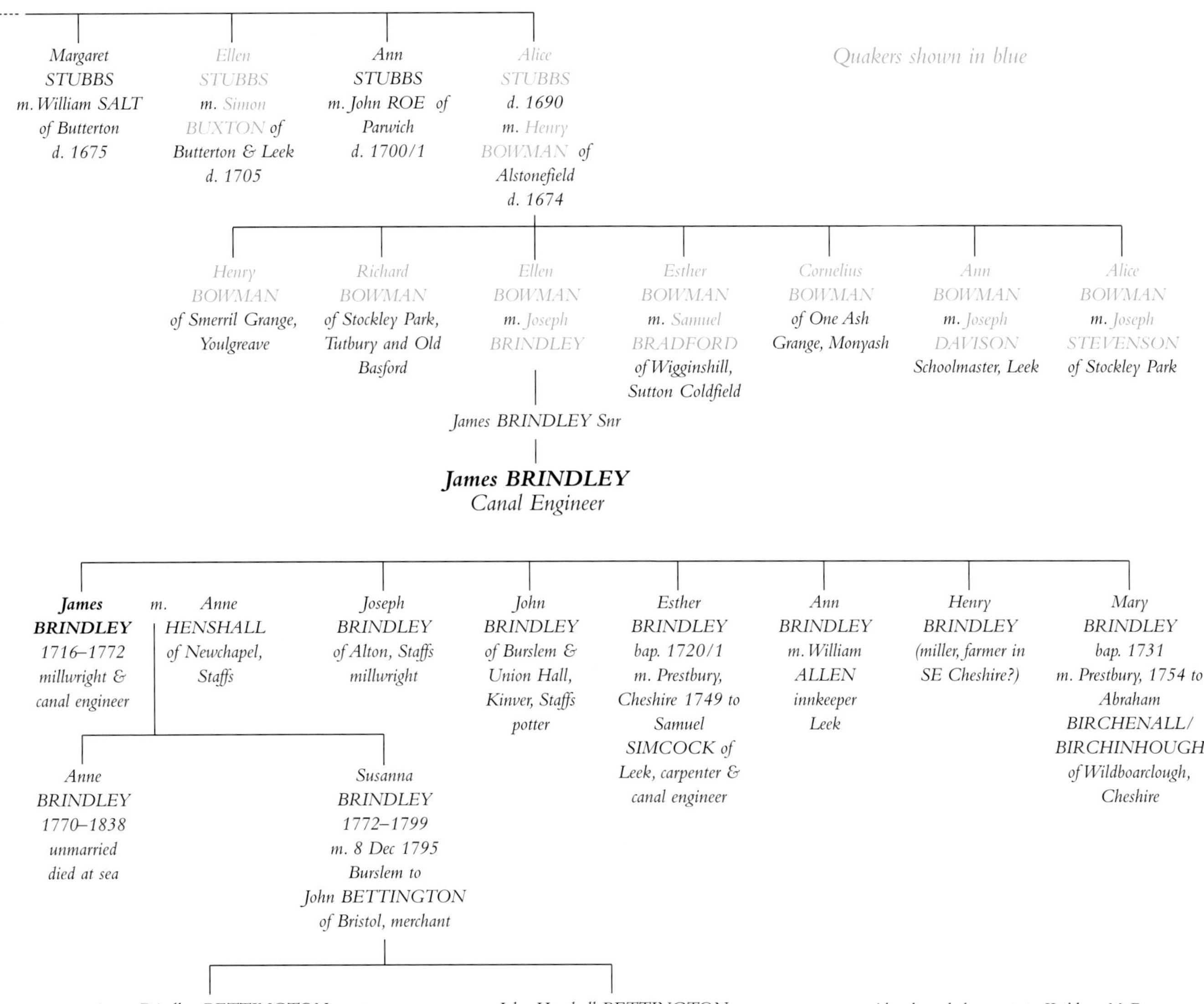

Two of Brindley's nephews, the sons of his brother Joseph, and his sister Ann Allen, went to the American colonies:

> The *Jett* from London is gone up the Rappahannock River. In her came John Ballendine Esq: with about forty ingenious mechanicks, who landed at Hampton. Mr Ballendine has made a tour of England, Scotland, Ireland and France, in order to make himself fully acquainted with inland navigation, and has also engaged and brought with him some of the best and most experienced artists in canals, locks, etc. that could be had in England; among them Mr James Brindley and Mr Thomas Allen, nephews to the celebrated engineer of that name, who were brought up with him and were well acquainted with all his works until his death. *The Virginia Gazette*, 7 July 1774.

Nephew James Brindley became involved in inland navigation in America and is mentioned a number of times in the correspondence of George Washington. On the morning of 11 September 1777 James, at his mansion near Wilmington, was host to Washington before the general left to lead the Battle of Brandywine later that day, in the American War of Independence.

The above information is from *Brindley Genealogy*, by Gordon Brindley, 2002, Churnet Valley Books, Leek, Staffordshire.

APPENDIX B

ORDNANCE SURVEY GRID REFERENCES FOR SIGNIFICANT SITES

Birthplace memorial stone, Tunstead, Derbyshire. Erected by the local history section of the Derbyshire Archaeological Society, unveiled on 1st November 1958. SK 109750

Lowe Hill Farm, Leek (substantially altered since Brindley's residence) SJ 997557

Sutton (site of apprenticeship workshop) SJ 925718

Wet Earth Colliery (in Clifton Country Park) SD 768042

Worsley Delph, Bridgewater Canal SD 748005

Turnhurst Hall (demolished 1929) SJ 865535

Barton Aqueduct (replaced by the Barton Swing Aqueduct in 1893). SJ 767975

Newchapel, Staffordshire. Brindley's gravestone and memorial tablet, in the churchyard of St James Church. Restored by public subscription, October 1958. SJ 864546

Wormhill, Derbyshire. Brindley memorial well. Installed in 1875 'in memory of James Brindley, civil engineer, born in this parish 1716'. SK 123742

Leek, Staffordshire. Brindley Mill Museum. The mill was designed and built by Brindley in c1752. The remaining building is two-thirds of the original, the rest demolished in 1948 for road-widening. Restored to working order by the Brindley Mill Museum Trust, and re-opened May 1974. On the Leek to Macclesfield road. The variable opening times are available from Leek Tourist Information (Telephone 01538 483741). SJ 978570

Birmingham. The James Brindley pub is by Gas Street Basin, and Brindleyplace, at the heart of the city's popular canal area.

Stoke-on-Trent, Staffordshire. Statue, erected 1990. At the junction of the Caldon and Trent & Mersey canals, near the Etruria Industrial Museum. SJ 873470

Coventry, canal basin. Statue, erected 1999. By James Butler R.A. Part of Coventry's Canal Art Trail.

Droitwich Canal. Statue, planned to be erected 2004. By John McKenna.

APPENDIX C

A typical flash-lock consisted of a single gate,

> made up of bars of wood called Rimers, set perpendicularly to the bottom of the passage and Lockgates [or paddles] put down between every two of them … which will keep a head of water … for the passage of a Barge; but must be pulled up at its arrival, and the water let go till there is an abatement of the fall, before the boat may pass either down or upwards; which, with the stream, is not without violent precipitation; and against it, at many places, not without the help of a Capstan at land, and sometimes neither of them without imminent danger.

Robert Plot, *The Natural History of Oxfordshire*, Oxford, 1677. Quoted in *The Engineers of the English River Navigations, 1620–1760*; Skempton, A, W,; *Transactions of the Newcomen Society*, Volume 29, p.25, illustration p.28.

APPENDIX D

PETITIONS FOR THE SALFORD CANAL, JANUARY–MARCH 1754

Journal of the House of Commons, Volume 26, pp905–77.

18 January Petition to bring in a Bill to construct a canal from Salford, through Eccles and Worsley to Leigh and Wigan. Water to be obtained from the river Irwell. Coal to be the major cargo. Referred to a Committee of the House.

4 February Mr Taylor has made a survey, from Salford to within half a mile of Wigan. Assisted by Robert Gibson. Leave given to bring in a Bill.

18 February Bill presented to the House by Lord Strange. First Reading.

25 February An opposing petition from those with land on the route. Claiming the survey had been done without landowners consent, and the whole project had been promoted privately without the knowledge of many in the area. Also two supporting petitions, from Leigh and Wigan.

28 February Opposing petition from Sir Oswald Mosley, Baronet, Lord of the Manor of Manchester.

5 March Opposing petitions from Manchester, Eccles, Leigh, and several private individuals.

Bill dropped as a result of the number of opposing petitions.

APPENDIX E

A description of a Brindley engine and boiler, sent in 1759 by Mr Spedding of Whitehaven to William Brown, the Tyneside engineer. From the dates, probably the one installed for Thomas Broad.

> the Cylinder 36 Ins. and lifts or forces the Water $26^{1}/_{2}$ Fa^{ms} to the Level & Dry Rods (or Spears) 17 Ins. more to the Top of the Pitts, and agreed to support the Engine with all Repairs & men to work her (exclusive of Coals) for 80£ p Annum for 15 Years, the Engine has now Wrought near three Years & Ans^{rs} very well …
> Expense on the Engine House was saved by building the cylinder into one wall and making the opposite wall act as the pivot bearing at the centre of the beam – the boilers were outside and made of Brick laid only in fine Lime is about 18ft long 12ft wide & 6ft deep in form of an Archd Vault, under it he has 4 small fireplaces like those of a Common Sett Pott, with Iron Doors & Brick instead of Iron for the Grate Bars which he does not clean from Clinkers above once in 10 or 12 Weeks his fires are so moderate as not to run the Coals. Above the Fire are laid Cast Iron Plates wch make the Boiler Bottom in that Part, the rest being paved with Brick the fire plays against the Iron Plates & goes into a Flue on the Backside the Boiler & is there recd in 4 Iron Pipes one for each Fire Place wch come thro' the Water & Steam in the inside of the Boiler & then are conveyed into the Chimney.

William Brown's Letter Book, p61. Manuscript collections, Institution of Mining Engineers, Newcastle-on-Tyne. Quoted by Arthur Raistrick, *Dynasty of Iron Founders*, revised 2nd edition, 1989, p147.

Extracts from Brindley's patent for a steam engine. No. 730, 1758.

> James Brindley, of Leek, in the County of Stafford, Millwright …
> … my Invention of A Fire Engine for Drawing Water out of Mines, or for Draining of Lands, or for Supplying of Cityes, Townes, or Gardens with Water, or which may be applicable to many other great and usefull Purposes in a better and more effectual Manner than any Engine or Machine that hath hitherto been made or used for the like Purpose …

The boyler or cistern for the water is to be made with brick or stone, arched over, and some part of the materials belonging thereto are to be of wood. The face of the fire at the bottom of one side of the boyler is to be made of stone or cast iron, and there is to be joined to it a plate of wrought iron to give way to expansion. In the centre of this plate is to be fixed the fire door, which is to be made of wrought or cast iron. The stove over the fire-place is to be made of cast iron, and is to be fixed within the boyler. At the top of the stove, in the center, an elbow pipe is to be fixed that lyes flat in the said boyler, and at the end of that elbow pipe is to be a short pipe screwed to it, which forms a right angle; and at the other end of this short pipe is to be screwed another pipe, which lies parallel to the elbow pipe; and at the end of the last pipe is to be screwed an upright pipe, which reaches to the top of the boyler; and joined to the top of the said upright pipe there is to be square cap of stone or cast iron, upon which cap of stone the chimney is to be built.

This is a great improvement upon the common method, according to which the boylers are made of iron, covered with lead or copper, which are often out of repair, and are apt to burst; and the fire to heat them consumes a much greater quantity of coal. At the top of the said boyler is to be fixed a pipe called the feeding pipe, which, by means of buoys in the boyler that rise and fall with the clack, supplys the boyler with water without attendance; but if the part be neglected by persons who attend on common fire engines, there boyler is often damaged, and sometimes destroyed.

The great arch chains for the engine are to be made of wood, with iron pins through them, which chains are more safe and durable than iron ones that are used in the common way. The pump trees are to be made of pipe staves hooped together, which come cheaper than iron pipes or bored trees, commonly used.

In witness whereof, I, the said James Brindley, have hereunto sett my hand and seal, this Twenty-sixth day of December, in the year of our Lord One thousand seven hundred and fifty-eight.

APPENDIX F

22 April 1769. At a special meeting of the Coventry Canal Company's committee Brindley gave the following instructions:

> That Bedworth Hill be laid open as far as the Surface is already laid open to the North of One Hundred Feet and upwards and not to proceed any further with the Tunnelling Channel till further Orders.
>
> That Timber be prepared for piles either Oak or Elm of the Dimensions of six or seven Inches Square or Twenty eight Inches in the Girth and not less than ten feet long.
>
> For every One Hundred Yards, two Hundred piles, the piles to be whole Timber Trees of the above Dimensions.
>
> That Coney Lane Bridge (No.11) be taken down as low as the surface of the Water, or lower if found necessary.
>
> That on the Towing Path side of the Bridge now begun by [??] all the Bricks be again taken up and the foundations dug to the bottom of the Canal; Some of the Wing Walls excepted.
>
> That a Sample of Barrow Lime be Ordered by way of making Experiments.
>
> That it be a standing order that the Undertakers forfeit sixpence for every Nitch they make in the Banks of the Canal for the wheeling planks.
>
> That the Soil dug out of the Canal be laid full three Yards from the Edge on the Towing Path side and from two to three feet on the other side according to the Soil.

APPENDIX G

BRIDGEWATER CANAL – RUNCORN LOCKS

Although not the work of James Brindley they do reflect the magnitude of the engineering work that could be done in his era if the finance was available.

Mersey

Runcorn Locks

Officially opened 1 January 1773. They were five sets of double-staircase locks linking the canal to the tidal Mersey estuary.
There are differing accounts of their dimensions:

> Each fell 7 feet but the lowermost had a fall of 22 feet 6 inches at low water, to enable craft to enter and leave on any tide.
>
> *Annual Register*, 1773, p65.

> five double descending locks each of which has a fall of 8 feet but all together have a 79 foot fall to low tide … each is 96 feet long and 16 feet wide and takes ships 80 feet in length and 15 feet broad … All these locks are supported on piles and are provided with beams laid lengthwise and crosswise, with double planks at the bottom. The side walls of brick are reinforced above and below and on the corners with dressed stone and in addition there is set in at every 12 feet on the side walls a layer of dressed stone.
>
> Johann Ludewig Hogrewe, captain of Engineers (British Museum MS.46).

Josiah Wedgwood took his children to see the locks in January 1773, later he wrote:

> I have seen a good deal of these matters before, but notwithstanding that, I was quite astonished at the vastness of the plan, & the greatness of stile in the execution. The walls of the locks are truly admirable, both for strength and beauty of workmanship. The front lock next to the sea (for such it seems when the tide is in) in particular, whose walls are composed of vast stones from 1 to 12 tons weight, & yet by the excellent machinery made use of, some of which is still left standing, they had a perfect command of these huge masses of rock as a common bricklayer of the brick in his hand. In short, to behold ten of these locks all at one view, with their gates, aqueducts, cisterns,

> sluices, bridges, etc, the whole seems to be the work of the Titans, rather than a production of our Pigmy race of beings, & I do not wonder that the Duke is so enamoured of his handiworks, that he is now in the fourth month of his stay at this place & is expected to divide his time between Runcorn & Trentham for the remainder of the summer.
>
> Eliza Meteyard, *The Life of Josiah Wedgwood*, p244.

In 1827 a second 'New Line' of locks was installed and was generally used for 'up' traffic. The original locks were closed in the 1930s and filled in, with the New Line closing in 1966. The whole area is now overwhelmed by redevelopment. (Hugh Malet, *The Bridgewater Canal – A Pictorial History*, 1990, p27). See also, 'Runcorn Revisited', John Wain, *Waterways World*, June 2002.

APPENDIX H

CHRONOLOGY

1716	Born, Tunstead, Derbyshire
1726	Family moved to Leek, Staffordshire
1734	Started millwright apprenticeship, Sutton, Cheshire
1742	Self-employed millwright, Leek
1750	Rented a Wedgwood workshop, Burslem, Staffordshire
1752	Clifton (Wet Earth) Colliery
1756	First steam engine commission
1758 Feb	Trent Canal – surveying route
1759 Jun	Bridgewater Canal – started work on
1760	Trent Canal – survey with Smeaton
1760 Mar	Bridgewater Canal – giving evidence to House of Lords
1760 May	Trent Canal – surveying from Harecastle
1760 Aug	Illegitimate son. Unproven
1761 Jul	Bridgewater Canal – official opening of Barton Aqueduct
1762	Dutch River – asked to convert three bridges into swinging type also Don Navigation – improvement advice on Tinsley area
1763	Stainforth & Keadby Canal – estimates for route
1764	Weaver, river – consulted on making Witton Brook navigable
1765	Droitwich Barge Canal – estimate for
1765	Chronic fever
1765 Jan	Calder & Hebble Navigation – appointed Engineer
1765 May	Potteric Carr – advice sought on drainage improvements
1765 Dec	Married Anne Henshall
1766	Calder & Hebble – resigned as Engineer
1766	Thames, river – opinion sought on waterworks at London Bridge
1766 Jan	Family moved to Turnhurst Hall
1766 May	Trent & Mersey Canal – appointed Surveyor-General
1766 May	Staffordshire & Worcestershire Canal – appointed Surveyor
1766 Jul	Trent & Mersey Canal – ceremonial cutting of first sod
1767	Birmingham Canal – asked to survey for
1767 Mar	Health suffering
1767 Nov	Bridgewater Canal – Bollin Aqueduct collapsed
1768	Chesterfield Canal – estimate for route to Bawtry
1768	Leeds & Liverpool Canal – asked to report on Longbotham's route

1768 Feb	Coventry Canal – appointed Engineer and Surveyor
1768 Mar	Droitwich Barge Canal – appointed Inspector of the Works
1768 Mar	Birmingham Canal – appointed Engineer
1768 Sep	Forth & Clyde Canal – in Glasgow discussing plans for. Also made a Burgess of Glasgow
1769 May	Oxford Canal – appointed Engineer and General Surveyor
1769 Sep	Coventry Canal – dismissed as Engineer
1769 Dec	First child born – Anne
1770 Jan	Thames, river – asked to plan navigational improvements
1770 Mar	Portrait painted by Francis Parsons
1770 May	Leeds & Liverpool Canal – appointed Chief Engineer, declined
1771 Mar	Droitwich Barge Canal – official opening
1771 Jun	Chesterfield Canal – appointed Engineer
1772 Jan	Second child born – Susanna
1772 May	Staffordshire & Worcestershire Canal – completed
1772 Sep	Caldon Canal – taken ill while surveying
1772 Sep	Birmingham Canal completed
1772 Sep 27	Died
1775	Norwood and Harecastle tunnels completed, each 2,880 yards long
1776	Bridgewater Canal – completed
1777 May	Trent & Mersey Canal – completed
1777 Jun	Chesterfield Canal – completed
1790	Coventry Canal – completed
1793	Oxford Canal – completed to the Thames

BIBLIOGRAPHY

Manuscript sources

Birmingham Central Library

MS 1633/3 and MS 1633/4. Letters, Josiah Wedgwood to Erasmus Darwin, 22 April 1765 and 10 July 1765. The latter includes a copy of a letter from the Mayor of Liverpool to Wedgwood about the Trent & Mersey's Liverpool plans. These letters originally formed part of a collection of autograph letters, compiled in the late 19th century by Elizabeth Wheeler. Many were addressed to her father S.T.Galton. Darwin was a close associate of the Galtons. They were purchased by Birmingham Central Libraries on 19 June 1991.

Matthew Boulton Papers, Letter Book D, pp.34–5, pp.40–3. Letters from Matthew Boulton to Thomas Gilbert and Samuel Garbett.

Brindley Mill Museum, Leek

Envelope 13 (Canal pamphlets), 'Facts and Reasons ... proposed canal ... ought not to terminate at Northwich and Burton ...' The original is given as ref. 32546-32 in University Library, Keele. Not dated, but circa 10 February 1766. Almost certainly written by Bentley and/or Wedgwood.

Envelope 8. Brindley and Whitworth, 'Report on Stockton, via Darlington, to Winston Canal'. The original is given as ref. OB STO Q in the Science Museum Library, London.

Derby Central Library

Pamphlet, 'Cursory View of the Advantages of an Intended Canal from Chesterfield to Gainsborough', 1769.

Stevenson, Seth Ellis, pamphlet, 'Seasonable Hints relating to the Intended Canal from Chesterfield to the River Trent below Gainsbrough', 8 December 1769.

Glasgow City Archives

AMJ/CB/F15/L3119. Brindley's admittance to the burgess-ship of the city, 9 September 1768.

House of Lords Record Office

Journal of the House of Commons, Vol 26, pages within the range 905–77. Petitions for the Salford Canal, January 1754 to March 1754.

House of Commons Journal, 24–25 November 1758, p.321.

33.Geo.II. No.13, Second Act for the Bridgewater Canal. Microfilm reference: Original Acts: Private. 33.Geo.II. No.7-93, reel 56. [Act is number 13].

Institution of Civil Engineers, Archives, London

Brindley's notebook, 1758–60.

Brindley's notebook, September 1761–November 1762.

Brindley's notebook, October/November 1763.

Also, see note, William Salt Library, ref. MS 85/1/42.

London School of Economics, Archives

Charles Hadfield's papers (Hadfield Collection).

National Archives (formerly **Public Record Office, Kew**)

RAIL 817/1. Minutes of the Chesterfield Canal Company, 18 April 1771 to 10 May 1780. An indexed transcript of this document, *Minutes of the Chesterfield Canal Company 1771–80*, has been published by the Derbyshire Record Society, Richardson, Christine, (ed) (1996).

RAIL 818/1. Minutes of the Coventry Canal Company, 9 March 1768.

RAIL 822/1. Minutes of the Droitwich Canal Company, 4 March 1768.

RAIL 825/1. Minutes of the Don Navigation Company 1729–1825, 14 June 1762.

RAIL 855/2. Minutes of the Oxford Canal Company, 12 May 1769 to 28 June 1775.

National Waterways Museum, Archives, Gloucester

BW 1080/95. Letter, E. Lingard to Hugh Henshall, 30 January 1768. Trent & Mersey progress report, work seems to be near Findern, Derbyshire. Includes details of clay deposits, and the allocation of the workmen.

Various database entries for the Trent & Mersey Canal. Recent acquisitions at the time of the author's visit.

BW 1083/95. Letter, W. Wyatt, to the Earl of Uxbridge, 27 February 1768.

BW 1084/95. Letter, from W. Wyatt, to the Earl of Uxbridge, 5 September 1768.

Northamptonshire Record Office

EB1459. Bridgewater Canal – detailed account of money paid for canal work, in Gilbert's handwriting.

EB1460. Bridgewater Canal – general account book of Agent.

EB1461, 'General State of His Grace the Duke of Bridgewater's Navigation, Colliery, Lime and Farm concerns in Lancashire and Cheshire, from Midsummer 1759'.

Nottingham University, Hallward Library, Department of Manuscripts and Special Collections

FR/73. Diary of the Reverend Seth Ellis Stevenson of Retford.

Patent Office, Newport, South Wales

No.730. Brindley's Patent for a Steam Engine, 26 December 1758.

Public Record Office, Kew (see **National Archives**)

Rotherham Library, Archives

Microfilm, Vol. 1 of the Platt letters, 'Journal of John Platt', Rotherham mason-architect, covers the years 1763–95.

Royal Society, London

Collected Reports of John Smeaton, vol 1, pp13–17. Report on the Practicability of the Trent & Mersey Canal, 11 July 1761.

Salford University Library

Canal Duke's Archives, Box 8, item 521a. Egerton, Francis Henry (8th Earl of Bridgewater), 'Letter to the Parisians', written in Paris, 24 March 1819 because he felt that public opinion, even in Paris, and publications such as the *Kippis Britannica* were giving an overblown importance to Brindley's role in the Bridgewater Canal at the expense of the Duke. He claimed to have heard the facts about Brindley direct from the Duke, who had died only 16 years before (8 March 1803), and had written them down at the time.

Duke of Bridgewater Archive, 12/556. Letter, John Gilbert to his brother, Thomas, 25 & 28 November 1767.

Sheffield Archives Office

MD3707. Chesterfield Canal, estimated tonnages via Bawtry, c1768. Document not dated, but quoted in *Two Centuries of Industrial Welfare*, by Arthur Raistrick, as part of the papers of the London Lead Company.

WWM.MP47.b and WWM.MP47.c. John Varley's estimates for the Greasbrough Canal. The matching manuscript map is ref. WWM.MP47.a.

Staffordshire Record Office

D593/v/3/6. Resolutions agreed at the Wolsley Bridge meeting, 30 December 1765.

D1368/1, D1368/2 and D1368/3. Staffordshire & Worcestershire Canal – Brindley's orders book, 3 volumes, 17 March 1767 to 9 August 1771.

D3186/1/1/1. Minute book of the Staffordshire & Worcestershire Canal Company.

D3186/1/6/4a. Staffordshire & Worcestershire Canal – list of all the structures. By John Green, 27 February 1770.

Stoke-on-Trent City Archives

SM6A. Brindley's and Smeaton's 'Plan for a Navigation chiefly by a Canal from Longbridge ... via Newcastle, Lichfield, Tamworth ... to Wilden'.

William Salt Library, Stafford

MS 85/1/42. This is a 20 page copy of one of Brindley's personal notebooks, the original is in a glass case at the Brindley Mill Museum, Leek, Staffordshire. Ref MS 85/2/42 is a transcript. A copy of this notebook is also held in the Archives of the Institution of Civil Engineers, London. There it is marked as 'Facsimile of a letter and part of one of the diaries of James Brindley, the great projector of Canal Navigation, in the collection of autographs of Joseph Mayer, [sig] Liverpool, June 20, 1844.'

tE9.2. Anon, pamphlet, 'The History of Inland Navigations. Particularly those of the Duke of Bridgewater in Lancashire and Cheshire; And the intended one promoted by Earl Gower and other Persons of Distinction in Staffordshire, Cheshire, and Derbyshire. Part the Second.' 18 November 1765. Thomas Bentley was responsible for the final draft. Its completion was delayed by the editorial hypercriticism of Erasmus Darwin. Dispersed by Wedgwood. 'Facts and figures on the movement and consumption of raw materials, the current costs and the savings to be anticipated, and the increased distribution and volume of trade which ought to ensue, were culled from all possible sources'. This was the edition with a map, unlike the first edition of November 1764.

bs 665. Congreve, Dr Thomas, (1717). Pamphlet, *A Scheme or Proposal for Making a Navigable Communication between the Rivers Trent and Severn*. Salt Pamphlets, v13. Written 6 February 1766. This copy was owned by John Barker.

Yorkshire Archaeological Society, Leeds

DD225 (Box 8). Worthington Jnr, J. S., letter to the Duke of Leeds, re payment for land by Canal Companies. Written from Dunham, 16 August 1771.

Journals, Magazines and Newspapers

Anon, 'James Brindley, Pioneer of the Cement Industry', in-house magazine of G&T Earle Ltd, Cement Manufacturers of Hull, November 1951. Matlock Local Studies Library.

Aris's Birmingham Gazette, 14 September 1767.

Biddle, Gordon, 'Early Days on the Leeds & Liverpool Canal', Railway & Canal Historical Society, *Journal*, January and September 1959. Contains extracts from 'Notes on the Early History of the Leeds & Liverpool Canal', by H. F. Killick, Law Clerk of the Leeds & Liverpool Canal Company. In June 1897 this was presented to the Bradford Historical and Antiquarian Society, and appeared in that Society's transactions, *The Bradford Antiquary*, Vol 3, 1896–1900.

Campbell, John H. D. M., Notes on James Brindley; *Derbyshire Miscellany*, the Bulletin of the Local History Section of Derbyshire Archaeological & Natural Historic Society, February 1959. Matlock Local Studies Library.

Chaloner, W. H., 'James Brindley (1716–72) and his Remuneration as a Canal Engineer', booklet reprinted from the *Transactions of the Lancashire and Cheshire Antiquarian Society*, Vols 75 & 76, 1965–6, 1969.

Derby Mercury newspaper, various.

Gittings, Derek, 'Legging It', *Waterways World*, February 2001.

Hamilton, Robert, 'Long Lost Loops of the Oxford Canal', *Waterways World*, June 1997.

Kirkham, Nellie, 'The Ventilation of Hillcarr Sough', *Transactions, Newcomen Society*, Vol 37, p.133.

Lewis, Christopher, 'Josiah Clowes, 1735–94', *Transactions, Newcomen Society*, Vol 50, p.155.

MacFarlane I. A., 'Mathew Dobson of Liverpool (1735–1784) and the History of Diabetes', *Practical Diabetes*, Vol 7, No.6, November/December 1990, p.251.

Moritz, Philip (1782), 'Description of the House of Commons', published in *English Historical Documents*, Vol X, 1714–1783.
Richardson, Christine, 'Brindley's Norwood Tunnel (1771–1775) – Twin of Harecastle', *Transactions, Newcomen Society*, Vol 72, pp.163–78.
Roberts, D., *History of the Quakers in Chesterfield and Derbyshire*, Chesterfield Local Studies Library. A folder of written-up notes done as a research project in 1970.
Sillitoe, Paul J., 'George Marchant's River Mersey Barrage', *Transactions of the Historic Society of Lancashire & Cheshire*, Vol 141, 1992, pp.329–37. Given source, SUL, Clifford Whitworth Library, Bridgewater Archive, ref. NA 5/409, December 1768.
Skempton, A. W., 'The Engineers of the English River Navigations, 1620–1760', *Transactions, Newcomen Society*, Vol 29.
Skempton, A. W., 'Engineering on the Thames Navigation, 1770–1845', *Transactions, Newcomen Society*, Vol 55, pp.153–76.
Skempton, A. W. and Clark Wright, Esther, 'Early Members of The Smeatonian Society of Civil Engineers', *Transactions, Newcomen Society*, Vol 44.
Tann, Jennifer, 'Makers of Improved Newcomen Engines in the Late 18th Century', *Transactions, Newcomen Society*, Vol 50.
Turner, Trevor, 'The Works of John Smeaton – A Chronological Survey', *Transactions, Newcomen Society*, Vol 50.
Vasey, Peter G., 'The Forth & Clyde Canal: John Adair, Progenitor of Early Schemes', Railway & Canal Historical Society, *Journal*, Vol 30, Part 7, March 1992.
Waterways Wolrd, magazine, various issues
Willan, T. S., 'Navigation of the River Weaver in the Eighteenth Century'. The Chetham Society, 1951.

Books

Aiken, Dr John, *A Description of the Country from Thirty to Forty Miles round Manchester*, 1795.
Ashton, Thomas Southcliffe, *Iron and Steel in the Industrial Revolution*, Manchester University Press, 1924.
Ashton, T. S., *The Industrial Revolution, 1760–1830*, Oxford University Press, 1973.
Atkinson, Glen, *The Canal Duke's Collieries – Worsley 1760–1900.*
Banks, A. G. and Schofield, R. B., *Brindley at Wet Earth Colliery – An Engineering Study*, David & Charles, 1968.
Barker, T. C., *The Sankey Navigation – The First Lancashire Canal*, reprint by the Sankey Canal Restoration Society, 1990, first published by the Historic Society of Lancashire & Cheshire, 1948.
Bayne-Powell, Rosamond, *Travellers in 18th Century England*, John Murray, London, 1951.
Berg, Torsten and Berg, Peter (trans), *R R Angerstein's Illustrated Travel Diary, 1753–1755*, Science Museum, London, 2001.
Blagrove, David, *At the Heart of the Waterways*, Sponsored by Braunston Marina and British Waterways. 1995.
Bloom, Dr Arnold, *Diabetes Explained*, MTP Press, Fourth edition 1982.
Body, Alfred H., *It Happened Round Manchester – Canals and Waterways*, University of London Press, 1969.
Boucher, Cyril T. G., *James Brindley, Engineer, 1716–1772*, Goose and Son Ltd, Norwich, 1968.
Boyes, John and Russell, Ronald, *The Canals of Eastern England*, David & Charles, 1977.
Brindley, Gordon, *Brindley Genealogy*, Churnet Valley Books, Leek, Staffordshire, 2002.
Carswell, John, *From Revolution to Revolution – England 1688–1776*, Development of English Society series, Routledge & Kegan Paul, London, 1973.
Cartwright, F. F., *A Social History of Medicine.*
Cook, Martin, *Medieval Bridges*, Shire Publications, 1998.
Copeland, Robert, *A Short History of Pottery, Raw Materials, and the Cheddleton Flint Mill*, Cheddleton Flint Mill Industrial Heritage Trust, 1972.
Currie, Ian, *Frosts, Freezes and Fairs*, Frosted Earth, 1996.
Daniel, Clarence, *Derbyshire Portraits*, Dalesman Books, 1978.
Deane, Phyllis, *The First Industrial Revolution*, Cambridge University Press, 2nd edition, 1990.
Delany, V. T. H. and Delany, D. R., *The Canals of the South of Ireland*, David & Charles, 1966.
Drabble, Margaret, *Arnold Bennett – A Biography*, Weidenfeld & Nicholson, London, 1974.
Dunicliff, J. W. S., *Three Staffordshire Canals*, J. H. Hall & Sons Ltd, Derby, 1992.
Evans, Kathleen M., *James Brindley – A New Perspective*, Churnet Valley Books, Leek, Staffordshire, 1997.
Finer, Ann and Savage, George (eds), *The Selected Letters of Josiah Wedgwood*, Cory, Adams & Mackay, 1965.
Fletcher, John C., *Waterways into Castlefield*, 1989.
Hadfield, Charles, *Rivers and Canals*, Originally published in *John Smeaton, FRS*, A. W. Skempton (ed), p103–29, London, 1981.
Hadfield, Charles, *The Canals of South and South-East England*, David & Charles, 1969.
Hadfield, Charles, *The Canals of South-West England*, David & Charles, 2nd edition, 1985.
Hadfield, Charles, *The Canals of the West Midlands*, David & Charles, 3rd edition, 1985.
Hadfield, Charles, *The Canals of Yorkshire & North East England* (2 vols), David & Charles, 1972.
Hadfield, Charles and Biddle, Gordon, *The Canals of North West England* (2 vols), David & Charles, 1970.
Heathcote, Evelyn D., *The Family of Heathcote*, 1899.
Hibbert, Christopher, *George III – A Personal History*, Viking, 1998.
Klemperer, William D. and Sillitoe, Paul J., *James Brindley at Turnhurst Hall*, No.6 Staffordshire Archaeological Studies, City Museum & Art Gallery, Stoke-on-Trent, 1995.
Labouchere, Rachel, *Abiah Darby of Coalbrookdale*, William Sessions Ltd, York, 1988.
Langford, J. Ian, *Staffordshire & Worcestershire Canal*, Towpath Guide No.1, Goose & Son, 1974.

Lead, Peter, *Agents of Revolution – John and Thomas Gilbert – Entrepreneurs*, Centre for Local History, University of Keele, 1989.
Lindsey, Jean, *The Canals of Scotland*, David & Charles, 1968.
Lindsey, Jean, *The Trent & Mersey Canal*, David & Charles, 1979.
Majdalany, Fred, *The Red Rocks of Eddystone*, White Lion, 1974.
Malet, Hugh, *Bridgewater – The Canal Duke, 1736–1803*, Manchester University Press, 1977.
Malet, Hugh, *Coal, Cotton and Canals*, 3rd edition, 1990.
Marshall, Dorothy, *Eighteenth Century England*, Longman, 2nd edition 1985.
McCutcheon, A.W., *The Canals of the North of Ireland*, David & Charles, 1965.
McIntyre, Ian, *Garrick*, Penguin Press, 1999.
Meteyard, Eliza, *The Life of Josiah Wedgwood*, re-print 1970, Cornmarket Press, London. 2 volumes. Original publication 1865.
Morton, Dr Alan Q., *Science in the 18th Century*, The King George III Collection, Science Museum, London, 1993.
Mullineux, Frank, *The Duke of Bridgewater's Canal*, Eccles and District History Society, 1959. Facsimile reprints in 1970, 1977.
Paget-Tomlinson, Edward, *The Illustrated History of Canal & River Navigations*, Sheffield Academic Press, 1993.
Phillips, John, *A General History of Inland Navigation, Foreign and Domestic*, David & Charles reprinted as *Phillips' Inland Navigation* – published 1970. First published 1792. The edition used for the reprint was the fifth, 1805.
Plumb, J. H., *England in the Eighteenth Century*, Pelican History of England, 1990.
Porter, Roy, *Enlightenment – Britain and the Creation of the Modern World*, Allen Lane, 2000.
Priestley, Joseph, *Navigable Rivers and Canals*, David & Charles, 1969. Originally published 1831 as a reference to Nichols, Priestley and Walker's *Map of the Inland Navigation, Canals and Rail Roads throughout Great Britain.*
Raistrick, Arthur, *Dynasty of Iron-Founders – The Darbys and Coalbrookdale*, revised 2nd edition, Sessions Book Trust in association with Ironbridge Gorge Museum Trust, 1989.
Raistrick, Arthur, *Quakers in Science and Industry*, David & Charles, 1968. First published 1950, The Bannisdale Press.
Raistrick, Arthur, *Two Centuries of Industrial Welfare, the London (Quaker) Lead Company, 1692–1905*, Moorland Publishing Co, 1977.
Richardson, Christine (ed), *Minutes of the Chesterfield Canal Company, 1771–80*, Derbyshire Record Society, vol XXIV, 1996. Transcript of PRO, RAIL 817/1.
Richardson, Christine, *The Waterways Revolution – From the Peaks to the Trent, 1768–1778*, 1992.
Riddell, John F., *Clyde Navigation.*
Roberts, Thomas R., *Arnold Bennett's Five Towns Origins*, Stoke-on-Trent Libraries, 1961.
Shill, Ray, *The Industrial Canal, vol. 1, The Coal Trade*, 1996.
Skempton, A. W. (ed), *John Smeaton, FRS*, London, 1981.
Sleigh, John, *History of the Ancient Parish of Leek*, 1862.
Smiles, Samuel, *Lives of the Engineers*, 1861.
Sykes, John, *The Quakers*, Allan Wingate Publishing, 1958.
Tames, Richard, *Josiah Wedgwood*, Shire Publications Ltd, 1995.
Ward, J. R., *The Finance of Canal Building in 18th Century England*, Oxford University Press, 1974.
Wheat, G., (1977), *On the Duke's Cut*, Transport Publishing Company, 22 Longmoor Road, Simmondley, Glossop, Derbyshire,in conjunction with Northern Counties Carriers Ltd.
Wickham, Helen, *Worsley in the Eighteenth Century*, 1984.
Willan, T. S., *River Navigation in England, 1600–1750*, Frank Cass & Co Ltd, 1964.
Willan, T. S., *The Early History of the Don Navigation,* Augustus M. Kelley, New York, 1968.

SOURCES

Source Locations

BCL	Birmingham City Libraries
BMM	Brindley Mill Museum, Leek, Staffordshire
DCL	Derby Central Library
GCA	Glasgow City Archives
HLRO	House of Lords Record Office
ICE	Archives of the Institution of Civil Engineers, London
NA	National Archives (formerly the Public Record Office, Kew)
NHRO	Northamptonshire Record Office
NUHL	Nottingham University, Hallward Library, Department of Manuscripts and Special Collections
NWM	National Waterways Museum, Gloucester
PRO	see NA
RLA	Rotherham Library and Archives
RS	The Royal Society, Library and Information Services, London
SAO	Sheffield Archives Office
SOTCA	Stoke-on-Trent City Archives
SRO	Staffordshire Record Office, Stafford
SUL	Salford University Library
TPO	The Patent Office, Newport, South Wales
WSL	William Salt Library, Stafford
YAS	Yorkshire Archaeological Society, Leeds

Chapter 1 – Potential Revealed

For much of the material contained in this chapter, regarding Brindley's wider family and Quaker connections, I am indebted to Kathleen M. Evans, and her book *James Brindley – A New Perspective*, 1997.

1 WSL, ref MS 85/1/42. This is a 20 page copy of one of Brindley's personal notebooks, the original is in a glass case at the Brindley Mill Museum, Leek, Staffordshire. Ref MS 85/2/42 is a transcript is a transcript of MS 85/1/42. A copy of this notebook is also held in the Archives of the Institution of Civil Engineers, London. There it is marked as 'Facsimile of a letter and part of one of the diaries of James Brindley, the great projector of Canal Navigation, in the collection of autographs of Joseph Mayer, [sig] Liverpool, June 20, 1844.'

2 Smiles, Samuel (1861), *Lives of the Engineers*. Smiles states that 'The life of Brindley has been derived almost entirely from original sources; amongst which may be mentioned the family papers in the possession of Robert Williamson Esq, of Ramsdell Hall, Cheshire; the documents relating to the engineer in the possession of Lord Ellesmere, proprietor of the Bridgewater Canal; and the valuable MS collection of Joseph Mayer Esq of Liverpool.' Also information from Robert Rawlinson, engineer Bridgewater Canal 'relative to certain interesting details as to the execution of the works of that undertaking.'

3 *Ibid.*

4 Aiken, Dr John (1795), *A Description of the Country from Thirty to Forty Miles Round Manchester.*

5 Lott, Graham, British Geological Survey. Letter to the author, 21 May 1998.

6 Skempton, A.W., 'The Engineers of the English River Navigations, 1620–1760', *Transactions, Newcomen Society*, Vol 29, p.25.

7 Willan T.S. (1964), *River Navigation in England, 1600–1750*, p.131.

8 WSL, ref bs 665. Congreve, Dr Thomas (1717), Pamphlet, 'A Scheme or Proposal for Making a Navigable Communication between the Rivers Trent and Severn'.

9 Willan, as before, this chapter, p.15.

10 *Ibid.*, pp.8–9.

11 Congreve, as before, this chapter.

12 Copeland, Robert (1983), *A Short History of Pottery Raw Materials and the Cheddleton Flint Mill.* Published by the Cheddleton Flint Mill Industrial Heritage Trust.

13 Atkinson, Glen. *The Canal Duke's Collieries – Worsley 1760–1900.*

14 Priestley, Joseph. *Priestley's Navigable Rivers and Canals.* David & Charles edition 1969.

15 Evans, as before, this chapter,

16 *Ibid.*, pp.21 and 30.

17 Sykes, John (1958), *The Quakers.* Allan Wingate Publishing.

18 *Ibid.*

19 Evans, as before, this chapter.

20 *Ibid.*

21 *Ibid.*, p.26.

22 Fletcher, John C (1989), *Waterways into Castlefield*, p.4.
23 Mullineux, Frank (1959), *The Duke of Bridgewater's Canal*. Eccles and District History Society.
24 Boucher, Cyril T.G. (1968), *James Brindley, Engineer, 1716–1772*, p.4.
25 Evans, as before, this chapter, p.27.

Chapter 2 – Theatre of Success

1 Deane, Phyllis (1990), *The First Industrial Revolution,* Cambridge University Press, p.4.
2 Carswell, John, *From Revolution to Revolution: England 1688–1776*, Development of English Society Series, p.75.
3 Deane, as before, this chapter, pp.11–15.
4 Marshall, Dorothy (1985), *Eighteenth Century England*, p.474.
5 Plumb, J.H. (1990), *England in the Eighteenth Century*, p.78.
6 Carswell, as before, this chapter, p.75.
7 Deane, as before, this chapter, p.123.
8 Carswell, as before, this chapter, p.82.
9 Morton, Alan Q. (1993), *Science in the 18th Century – The King George III Collection.*
10 Sleigh, John (1862), *History of the Ancient Parish of Leek.*
11 Bayne-Powell, Rosamond (1951), *Travellers in 18th Century England.*
12 Marshall, as before, this chapter, p.68.
13 *Ibid.*, pp.7–8.
14 Deane, as before, this chapter, p.17.
15 Carswell, as before, this chapter, p.107.
16 Deane, as before, this chapter, p.17.
17 Marshall, as before, this chapter, p.227.
18 Bayne-Powell, as before, this chapter, p.189.
19 Carswell, as before, this chapter, p.78.

Chapter 3 – The Millwright

1 Majdalany, Fred (1974), *The Red Rocks of Eddystone*, p.110.
2 *Ibid.*, p.107–11.
3 Smiles, Samuel (1861), *Lives of the Engineers.*
4 Evans, Kathleen M. (1997), *James Brindley – A New Perspective*, pp.28, 94.
5 Meteyard, Eliza (1865), *The Life of Josiah Wedgwood*, p.278.
6 Copeland, Robert (1972), *A Short History of Pottery Raw Materials and the Cheddleton Flint Mill.*
7 *Ibid.,* pp.2–6, 13.
8 Finer, Ann & Savage, George (1965), *The Selected Letters of Josiah Wedgwood*, p.342.
9 *Ibid.,* pp.201, 205.
10 *Ibid.,* p.6.
11 Meteyard, as before, this chapter, pp.220, 228.

Chapter 4 – Expanding Horizons

1 Evans, Kathleen M (1997), *James Brindley – A New Perspective*, p.28.
2 Heathcote, Evelyn D. (1899), *The Family of Heathcote.*
3 *Derby Mercury* newspaper, 4 November 1775, p.4.
4 Morton, Dr A.Q., 'Men and Machines in Mid Eighteenth Century London', p.6. Newcomen Society. Paper read, Science Museum, London, 12 January 1994.
5 Banks, A.G. & Schofield, R.B. (1968), *Brindley at Wet Earth Colliery – An Engineering Study*, p.36.
6 Preece, Geoff (1984), *Exploring Wet Earth Colliery*, p.3.
7 Atkinson, Glen. *The Canal Duke's Collieries – Worsley 1760–1900*, p.7.
8 Preece, as before, this chapter, p.3.
9 Schofield, R.B. Letter to the author, 20 May 2002.
10 Banks & Schofield, as before, this chapter, p.40.
11 Morton, as before, this chapter, p.6.
12 Skempton, A.W., 'The Engineers of the English River Navigations, 1620–1760', *Transactions, Newcomen Society*, Vol 29, p.52.
13 Morton, as before, this chapter, p.7.
14 Barker, T.C. (1948), *The Sankey Navigation – The First Lancashire Canal*, p.13.
15 Banks & Schofield, as before, this chapter, p.128.
16 Deane, Phyllis (1990), *The First Industrial Revolution*, p.4
17 *Ibid.,* p.74.

18 *Ibid.,* p.74.
19 Skempton, as before, this chapter, p.27.
20 *Ibid.,* pp.1, 36.
21 Barker, as before, this chapter, pp.7–8.
22 HLRO, *Journal of the House of Commons*, Vol 26, pages within the range 905–77. Petitions for the Salford Canal, January 1754 to March 1754.
23 Barker, as before, this chapter, pp.22–9.
24 Lindsey, Jean (1979), *The Trent & Mersey Canal*, p.18.

Chapter 5 – On the Brink of Fame

1 WSL, ref MS 85/1/42. Copy of Brindley's notebook 1755–8. See chapter 1, note 1.
2 Tann, Jennifer, 'Makers of Improved Newcomen Engines in the Late 18th Century'. *Transactions, Newcomen Society*, Vol 50, p.181.
3 Ashton, T.S. (1973), *The Industrial Revolution 1760–1830*, p.29.
4 Brindley's notebook 1755–8, as above.
5 *Ibid.*
6 *Ibid.*
7 *Ibid.*
8 Boucher, Cyril T.G. (1968), *James Brindley, Engineer, 1716–1772*, pp.39–40.
9 ICE, James Brindley's notebook, 1755–58.
10 *Ibid.*
11 TPO, No.730. Brindley's Patent for a Steam Engine, 26 December 1758.
12 Bayne-Powell, Rosamond (1951), *Travellers in 18th Century England*, p.41.
13 Raistrick, Arthur (1968), *Quakers in Science and Industry*, p.47.
14 Raistrick, Arthur (1989), *Dynasty of Iron-Founders – The Darbys and Coalbrookdale*, p.2.
15 *Ibid.*, p.4.
16 Raistrick (1968), as before, this chapter, p.142.
17 Evans, Kathleen M. (1997), *James Brindley – A New Perspective*, p.32.
18 Roberts, D. (1970), *History of the Quakers in Chesterfield and Derbyshire*, p.18.
19 Raistrick, Arthur (1977), *Two Centuries of Industrial Welfare, the London (Quaker) Lead Company, 1692–1905.*
20 Brindley's notebook 1755–8, as before, this chapter.
21 *Ibid.*
22 *Ibid.*
23 TPO, as before, this chapter.
24 Atkinson, Glen. *The Canal Duke's Collieries – Worsley 1760–1900*, p.8.

Chapter 6 – A Canal for the Nation

1 Willan, T.S. (1964), *River Navigation in England, 1600–1750*, p.5.
2 Skempton, A.W. (ed) (1981), *John Smeaton, FRS*, pp.103–29.
3 *Derby Mercury*, newspaper, 8–15 December 1758. No.39 Vol XXVII, p.1.
4 WSL, ref MS 85/1/42. Copy of Brindley's notebook 1755–8. See chapter 1, note 1.
5 *Derby Mercury*, as before, this chapter.
6 *Ibid.*
7 WSL, ref bs 665. Congreve, Dr Thomas (1717), Pamphlet, *A Scheme or Proposal for Making a Navigable Communication between the Rivers Trent and Severn.*
8 *Derby Mercury*, as before, this chapter.
9 *Ibid.*
10 Turner, Trevor. 'The Works of John Smeaton – A Chronological Survey'. *Transactions, Newcomen Society*, Vol 50, p.37.
11 Meteyard, Eliza (1865), *The Life of Josiah Wedgwood*, pp.152, 279.
12 WSL, ref MS 85/1/42. Copy of Brindley's notebook 1755–8. See chapter 1, note 1.
13 Finer, Ann & Savage, George (1965), *The Selected Letters of Josiah Wedgwood*, p.6.
14 Meteyard, as before, this chapter, pp.279–81.
15 Boucher, Cyril T.G. (1968), *James Brindley, Engineer, 1716–1772*, p.44.
16 ICE. James Brindley's notebook, 1758–60.
17 Malet, Hugh (1977), *Bridgewater – The Canal Duke, 1736–1803*, p.94.
18 WSL, ref MS 85/1/42. Copy of Brindley's notebook 1755–8. See chapter 1, note 1. Also, ICE, James Brindley's notebook, 1758–60.
19 Majdalany, Fred (1974), *The Red Rocks of Eddystone.*
20 Bayne-Powell, Rosamond (1951), *Travellers in 18th Century England.*

Chapter 7 – A Canal for the Duke of Bridgewater

1 Body, Alfred H. (1969), *It Happened Round Manchester – Canals and Waterways*, p.14.

2 Atkinson, Glen. *The Canal Duke's Collieries – Worsley 1760–1900*, p.2.
3 Wheat, G. (1977), *On the Duke's Cut*, p.5.
4 Paget-Tomlinson, Edward (1993), *The Illustrated History of Canal & River Navigations*, p.165.
5 Atkinson, as before, this chapter, p.9.
6 Malet, Hugh (1977), *Bridgewater – The Canal Duke, 1736–1803*, pp.39, 41. Given source, *Rees Cyclopaedia*, 1819.
7 *Ibid.*, p.32. Given source, a letter, Francis Reynolds of Strangeways to Edward Chetham, 1758.
8 Malet, Hugh (1961), *The Canal Duke*, p.57.
9 HLRO, *House of Commons Journal*, 24–25 November 1758, p.321.
10 NHRO, ref EB1459. Bridgewater Canal – detailed account of money paid for canal work, in Gilbert's handwriting.
11 ICE, James Brindley's notebook, 1758–60.
12 NHRO, EB1459, as before, this chapter.
13 Malet (1977), frontispiece.
14 *Ibid.*, p.42.
15 *Ibid.*, p.76.
16 *Ibid.*, pp.63, 115–16.
17 *Ibid.*, p.94.
18 Lead, Peter (1989), *Agents of Revolution – John and Thomas Gilbert – Entrepreneurs*, p.35.
19 *Ibid.*, p.46.
20 Malet (1977) as before, this chapter. Given source, a letter, R. Lansdale to J. Loch, Worsley, 21 December 1843.
21 NHRO, refs. EB 1459, and EB 1461.
22 NHRO, ref. EB 1459.
23 HLRO, *House of Commons Journal*, Volume 28.
24 NHRO, ref. EB 1459.
25 ICE, James Brindley's notebook, 1758–60.
26 Carswell, John (1973), *From Revolution to Revolution: England 1688–1776*, p.132.
27 *Ibid.*, p.120.
28 Ashton, Thomas Southcliffe (1924), *Iron and Steel in the Industrial Revolution*, p.131.
29 ICE, James Brindley's notebook, 1758–60.
30 HLRO, *House of Commons Journal*, Volume 28.
31 *Ibid.*
32 *Ibid.*
33 *Ibid.*
34 HLRO, 33.Geo.II. No.13, Second Act for the Bridgewater Canal. Microfilm reference: Original Acts: Private. 33.Geo.II. No.7–93, reel 56. [Act is number 13].
35 Priestley, Joseph. *Priestley's Navigable Rivers and Canals*. David & Charles edition 1969.
36 HLRO, 33.Geo.II. No.13, as before, this chapter.
37 Skempton, A.W., *Canals and River Navigations before 1750*, p.467. Originally published in *History of Technology*, Vol 3, pp.438–70. Oxford, 1957.
38 Phillips, John (1970), *A General History of Inland Navigation, Foreign and Domestic*, pp.106–7.
39 ICE, James Brindley's notebook, 1758–60.
40 *Ibid.*
41 Roberts, Thomas R. (1961), *Arnold Bennett's Five Towns Origins*, p.2.
42 Drabble, Margaret (1974), *Arnold Bennett – A Biography*, pp.23–4.
43 Brindley, Gordon (2002), *Brindley Genealogy*, pp.39, 142.
44 Skempton, A.W., 'The Engineers of the English River Navigations, 1620–1760', p.36. *Transactions, Newcomen Society*, Vol 29, p.25.
45 *Ibid.*, p.41.
46 ICE, James Brindley's notebook, 1758–60.
47 Meteyard, Eliza (1970), *The Life of Josiah Wedgwood*, p.277.
48 RS, *Collected Reports of John Smeaton*, vol 1, pp.13–17. Report on the Practicability of the Trent & Mersey Canal, 11 July 1761.
49 *Ibid.* Also SOTCA, ref. SM6A. Brindley's and Smeaton's 'Plan for a Navigation chiefly by a Canal from Longbridge...via Newcastle, Lichfield, Tamworth … to Wilden'
50 *Ibid.*
51 Cook, Martin (1998), *Medieval Bridges*, p.6.
52 RS, *Collected Reports of John Smeaton …*, as before, this chapter.
53 Skempton, A.W., 'The Engineers of …', as before, this chapter, p.49.
54 Hadfield, Charles (1981), *Rivers and Canals*, p.105.

Chapter 8 – A Phenomenal Success

1 Bayne-Powell, Rosamond (1951), *Travellers in 18th Century England*, p.189.
2 Smiles, Samuel (1861), *Lives of the Engineers*. p390.

3 Malet, Hugh (1977), *Bridgewater – The Canal Duke, 1736–1803*, p.62.
4 NHRO, ref. EB 1459.
5 Phillips, John (1970), *A General History of Inland Navigation, Foreign and Domestic*, pp.90–1.
6 Atkinson, Glen. *The Canal Duke's Collieries – Worsley 1760–1900*, p.10.
7 ICE, James Brindley's notebook, 1758–60.
8 SUL, Canal Duke's Archives, Box 8, item 521a. Egerton, Francis Henry (8th Earl of Bridgewater), 'Letter to the Parisians', Written in Paris, 24 March 1819.
9 Malet, Hugh, as before, this chapter, p.63.
10 SUL, 'Letter to the Parisians', as before, this chapter.
11 *Ibid.*
12 Mullineux, Frank,(1959), *The Duke of Bridgewater's Canal*, p.13. Given source, the *Manchester Mercury* newspaper, 21 July 1761.
13 WSL, ref. tE9.2., pamphlet, 'The History of Inland Navigations. Particularly those of the Duke of Bridgewater in Lancashire and Cheshire; And the intended one promoted by Earl Gower and other Persons of Distinction in Staffordshire, Cheshire, and Derbyshire. Part the Second'. 18 November 1765, pp.46–9.
14 *Ibid.*, p.36.
15 Malet, Hugh, as before, this chapter, p.68.
16 ICE, James Brindley's notebook, September 1761–November 1762.
17 *Ibid.*
18 Hibbert, Christopher (1998), *George III – A Personal History*, pp.42–50.
19 ICE, James Brindley's notebook, September 1761–November 1762.
20 Malet, as before, this chapter, p.74. Given source, Huntingdon Library, California, evidence for the 3rd Act.
21 ICE, James Brindley's notebook, September 1761–November 1762.
22 Manchester Ship Canal Company (1961), *The Bridgewater Canal – Bi-centenary of the Canal*, p.89.
23 ICE, James Brindley's notebook, September 1761–November 1762.
24 Aiken, Dr John (1795), *A Description of the Country from Thirty to Forty Miles Round Manchester.*
25 Bayne-Powell, Rosamond (1951), *Travellers in 18th Century England*, p.78.
26 McIntyre, Ian (1999), *Garrick*, pp.1–6.
27 ICE, James Brindley's notebook, September 1761–November 1762.
28 *Ibid.*
29 *Ibid.*
30 Malet, as before, this chapter, p.75.
31 *Ibid.*, pp.121–3.
32 Lead, Peter (1989), *Agents of Revolution – John and Thomas Gilbert – Entrepreneurs*, p.61.
33 Malet, as before, this chapter. Given source, Huntingdon Library, California, evidence for the 3rd Act.
34 *Ibid.*, p.71.
35 *Ibid.*, p.74.
36 *Ibid.*
37 ICE, Brindley's notebook, September 1761–November 1762.
38 *Ibid.*
39 *Ibid.*
40 *Ibid.*

Chapter 9 – Growing Fame

1 ICE, James Brindley's notebook, September 1761–November 1762.
2 Skempton, A.W. and Clark Wright, Esther, 'Early Members of The Smeatonian Society of Civil Engineers', *Transactions, Newcomen Society*, Vol 44, p.23.
3 Smiles, Samuel (1861), *Lives of the Engineers*, p.193.
4 NA, ref. RAIL 825/1., Minutes of the Don Navigation Company, 1729–1825. 14 June 1762
5 Hadfield, Charles. *The Canals of Yorkshire & North East England, p.77.*
6 *Ibid.*
7 NA, ref. RAIL 825/1, as before, this chapter.
8 Willan, T.S. (1968), *The Early History of the Don Navigation*. Map.
9 ICE, James Brindley's notebook, September 1761–November 1762.
10 NHRO, ref. EB1460. Bridgewater Canal – general account book of Agent.
11 ICE, James Brindley's notebook, September 1761–November 1762.
12 NA, ref. RAIL 825/1, as before, this chapter. 26 January 1763.
13 NA, ref. RAIL 817/1. Minutes of the Chesterfield Canal Company, 18 April 1771 to 10 May 1780. See note in Papers section of Bibliography. Also, Richardson, Christine (1992), *The Waterways Revolution*, pp.46–59.
14 RLA, Microfilm, Vol. 1 of the Platt letters, 'Journal of John Platt', Rotherham mason-architect, covers the years 1763–95. Also, Currie,

Ian (1996), *Frosts, Freezes and Fairs*, p.10.
15 Finer, Ann & Savage, George (1965), *The Selected Letters of Josiah Wedgwood*, p.24.
16 Carswell, John (1973), *From Revolution to Revolution: England 1688–1776*, p.135.
17 Hadfield, Charles and Biddle, Gordon. *The Canals of North West England*, p.26.
18 ICE, Brindley's notebook (October/November 1763), This is the source for all of Brindley's activities in this chapter.
19 Mullineux, Frank (1959), *The Duke of Bridgewater's Canal*, p.17.
20 Wickham, Helen (1984), *Worsley in the Eighteenth Century*, p.5.
21 Phillips, John (1970), *A General History of Inland Navigation, Foreign and Domestic*, p.37.
22 Mullineux, as before, this chapter.
23 Malet, Hugh (1977), *Bridgewater – The Canal Duke, 1736–1803*, p.46.
24 NHRO, ref. EB1461, 'General State of His Grace the Duke of Bridgewater's Navigation, Colliery, Lime and Farm concerns in Lancashire and Cheshire, from Midsummer 1759'.
25 ICE, Brindley's notebook (October/November 1763), This is the source for all of Brindley's activities in this chapter.
26 Ashton, Thomas Southcliffe (1924), *Iron and Steel in the Industrial Revolution*, p.133.
27 Mullineux, as before, this chapter, p.14. Given source, a letter published in the *Annual Register*.

Chapter 10 – A National Network Begins

1 The 'Mechanic Arts' section of *The Complete Dictionary of Arts and Sciences*. Quoted by Morton, Dr A.Q., 'Men and Machines in Mid Eighteenth Century London'. Newcomen Society paper, read at the Science Museum, London, 12 January 1994.
2 Malet, Hugh (1977), *Bridgewater – The Canal Duke, 1736–1803*, p.97.
3 Hadfield, Charles. *The Canals of Yorkshire & North East England*, p.48. Given source, the Calder & Hebble minute-book, 6 December 1764.
4 *Ibid.*, p.51.
5 *Ibid.*
6 *Ibid.*, pp.51–3.
7 Boyes John and Russell, Ronald,. *Canals of Eastern England*, p.49.
8 Hadfield, Charles (1981), *Rivers and Canals*, p.114.
9 Ashton, Thomas Southcliffe (1924), *Iron and Steel in the Industrial Revolution*, p.48.
10 Meteyard, Eliza. *The Life of Josiah Wedgwood*, p.411.
11 Vasey, Peter G., 'The Forth & Clyde Canal: John Adair, Progenitor of Early Schemes'. Railway & Canal Historical Society, *Journal*, Vol 30, Part 7, March 1992.
12 Hadfield, Charles (1981), as before, this chapter, p.64. Given source, , Smeaton's reports, vol 2, pp.98–120, 28 October 1768.
13 *Ibid.*, p.65.
14 Tames, Richard (1995), *Josiah Wedgwood*, pp.7–9.
15 *Ibid.*
16 Meteyard, as before, this chapter, p.305.
17 Finer, Ann & Savage, George [eds] (1965), *The Selected Letters of Josiah Wedgwood*, pp.7, 28.
18 *Ibid.*, pp.11, 14.
19 Meteyard, as before, this chapter, pp.345, 354.
20 Finer & Savage, as before, this chapter, p.9.
21 Bleasdale, W.J., letter to the author, 18 January 1996.
22 Willan, T.S., 'Navigation of the River Weaver in the Eighteenth Century', The Chetham Society, 1951.
23 Meteyard, as before, this chapter, p.305.
24 *Ibid.*, p.347.
25 *Ibid.*, p.346.
26 Porter, Roy (2000), *Enlightenment – Britain and the Creation of the Modern World*, p.93.
27 *Ibid.*, p.79.
28 *Ibid.*, pp.85–6, 92.
29 *Ibid.*, p.76.
30 Aiken, Dr John (1795), *A Description of the Country from Thirty to Forty Miles Round Manchester.*
31 *Dictionary of National Biography,* 1921.
32 Lead, Peter (1989), *Agents of Revolution – John and Thomas Gilbert – Entrepreneurs*, p.72.
33 Meteyard, as before, this chapter, p.347.
34 *Ibid.*, p.351.
35 Carswell, John (1973), *From Revolution to Revolution: England 1688–1776*, p.175.
36 Finer & Savage, as before, this chapter, p.31.
37 Hadfield, Charles. *Canals of the West Midlands*, p.20.
38 WSL, ref. tE9.2., pamphlet, 'The History of Inland Navigations. Particularly those of the Duke of Bridgewater in Lancashire and Cheshire; And the intended one promoted by Earl Gower and other Persons of Distinction in Staffordshire, Cheshire, and Derbyshire. Part the Second'. 18 November 1765, p.58.

39 Hadfield, Charles. *Canals of the West Midlands*, p.20.
40 Gittings, Derek. 'Legging It'. In *Waterways World*, February 2001, p.63.
41 Hadfield, Charles. *Canals of the West Midlands*, p.21.
42 WSL, ref. tE9.2., pamphlet, 'The History of Inland Navigations …' as before, this chapter, p.85.
43 Meteyard, as before, this chapter, p.409.
44 *Ibid.*, pp.409–12.
45 *Ibid.*, p.412.
46 *Ibid.*, p.410.
47 WSL, ref. tE9.2., as before, this chapter, p.40.
48 Phillips, John (1970), *A General History of Inland Navigation, Foreign and Domestic,* p.91. Also, WSL, ref. tE9.2., as before, this chapter, pp.39–40, 47, 54.
49 WSL, ref. tE9.2., as before, this chapter, pp.39–40, 54.
50 *Ibid.*, p.48.
51 *Ibid.*, p.40.
52 *Ibid.*, p.54.
53 Meteyard, as before, this chapter, p.408.
54 *Ibid.*, p.403.
55 Porter, Roy (2000), *Enlightenment – Britain and the Creation of the Modern World, p.*439. Given source, Darwin's *Zoonomia*, 3rd edition, vol.ii, p.505.
56 *Ibid.*, p.439.
57 Hadfield, Charles. *Canals of the West Midlands*, p.21. Given source, a letter, Wedgwood to Darwin, April 1765.
58 Meteyard, as before, this chapter, p.414.
59 WSL, ref. tE9.2., as before, this chapter, p.36.
60 Meteyard, as before, this chapter, p.418.
61 Lead, Peter (1989), *Agents of Revolution – John and Thomas Gilbert – Entrepreneurs*, p.75.
62 *Ibid.*
63 Lindsey, Jean (1979), *The Trent & Mersey Canal*, p.18.
64 BCL, ref. MS 1633/3-4. Letters, Josiah Wedgwood to Erasmus Darwin, 22 April 1765, and 10 July 1765. The latter includes a copy of a letter from the Mayor of Liverpool to Wedgwood about the Trent & Mersey's Liverpool plans.
65 Meteyard, as before, this chapter, p.424.
66 Malet, Hugh (1977), *Bridgewater – The Canal Duke, 1736–1803*, p.113.
67 Lindsey, as before, this chapter, p.18.
68 *Ibid.*, p.19.
69 Meteyard, as before, this chapter, p.427.
70 Finer & Savage, as before, this chapter, p.25. Given source, letter E18102-25 of the Wedgwoood archives.
71 *Ibid.*
72 Phillips, John, as before, this chapter, p.165.
73 *Ibid.*
74 SRO, ref. D593/v/3/6. Resolutions agreed at the Wolsley Bridge meeting, 30 December 1765.
75 Meteyard, as before, this chapter, p.430.
76 Evans, Kathleen M (1997), *James Brindley – A New Perspective*, p.50. Also, NHRO, ref. EB1460, Bridgewater Canal – general account book of Agent.
77 Klemperer, William D. and Sillitoe, Paul J. (1995), *James Brindley at Turnhurst Hall (An Archaeological and Historical Investigation)*, p.10. Given source, , SRO, ref. F3534/1/16.
78 *Ibid.*, pp.11–13.
79 BMM, Envelope 13 (Canal pamphlets), 'Facts and Reasons … proposed canal … ought not to terminate at Northwich and Burton …' The original is ref 32546-32 in University Library, Keele. Not dated, but circa 10 February 1766. Almost certainly written by Bentley and/or Wedgwood.
80 Meteyard, as before, this chapter, pp.432–4.
81 Malet, Hugh (1977), *Bridgewater – The Canal Duke, 1736–1803*, p.115.
82 WSL, Salt Pamphlets, v13. Written 6 February 1766. This copy was owned by John Barker.
83 Meteyard, as before, this chapter, p.434.
84 *Ibid.*, p.431.
85 Moritz, Philip (1782), 'Description of the House of Commons'. Published in *English Historical Documents*, Vol X, 1714–1783.

Chapter 11 – Personification

1 Berg, Torsten and Berg, Peter (trans) (2001), *R R Angerstein's Illustrated Travel Diary, 1753–1755.* p xv.
2 Hadfield, Charles. *Canals of the West Midlands*, p.49.
3 SRO, ref. D1368/1-3. Staffordshire & Worcestershire Canal – Brindley's orders book, 3 volumes, 17 March 1767 to 9 August 1771.

4 *Ibid.*, p.11.
5 *Ibid.*
6 *Ibid.*
7 SRO, ref. D3186/1/6/4a. Staffordshire & Worcestershire Canal – list of all the structures. By John Green, 27 February 1770.
8 Meteyard, Eliza. *The Life of Josiah Wedgwood*, p.497.
9 Lindsey, Jean (1979), *The Trent & Mersey Canal*, p.33.
10 *Ibid.*, p.44.
11 Ward, J. R. (1974), *The Finance of Canal Building in 18th Century England*, pp.78, 128.
12 Malet, Hugh (1977), *Bridgewater – The Canal Duke, 1736–1803*, p.96. Given source, Cambridge University Library, Additional MS 6294,NP, p.107.
13 Meteyard, as before, this chapter, p.455.
14 Biddle, Gordon. 'Early Days on the Leeds & Liverpool Canal', Railway & Canal Historical Society, *Journal*, January and September 1959, p.66.
15 Hadfield, Charles. *The Canals of Yorkshire & North East England*, p.51.
16 Hadfield, Charles and Biddle, Gordon, *The Canals of North West England*, p.263. Given source, John Rennie's manuscript notebooks, Library of the Institution of Civil Engineers, London.
17 Finer, Ann & Savage, George [eds] (1965), *The Selected Letters of Josiah Wedgwood*, p.48.
18 Paget-Tomlinson, Edward (1993), *The Illustrated History of Canal & River Navigations*, p.159.
19 Lewis, Christopher. 'Josiah Clowes, 1735–94.' *Transactions, Newcomen Society*, Vol 50, 1978–9, p.155.
20 Kirkham, Nellie, 'The Ventilation of Hillcarr Sough', *Transactions, Newcomen Society*, Vol 37, p.133.
21 *Aris's Birmingham Gazette*, 14 September 1767.
22 Malet, Hugh (1990), *Coal, Cotton and Canals*, p.10. Also, Lindsey, as before, this chapter, pp.36–7.
23 Lindsey, as before, this chapter, p.37.
24 BBC Radio 4, April 2000. Conversation with a lime mortar user.
25 Majdalany, Fred (1974), *The Red Rocks of Eddystone*, p.153.
26 Anon. 'James Brindley, Pioneer of the Cement Industry'. In-house magazine of G&T Earle Ltd, Cement Manufacturers of Hull. November 1951. Matlock Local Studies Library.
27 NHRO, ref. EB1461, 'General State of His Grace the Duke of Bridgewater's Navigation, Colliery, Lime and Farm concerns in Lancashire and Cheshire, from Midsummer 1759'.
28 Bloom, Dr Arnold (1982), *Diabetes Explained*, pp.18, 25.
29 MacFarlane I.A., 'Mathew Dobson of Liverpool (1735–1784) and the History of Diabetes', *Practical Diabetes*, Vol 7, No.6, November/December 1990, p.251.
30 Meteyard, as before, this chapter, p.429.
31 Finer & Savage, as before, this chapter, pp.41, 50, 58.
32 *Ibid.*, pp.52, 62. Also, Tames, Richard (1995), *Josiah Wedgwood*, p.19.
33 Meteyard, as before, this chapter, p.38.
34 *Ibid.*, p.220.
35 Cartwright, F.F., *A Social History of Medicine*.
36 Finer & Savage, as before, this chapter, p.48.
37 *Ibid.*, pp.56, 60, 104.
38 Lindsey, as before, this chapter, p.35.
39 Meteyard, as before, this chapter, p.503.
40 *Ibid.*
41 Hadfield, Charles. *Canals of the West Midlands*, p.64.
42 Anon. *Coventry's Waterway*, p.6, Coventry Canal Society.
43 Blagrove, David (1995), *At the Heart of the Waterways*, p.7.
44 Meteyard, as before, this chapter, p.27.
45 Porter, Roy (2000), *Enlightenment – Britain and the Creation of the Modern World*, pp.206, 436.
46 Meteyard, as before, this chapter, pp.13, 503.
47 RLA, Microfilm, Vol.1 of the Platt letters, 'Journal of John Platt', Rotherham mason-architect, covers the years 1763–95.
48 Priestley, Joseph. *Priestley's Navigable Rivers and Canals*. p121.
49 SUL. Duke of Bridgewater Archive, 12/556. Letter, John Gilbert to his brother, 25 & 28 November 1767.
50 Meteyard, as before, this chapter, p.498.
51 Meteyard, as before, this chapter, p.497.
52 Currie, Ian (1996), *Frosts, Freezes and Fairs*, p.10.
53 SAO, ref. MD3707. Chesterfield Canal, estimated tonnages, via Bawtry, c1768. Document not dated, but quoted in *Two Centuries of Industrial Welfare*, by Arthur Raistrick, as part of the papers of the London Lead Company.

Chapter 12 – Brindley & Co.

1 NWM, ref. BW 1080/95. Letter, E Lingard to Hugh Henshall, 30 January 1768. Trent & Mersey progress report, work seems to be

near Findern, Derbyshire. Includes details of clay deposits, and the allocation of the workmen.

2 NA, ref. RAIL 818/1. Minutes of the Coventry Canal Company. 9 March 1768.

3 *Ibid.* Also, Hadfield, Charles. *Canals of the West Midlands*, p.60.

4 NWM, ref. BW 1080/95, as before, this chapter.

5 Skempton, A.W. and Clark Wright, Esther, 'Early Members of The Smeatonian Society of Civil Engineers'. *Transactions, Newcomen Society*, Vol 44. Page 23.

6 BMM, Envelope 8. Brindley and Whitworth, 'Report on Stockton, via Darlington, to Winston Canal'. The original is given as ref. OB STO Q in the Science Museum Library, London.

7 Hadfield, Charles. *Canals of South West England*, p.37. Also, Hadfield, Charles. *The Canals of South and South East England*, pp.169, 178. Skempton & Clark Wright, as before, this chapter, p.29. Hadfield, Charles and Biddle, Gordon, *The Canals of North West England*, p.183.

8 McCutcheon, A.W. *Canals of the North of Ireland*, p.42. Also, Skempton & Clark Wright, as before, this chapter, p.29.

9 NWM, various database entries for the Trent & Mersey Canal. Recent acquisitions at the time of the author's visit.

10 NWM, ref. BW 1083/95. Letter, W. Wyatt, to the Earl of Uxbridge, 27 February 1768. Also, NWM, ref. BW 1080/95. Letter, E. Lingard to Hugh Henshall, 30 January 1768.

11 NWM, ref. BW 1084/95. Letter, from W. Wyatt, to the Earl of Uxbridge, 5 September 1768.

12 Lindsey, Jean (1979), *The Trent & Mersey Canal*, p.38. Given source, the *Derby Mercury* newspaper, 6 October 1768.

13 *Ibid.*, p.38. Given source, Young, Arthur. *Tour Through the North of England.*

14 Chaloner, W.H., 'James Brindley (1716–72) and his Remuneration as a Canal Engineer'. Booklet reprinted from the *Transactions of the Lancashire and Cheshire Antiquarian Society*, Vols.75 & 76, 1965–6. 1969.

15 *Ibid.* Given source, PRO Northern Ireland, ref. T.2541/IA/1/8/96A. The Duke of Abercorn's archives.

16 NA, ref. RAIL 818/1. Minutes of the Coventry Canal Company.

17 *Ibid.* Also, Lindsey, Jean, *The Canals of Scotland*, p.20.

18 Ward, J.R., *The Finance of Canal Building in 18th Century England*, pp.30–1.

19 NA, ref. RAIL 818/1, as before, this chapter.

20 NA, ref. RAIL 822/1. Minutes of the Droitwich Canal Company. 4 March 1768.

21 Meteyard, Eliza. *The Life of Josiah Wedgwood*, p.240.

22 Tames, Richard. *Josiah Wedgwood*. Shire Lifelines series, No 4. Shire Publications Ltd, 1995

23 Meteyard, as before, this chapter, p.504.

24 *Ibid.*, p.38.

25 Lead, Peter (1989), *Agents of Revolution – John and Thomas Gilbert – Entrepreneurs*, p.77.

26 Lindsey, Jean (1979), *The Trent & Mersey Canal*, p.42. Given source, Picton, Sir James A., *City of Liverpool Municipal Archives and Records from 1700 to 1835*, p.244. 1886.

27 Sillitoe, Paul J., 'George Marchant's River Mersey Barrage'. *Transactions of the Historic Society of Lancashire & Cheshire*, Vol 141. 1992, pp.329–37. Given source, SUL, Clifford Whitworth Library, Bridgewater Archive, ref. NA 5/409, December 1768.

28 Lindsey, as before, this chapter, p.40.

29 Meteyard, as before, this chapter.p.39. Also, Finer, Ann & Savage, George [eds] (1965), *The Selected Letters of Josiah Wedgwood*, p.63.

30 Finer, Ann & Savage, George [eds] (1965), *The Selected Letters of Josiah Wedgwood*, pp.65, 102.

31 GCA, ref. AMJ/CB/F15/L3119. Brindley's admittance to the burgess-ship of the city, 9 September 1768.

32 Phillips, John (1970), *A General History of Inland Navigation, Foreign and Domestic*, p.200.

33 Raistrick, Arthur (1977), *Two Centuries of Industrial Welfare, the London (Quaker) Lead Company, 1692–1905.*

34 Labouchere, Rachel (1988), *Abiah Darby of Coalbrookdale*, p.165. Taken from the Journal of Abiah Darby (1716–1794), second wife of Abraham Darby II. The Journal is now in the archives at Friends House, London.

35 Evans, Kathleen M. (1997), *James Brindley – A New Perspective*, p.32.

36 Raistrick, Arthur (1968), *Quakers in Science and Industry*, p.47.

37 *Ibid.*, pp.33, 43.

38 SRO, ref. D1368/1-3. Staffordshire & Worcestershire – Brindley's orders book, vol.2, p.50. 3 volumes, 17 March 1767 to 9 August 1771.

39 Langford, J. Ian (1974), *Staffordshire & Worcestershire Canal* – Towpath Guide No.1, p.99.

40 ICE, James Brindley's notebook, September 1761 – November 1762.

41 Droitwich Canal, handwritten estimate, dated 5 October 1767, at Newchapel. Photocopy sent to the author by Max Sinclair – 'original was in private ownership, now lost'.

42 Sillitoe, Paul J. Letter to the author, 21 April 1995. Had searched the minutes (NA, RAIL 822/1) from the first meeting, 4 March 1768, to 3 September 1773. He found only two references to Brindley – at the first General Meeting (4 March 1768), appointed 'Inspector of the Works', annual salary £60. Priddey's salary confirmed at £90. The only other reference was a General Meeting on 2 September 1768 where it was 'Ordered that Mr Brindley's demand for attending the soliciting the Act be paid by the Treasurer'.

43 Droitwich Canals Trust (2000), *A Guide to the Droitwich Canals*, p.30.

44 *Ibid.*, p.31.

45 *Ibid.*

46 *Ibid.*, pp.10–11.

47 Richardson, Christine (1992), *The Waterways Revolution – From the Peaks to the Trent (1768–78).* The source for information on the construction of the Chesterfield Canal. Also Richardson, Christine (ed) (1996), *Minutes of the Chesterfield Canal Company (1771–80),* transcription of NA, RAIL 817/1.
48 DCL, pamphlet, 'Cursory View of the Advantages of an Intended Canal from Chesterfield to Gainsborough'. 1769.
49 DCL, Stevenson, Seth Ellis, pamphlet, 'Seasonable Hints relating to the Intended Canal from Chesterfield to the River Trent below Gainsbrough'. 8 December 1769. Also, NUHL, ref. FR/73, diary of the Reverend Seth Ellis Stevenson.
50 DCL, pamphlet, 'Cursory View …' as before, this chapter.
51 *Derby Mercury* newspaper, 17 May 1771, p.4.
52 *Ibid.*, 21 June 1771, p.4.
53 *Ibid.*, 5 July 1771, p.4.
54 Hadfield, Charles. *Canals of the West Midlands*, p.69.
55 *Ibid.*, p.65.
56 Coventry Canal Society. *Coventry's Waterway*, p.63. Given source, the minutes of the Coventry Canal Company.
57 *Ibid.*, p.7.
58 NA, ref. RAIL 855/2. Minutes of the Oxford Canal Company. From 12 May 1769 to 28 June 1775.
59 Paget-Tomlinson, Edward (1993), *The Illustrated History of Canal & River Navigations*, p.119.
60 NA, ref. RAIL 855/2, as before, this chapter. 15 August 1769.
61 Paget-Tomlinson, as before, this chapter, p.345.
62 SAO, refs. WWM.MP47.b and WWM.MP47.c. John Varley's estimates for the Greasbrough Canal. The matching manuscript map is ref. WWM.MP47.a. Also, NU, ref. FR/73. Diary of the Reverend Seth Ellis Stevenson. 15 June 1769.
63 NA, ref. RAIL 855/2, as before, this chapter. 2 January 1770.
64 Evans, as before, this chapter, pp.25, 73.
65 NA, ref. RAIL 855/2, as before, this chapter.
66 Skempton, A.W., 'Engineering on the Thames Navigation, 1770–1845'. *Transactions, Newcomen Society*, Vol 55.
67 Peltz, Dr Lucy, National Portrait Gallery, Curator of 18th Century Collections. Letter to the author, January 2002.
68 Meteyard, as before, this chapter, p.241.
69 Charles Hadfield's papers at the London School of Economics, Archives (Hadfield Collection). Also, SRO, ref. D1368/1-3. Staffordshire & Worcestershire Canal – Brindley's orders book, vol.2, p.75.
70 Biddle, Gordon, 'Early Days on the Leeds & Liverpool Canal', p.68. Railway & Canal Historical Society, *Journal*, January and September 1959.
71 Lindsey, Jean (1979), *The Trent & Mersey Canal*, p.39. Given source, House of Commons evidence given by Brindley.
72 SRO, ref. D3186/1/1/1. Minute book of the Staffordshire & Worcestershire Canal Company.
73 DCL, 'Seasonable Hints …' as before, this chapter.
74 NA, ref. RAIL 855/2, as before, this chapter. 26 July 1770.
75 *Ibid.*
76 Blagrove, David (1995), *At the Heart of the Waterways*, p.12.
77 NA, ref. RAIL 855/2, as before, this chapter. 12 September 1770.
78 *Ibid.*, 6 April 1772.
79 Hadfield, Charles. *The Canals of South and South-East England*, p.190.
80 BCL, Matthew Boulton Papers, Letter Book D, p.34–5, p.40–3. Letters from Matthew Boulton to Thomas Gilbert, and Samuel Garbett.
81 *Ibid.*
82 Young, Arthur. *Six Months Tour through the North of England*, Volume III, p.251 onwards.
83 Smiles, Samuel (1861), *Lives of the Engineers.*
84 Richardson, Christine, 'Brindley's Norwood Tunnel (1771–1775) – Twin of Harecastle'. *Transactions, Newcomen Society*, Vol 72, pp.163–78.
85 Shill, Ray (1996), *The Industrial Canal, Volume 1 – The Coal Trade*, p.3.
86 Hadfield, Charles. *Canals of the West Midlands*, p.69.
87 NA, ref. RAIL 855/2, as before, this chapter. Also, Hamilton, Robert, 'Long Lost Loops of the Oxford Canal', published in *Waterways World*, June 1997.
88 Lindsey, Jean, as before, this chapter, p.43.
89 Hadfield, Charles. *Canals of the West Midlands*, p.31
90 Finer & Savage, as before, this chapter, p.13.
91 Meteyard, as before, this chapter, pp.116, 239.
92 YAS, ref. DD225 (Box 8). Worthington Jnr, J.S., letter to the Duke of Leeds, re payment for land by Canal Companies, written from Dunham, 16 August 1771.
93 Hadfield, Charles and Biddle, Gordon, *The Canals of North West England*, p.183.
94 Hadfield, Charles. *Canals of the West Midlands*, p.32.
95 NA, ref. RAIL 817/1. Minutes of the Chesterfield Canal Company, 1771–80. 26 June 1772. See above for transcript note.
96 *Ibid.*

97 Meteyard, as before, this chapter, p.241.
98 *Ibid.*
99 Lower, Dr Barbara. Letter to the author re the symptoms of Brindley's final illness, 19 January 2002.
100 Meteyard, as before, this chapter, pp.241, 244.
101 *Ibid.*, p.242.
102 *Ibid.*
103 *Ibid.*, p.243.
104 NUHL, ref. FR/73. Diary of the Reverend Seth Ellis Stevenson.
105 *Derby Mercury* newspaper, 9 October 1772.
106 NA, ref. RAIL 817/1. Minutes of the Chesterfield Canal Company, 1771–80, 12 May 1774. Also, Evans, Kathleen M. (1997), *James Brindley – A New Perspective*, p.76.
107 *Ibid.,* Evans.
108 Campbell, John H.D.M., Notes on James Brindley; *Derbyshire Miscellany*, the Bulletin of the Local History Section of Derbyshire.Archaeological & Natural Historic Society. February 1959. Matlock Local Studies Library.
109 Duke, Timothy H.S. (Chester Herald), on behalf of the College of Arms, London. Letter to the author, 19 March 2001.

Chapter 13 – Enduring Fame

1 *Biographia Britannica*, second edition, London 1778–93.
2 The poem 'Monument for Mr Brindley' is Part 1, Canto III, poem IX (p.414).

> So with strong arm immortal Brindley leads
> his long canals and parts the velvet meads;
> Winding in lucid lines, the watery mass
> minds the firm rock, or loads the deep morass.
>
> While rising locks a thousand hills alarm,
> flings o'er a thousand streams its silver arms;
> Feeds the long vale, the nodding woodland laves,
> and plenty, arts and commerce freight the waves.
>
> Nymphs! who erstwhile round Brindley's early bier,
> on snow-white bosoms showered the incessant tear;
> Adorn his tomb! Oh raise the marble bust,
> proclaim his honours, and protect his dust.
>
> With urns inverted round the sacred shrine
> their ozier wreaths let weeping Naiads twine;
> While on the top mechanic genius stands,
> counts the fleet waves, and balances the lands.

3 Ebenezer Elliott, 'Steam at Sheffield', c1830s. Quoted by Jeremy Warburg (ed), *The Industrial Muse*, Oxford University Press, 1958, pp.17–21.

> How oft of Brindley's deeds th' apprenticed boy
> Would speak delighted, long ere freedom came!
> And talk of Watt! while, shedding tears of joy,
> His widow'd mother heard, and hoped the name
> Of her poor boy, like theirs, would rise to fame …

INDEX